# A JOURNEY NORTH

# A Journey North

One Woman's Story of Hiking
the Appalachian Trail

By Adrienne Hall

APPALACHIAN MOUNTAIN CLUB BOOKS
BOSTON

Cover Photograph: Jerry and Marcy Monkman
Cover Design: Ola Frank and Belinda Desher
Book Design: Eva Ruutopõld

Text copyright © 2000 Adrienne Hall. All rights reserved.
First paperback edition 2001
Distributed by The Globe Pequot Press, Inc., Guilford, CT.

*The Library of Congress has cataloged the hardcover edition as follows:*

*Hall, Adrienne*
*A journey north : one woman's story of hiking the Appalachian Trail / Adrienne Hall*
*p.   cm.*
ISBN 1-878239-91-0 *(hardcover)*  ISBN 1-929173-05-9 *(paperback)*
*1. Hiking—Appalachian Trail. 2. Backpacking—Appalachian Trail. 3. Hall,*
*Adrienne—Journeys—Appalachian Trail. 4. Appalachian Trail—Description and*
*travel. I. Title.*
*GV199.42.A68 H24 2000*
917.404'43'092—dc21                                   00-021504
[B]

The paper used in this publication meets the minimum requirements of the
American National Standard for Information Sciences—Permanence of Paper
for Printed Library Materials,
ANSI Z39.48—1984.∞

Printed on recycled paper using soy-based inks.

Printed in the United States of America.

10  9  8  7  6  5  4  3  2  1                    01  02  03  04  05

# TABLE OF CONTENTS

For Craig

# ACKNOWLEDGMENTS

I am greatly indebted to the following people, who shared with me their expertise and who often spoke candidly about difficult issues: Glen Cardwell, Dr. Andy Friedland, Gary Henry, Bruce Hill, Vicky Hoover, Andrew Hyman, Brian King, Dr. Joseph Mitchell, Dr. Tom Pauley, Dr. John Peine, Mary Anne Peine, Jim Renfro, Scott Silver, Dr. Miranda Shaw, and Pamela Underhill.

For having faith in my idea and my prose, and for his dedication to this project, I extend a sincere thank you to Mark Russell at AMC Books.

I'd also like to acknowledge the faculty of the Environmental Studies Program at the University of Montana. Thank you to Bill Chaloupka and Norma Nickerson for reviewing the manuscript. I am especially grateful to Don Snow, my invaluable advisor, for sharing his knowledge of the craft and, in the process, renewing my love of language.

To Mom, Dad, and Scott, and also to Craig and Holly, I am forever appreciative of your unconditional love and support.

Finally, I'd like to thank the Appalachian Trail hikers who made me smile and inspired me to keep walking. It fills me with pleasure to know that so many people love the Appalachian Trail, and I am grateful for the thousands of people who are dedicated to caring for America's original long-distance footpath.

# A SIX MONTH DATE

Hiking 2,159 miles from Georgia to Maine was not my idea. In fact, when my boyfriend, Craig, asked me to hike the Appalachian Trail, I had to admit that I didn't know such a corridor of wilderness existed. It becomes apparent, then, that I did not hike the Appalachian Trail for the same reasons that have inspired many people to attempt a thru-hike of America's oldest National Scenic Trail. It was not my lifelong dream. I was not a lost youth searching for an identity. I was not retired and looking for a new way to spend my time. I was not sorting through a death or divorce. I was not recently fired from a job. The truth is that my boyfriend asked me on a date.

In the fall of 1994 I was in my senior year of college in Virginia. Most of my time was spent attending classes, applying to graduate school, playing soccer, and identifying beetles (3,000 beetles, to be exact) for a tedious research project in biology. Instead of partying into the wee hours, I made stress-releasing trips to the Little Yogurt Shop with my roommate, who was trudging through a similar application process. I was clinging to a way of life that was inevitably going to end, while trying to develop some relatively acceptable plan for life after graduation. When I had a free afternoon I would grab my mountain bike and scout out patches of green that were tucked away in the urban outskirts. The trails I found were not very challenging—too flat and too cramped. Still, bike rides revived Rocky Mountain memories—memories of the past summer that I spent in Colorado—memories of the best summer of my life.

That summer the world made sense. Every morning I rode my bike to work along a dirt road that wrapped around the base of 13,000-foot peaks. Most afternoons I climbed mountains and glissaded down their snowy chutes. Some nights my friends and I lit candles and slept on the roof. It was the summer when I fell in love with mountains, and when I fell in love with Craig.

Craig and I spent the summer playing frisbee in wildflower meadows, camping in rainstorms, and singing John Denver classics from the back of a pickup. We danced and laughed and loved, and then the summer was over. Like any storybook summer fantasy, it ended too soon. I returned to Virginia in late August to begin my senior year, and Craig continued working as a heavy-equipment operator in Colorado. We talked every couple weeks, but I wasn't sure if our paths would merge again. That was before he asked me out.

One November night Craig called to tell me about his hectic work schedule and about his new Alaskan malamute puppy. He asked what I thought about the name Diesel.

"If you were in a park," I said, "and there were a lot of people around, would you feel comfortable yelling, 'Come, Diesel! Diesel, get over here!'? I don't know; I couldn't say that with a straight face."

"I see your point. I guess Switchback and Duct Tape are out of the question too," he said. "How about Kodiak, after the Alaskan island?"

"Yeah, I like that. Kodiak."

Then his voice became soft and serious. "You know, I've been thinking a lot about hiking the Appalachian Trail. I seriously want to do it. I know if I don't go for it now, I'll never do it . . . and I'd like you to go with me."

"Sure," I gasped, having no idea what such a trip would entail.

Craig began filling me in. The trail is more than 2,000 miles long, a minor detail I had not been aware of. He continued, "That means backpacking for six months, fording rivers, sleeping in mice-infested shelters, climbing Mount Washington—which claims the worst weather conditions on the planet—encountering black bears and snakes, and being wet for days at a time." Craig informed me that every year about 2,000 people attempt to hike the trail in its entirety and only 10 percent make it. I later learned that only 10 percent of that 10 percent are women. He hung up, leaving me to contemplate a life of hiking and camping for half a year. A week later I called him back and accepted. "You've got a date."

I graduated from college, spent three months backpacking through Europe, and moved to Boulder, Colorado, in the fall of 1995 to live with

Craig. We began accumulating information about the trail: guidebooks, how-to books, narrative books, handbooks, and maps. I remember Craig telling me that hiking the trail had been his dream since he was thirteen, when he volunteered to paint blazes on the trees of the Appalachian Trail just five miles from his Connecticut home. I was apprehensive about committing to a journey that wasn't *my* lifelong dream, but I was open to adventure and figured my perseverance would get me through. During my time in Boulder, every day was visited by thoughts of life in the woods. We were itching to muddy our boots.

I was excited to go with Craig because, to be quite honest, I thought he was a real mountain man, and I was drawn to his rugged character. When we went camping with a group, he'd sneak away and go fishing or exploring by himself. Sometimes he'd wink at me before he left, which meant that it was okay if I followed. Eager for adventure, I always did. When I daydreamed about the Appalachian Trail, I pictured romantic scenes of us skinny-dipping in secluded ponds, bathing under waterfalls, taking naps in springtime flower meadows, creating a layer of condensation on the tent wall as we made love all night long, and holding each other during stormy nights in the shelters.

When my friends told me this experience would make us or break us, I laughed politely and agreed. But I never envisioned a future together beyond romantic backpacking trips, and I had no idea that Craig, who was five years older at twenty-eight, had given considerable thought to the consequences of our making it to Maine. Although he never said it, I came to understand that hiking the length of the nation was a prerequisite for a wife.

Craig loved his job as a heavy-equipment operator; sometimes I felt he loved it more than me. He worked fourteen-hour days, six days a week, in hopes of stashing away enough money to pay for the trip. At the time, I was pursuing life, not a career, and I spent more time volunteering for environmental groups than I did working for money. I was convinced that Craig worked enough for both of us. He'd come home with dirt ground into his Carhartt overalls and grease smeared over his rough hands and forearms. I liked to think that he worked long hours for the money, but in my heart I knew he devoted his time to excavators and backhoes and loaders because he loved them; he loved to get dirty and control equipment that had the power to crush a building in a single blow.

After work Craig would strut into the kitchen, take off his Leatherman and beeper, and give me a kiss. Then he'd wrestle Kodiak to the ground, wipe the crusties out of the corners of Kodi's eyes, and kiss his forehead. He'd turn to me, give me a bear hug, and press his unshaven cheek against mine. I would ask him if he would please take the weekend off to go camping with me, or I'd ask him to come home early on Thursday so we could go out, but the answer was usually no. He wouldn't turn down work, he'd say; and I would just have to accept that. It was then that I understood it would take something huge, something more important than me, for him to quit his job. I understood that he wanted to hike this trail more than anything, and the reasons had a lot to do with his past and little to do with me. In late December 1995 Craig quit his job and the two of us headed east to prepare for the trip.

We spent all of January alternating between Pennsylvania, at my parents' house, and Connecticut, at his. Both locations were getting blasted with severe winter weather, and we assumed that if we trained in those conditions, the actual hike in February would seem easy. For days the temperature never rose above nine degrees, and we headed out daily into three feet of snow and tromped a few miles through the woods carrying backpacks filled with books and five-pound bags of flour. Eventually I got used to the strange looks (the confused "there's a girl with a large backpack trekking through the parks of suburban Philadelphia" look), and I learned to respond politely to the comments: "Now, just where do you think *you're* going?", "You out for a big hike today?", and my favorite from a guy taking out his cell phone at the trailhead: "That's quite a big pack for a little girl." I cinched the straps on my snowshoes, and the little girl with the big pack left him in the dust.

My legs got stronger. I lifted weights in the basement and went for three-mile runs when the roads were plowed. My boots were breaking in and my pack straps, although not entirely comfortable, were feeling less like dull knives against my shoulders and more like they belonged on my body. Craig made a fair effort to get in shape, but he viewed home-cooked meals the same way he viewed work: they both fell into the category of "things not to be passed up." He preferred apple pie to the three-mile runs and decided to implement the Get In Shape Once I'm On The Trail strategy. Although this philosophy would never work for me and would probably not work for most people, there are some individuals who are, somehow, in good enough shape in the beginning to swing it, and who not only can handle, but seem to prefer, a week or two of intense pain that compensates for months of not training. It works for some people, and Craig was one of them.

Craig had saved about $2,000 and I had $1,000. "The books say it'll cost about a dollar a mile," he said. "Since we already own most of the equipment and we'll buy our food in bulk, I think we should have enough to cover our expenses if we don't spend too much time in towns."

"I still think we're a couple thousand dollars short," I said. "I don't see how we can do it with less than $5,000. And don't forget about Kodiak." We knew we'd need dog food and a little extra money to bail him out of whatever trouble he got into.

We arranged to hike without Kodiak until Virginia for a number of reasons. Most importantly we felt we should get accustomed to long-distance hiking and to each other before we assumed responsibility for a dog. It would also be necessary to board him and have him shuttled around Great Smoky Mountains National Park, since dogs are not allowed inside the park's boundaries. Hiking with a dog and hiking *responsibly* with a dog are two very different things. We knew we would have to control him at all times so he wouldn't disturb other hikers, chase wildlife, attack other dogs, or muddy water sources. We knew that the additional stress of worrying about his pack, which we modified with extra straps and safety pins so it wouldn't slide up on his neck when he ran, might be more than we could handle. During our first couple weeks, we certainly didn't need to worry about keeping his dog food dry in the snow and keeping him from wading in streams with his pack on. Although we weren't quite sure what unforeseen trouble Kodiak would get into, we knew he would find a way to create what

I fondly call "situations." In retrospect, leaving Kodiak at home was one of the very few good decisions we made in the entire planning process. We planned on reuniting with Kodiak whenever one of our families could drive south and bring him to us.

Before we started the AT, a friend of ours bet us each $100 that we wouldn't finish. "You both have to hike the entire trail and you can't split up. You have to finish together. It's nothing against you," he said, "I'm a gambler; I'm just playing the odds." Before we departed he said as an afterthought, "You know what might keep you two together? Kodiak." Our friend looked at Kodi and at the dog's proud parents. "He just might be the glue that holds you together." Craig immediately began calling the dog "Glue," and Kodi looked more confused than ever. For a dog that after two years still had trouble with "sit" and "stay," "glue" was light-years beyond the range of his comprehension.

Craig and I estimated how long it would take to complete certain sections of the trail, and we planned our food drops accordingly. We collected eight corrugated boxes and lined them up on the floor. We labeled each box with its destination and the number of days it would take to reach our next supply box. For example, box #1 would be sent to Fontana Dam, North Carolina. We estimated it would take eight days to hike the 106 miles from Fontana Dam to our next mail drop at Hot Springs, North Carolina. So into the box went eight breakfasts, lunches, and dinners, and eight days' of snacks. We filled each box with rations of pasta, oatmeal, rice, dehydrated fruits and vegetables, energy bars, trail mix, and chocolate. We addressed the boxes to ourselves, general delivery, to each post office near the trail.

From a pile that represented an accumulation of five years' worth of camping gear, we selected the necessary items to fill our packs. Since I worked at an outdoors outfitter in Boulder, we were able to buy any gear we needed at a substantially discounted price. We both added leather boots and thick fleece jackets to our growing gear collection, but we already owned most of the gear we would need for the AT. We stuffed our packs, unstuffed them, and threw out half of the gear. We packed again, and again, and threw a few more things back in the closet. We still managed to pack too much.

We knew the trail in Georgia traversed forested mountains, but we didn't know what the conditions would be like. It might be warm; it might be cold. It might snow. It might be difficult to find water. It might be difficult to find the trail. The trail might be flat and smooth or it might be steep and rocky. It was difficult to choose the appropriate gear when neither of us had ever been to Georgia.

In the end we narrowed it down to a still-too-large equipment list. We both carried Dana Designs backpacks and wore Vasque Alpine boots. We began the trip with a Peak 1 camp stove and switched to my trusty MSR Whisperlite after the Peak 1 froze in the Smokies. Our clothes were all synthetic: waterproof jacket and pants, two layers of fleece, two pairs of long johns, two pairs of socks and liners, gaiters, and snowshoes. We started with a week's worth of food, a personal hygiene kit, a first-aid kit, a pencil and journal, sandals to wear around camp, cookware, headlamps, the Sierra Designs Polaris two-person tent, sleeping pads, a fleece blanket to line the tent, a twenty-degree synthetic sleeping bag for me (which would not even come close to keeping me warm) and a zero-degree down bag for Craig.

During the days before our departure we snuggled on the sofa with piles of blankets and read more books about the Appalachian Trail. The stories painted a picture of a trail that was lined with soft ferns and wildflowers and hiked by radiant and spirited hikers. I read about hikers meeting friends they would stay in touch with for life, and hikers meeting a companion they'd marry when it was all over. There were tales of astounding kindness, of locals bringing platters of homemade food to hungry trekkers, of hostels opening their doors to the ragged and weary. Veteran thru-hikers recalled the joys of getting a ride into town and sharing an all-you-can-eat restaurant with new acquaintances, sleeping under the stars, experiencing a spiritual awakening, basking in the beauty of springtime foliage and soft rays of sunshine, fulfilling their dreams and glorying in their triumphs.

Darrell Maret in *Walking the Appalachian Trail* describes the AT experience as "a life more worthwhile even the gods could not dream of." In an article titled "The AT: Trailblazing for Tomorrow," Joseph Keyser writes of the AT experience as "unique and compelling, a journey through lush wilderness and historic towns, along ridgelines, and past glistening lakes." Ann and Myron Sutton write, "The A.T. will always be, God and the public willing, a high road to paradise where we may walk and dream to our heart's content." Our minds were filled with accounts of hikers who never wanted to leave the trail, and about the agonizing transition back into civilization. The trail posed a challenge to us but it was not overly daunting. "It's nothing we can't handle," said Craig, and I pictured miles and miles of fun.

Of course, there were hints of pain and exhaustion, but the stories always seemed to end on a positive note, and Craig and I, already a little apprehensive, didn't let the details of pain and suffering penetrate too deeply. The one publication we should have taken more seriously (but didn't because we assumed it was written for beginners), was a booklet called *Walking the Appalachian Trail Step by Step*. The booklet was published by the Appalachian Trail Conference (ATC), the official headquarters and information distributors for the trail. We spent two minutes glossing over the Hazards on the Trail section and two hours studying the temperature and precipitation data for the fourteen states through which the trail passes; charts of average monthly temperatures are interesting, but they are virtually useless when planning a thru-hike.

The point of the booklet we missed was essentially this: Every year thousands of people start at Springer Mountain and believe they will walk to Maine, but most people drop out. Many quit at the first town twenty miles up the trail. After spending months preparing for and investing in a thru-hike, to quit after twenty miles would, obviously, be disappointing. The booklet lists common reasons for hikers quitting: starting too early, heavy rains, too strenuous a schedule, unexpectedly rugged terrain, loneliness, disagreeable food, poor physical shape, ill-fitting boots and equipment, and no sense of humor. If you are considering a thru-hike, the booklet says, you should ask yourself these questions: Do you have a tendency toward homesickness and loneliness? Are you willing to endure days of rain, trudging through mud and puddles in wet hiking boots? Are you willing to plod up seemingly endless mountains with muscles that ache, only to see another grind still to come? Will occasional days without sufficient water or the monotony of trail meals discourage you? I'm fairly certain I missed those questions. I'm also fairly certain that had I answered those questions, the ATC would have recommended that I stay home.

In our selective quest for information, we chose not to focus on the ATC's warnings about hazards on the trail. It said weather is often unpredictable and there can be snow in the South until May. Be wary of strangers, ticks that transmit Lyme disease, poisonous snakes, porcupines, skunks, raccoons, and black bears. Bring appropriate clothing and understand the conditions that are likely to lead to hypothermia. Also be aware of the symptoms and treatment for heat exhaustion, heat cramps, and heat stroke. Treat water or risk contracting *Giardia*. Know basic first aid, especially what to do for twisted or sprained ankles, abrasions, and lacerations. It may have been fortunate that we didn't have a realistic vision of the trail or we might have been more apprehensive about hiking it.

We were not novice hikers, so why were our expectations so far from reality? Why did we pay attention only to the parts of the books that made it sound easy? When I look at pictures of us gearing up for the trail, with bulky items like snowshoes and a fleece blanket strapped to the outside of our packs, I can only shake my head and laugh. What on earth were we thinking?

I had an enormous sleeping mattress, which Craig affectionately named Big Red because of its red stuff sack. Our entire tent, tent poles, and tent rainfly fit in a stuff sack that was smaller than Big Red's. I strapped Big Red to the outside of my pack. "There's no point in buying another when this one is perfectly functional," I said. "Honey, you can't even fit between two trees that are close together," said Craig. Sure enough, on the trail Craig turned around laughing with an "I told you so" expression on his face when Big Red got wedged between two tree trunks. I had to pull out, get a running start, and shove me, my pack, and Big Red through the tight trees.

By mid-January we had told many people of our plans. The more people we told, the less confident we became. People were congratulating us and we hadn't taken one step. Our plans to leave by the first of February were blown away in a series of blizzards and ice storms and pleas from our families to postpone the trip until March or April, when most people begin the trek north. To us, hiking with hundreds of people was unacceptable. We were looking for a wilderness experience, not a social gathering. Our plan was to beat the masses. A combination of boredom and anxiety spurred us to set the departure date for February 12.

The night before we set out for the AT we were lying in bed and Craig rolled over on me, gently turned my face towards his huge blue eyes, and gave me his most earnest look. It must have taken him a while to muster the courage to tell me that he loved me, but he did it with such sincerity I felt tears filling the corners of my eyes. I had said those words to only one other person, and that was back in high school and I didn't really mean it; I just didn't want to make him feel bad since he was hanging out there with a naked soul and an unprotected heart. The old "you too" comes in handy during those awkward moments. But this time it was real. This time I felt it in my toes.

A knock at the door. "Raindrop, Hibird," Mom called, "I just heard the weather forecast and it looks like another storm is going to hit the South. Why don't you stay here another week?" My mother, fully aware of how corny it sounded to call us by our trail names, still insisted on "getting into it"; it is part of the Appalachian Trail culture to identify yourself with a name other than the one you use in society. Sometimes trail names describe the person, like Walks with Two Sticks (a man who carried two long hiking sticks) or Papa Smurf (a short man with a thick white beard who dressed in blue long johns and a red vest). Other times you'll meet a hiker named Blue Iggy or Zappa and you can only guess what the name refers to.

Craig's name, Hibird, referred to a term that was born in Boulder and was used exclusively by our group of friends to describe someone who was crazy enough to rock-climb a thousand-foot wall, or spend weekends sky diving, or, in this case, walk more than 2,000 miles up the Appalachian Trail.

Craig gave me my name. He thought Raindrop was appropriate because "it is something pure and simple and natural, like you." I was flattered and the name stuck. Months later he confessed that he got the idea for the name from a guy he met at work who had a horse named Raindrop. So I was named after a horse. Terrific.

"I'm serious," my mother said, "I can't imagine you two hiking in this weather. I wish you'd stay here a while longer till it warms up." Craig and I looked at each other. We both knew that even if it snowed ten feet and was twenty below zero we were much too stubborn to change our plans. The next day we rented a car and drove from Philadelphia to Atlanta. It was colder than we thought. We stopped at a gas station in Atlanta to fill up and get a hot drink. A woman who had an accent that was the female version of Arnold Schwarzenegger pulled up and was immediately excited to see our backpacks.

"Ah," she said, "You do the backpacking?"

"Yes," we said.

"Because I do the backpacking," she said. "So good for you. The backpacking is fun, eh?"

"Yes," we said a bit apprehensively, "we like the backpacking."

"Ooooh, it is very cold for the backpacking now, eh?" she giggled. "You must know what you're doing. You very brave. It is fun, the backpacking." And she waved goodbye.

As she drove away, I held on to my forty-five-pound backpack and rocked back and forth to keep warm. I felt my confidence growing weaker by the minute. I shot Craig a look that I had hoped would make him tell me that everything was going to be okay, but he said nothing and studied the map.

From Atlanta we hitched a ride with my cousin into the country-side two hours north of the city. "Two hours," I thought to myself over and over, "two hours left of being warm, two hours left of roads and gas stations and houses with cozy beds." Around 11 P.M. on Valentine's Day, my cousin dropped us off at a dark and deserted Amicalola State Park.

## CHAPTER ONE

# STEPPING INTO THE WILDERNESS

Craig and I signed in at Amicalola State Park as the thirteenth and fourteenth thru-hikers of 1996 and began sloshing through the thawing mud on the Approach Trail to the top of Springer Mountain. Hundreds of trees lay on their sides, torn from the ground by Hurricane Opal. Roots of scraggly shrubs clenched the soil like bony, arthritic hands. Twisted trees, like ancient totems, told their story of wind, rain, disease, and parasites. I wondered if we would feel like those trees after six months on the trail—weathered and frayed but strong all the same. Would we collect blisters and bruises and bulging muscles as the trees collect nicks and broken limbs and lightning scars? After six months, would a stranger be able to narrate our story by looking in our eyes? I felt like a clean slate, waiting for the trail to write my story.

The Georgian Appalachian sprawl was impressive; I never expected the Peach State to possess such steep, enormous mountains. The first mile slipped behind us rather quickly, but as the next hour passed our eager feet gradually slowed to a trudge. I was suddenly struck with the feeling that I was going to have to walk forever to get to Maine. Maine was an unfathomably remote distance from where I stood; all I could think to do was connect the shelters and hope that one day I would wake up in a state farther to the north. This was Day One and I felt I had made a good effort; I felt like I had put up a good fight. I had made some progress and might even deserve some recognition for my hard work. But reality was grim: despite the effort I had exhibited that first day, I hadn't seen even the first inch of the Appalachian Trail, since the actual terminus is a day's hike to the top of Springer Mountain. Day One really meant Day Zero. It meant, "That was your chance to warm up, now you may begin."

The Approach Trail twists up and over 3,000- and 4,000-foot mountains for eight miles and leads to the bronze plaque that marks the southern terminus of the Appalachian Trail. The figure on the plaque is a stout man with a driven, solitary grimace and dated attire. He sports a bell-shaped cap, a small pack slung over a comfortable collared shirt, a knife on his hip, and baggy pants that end about midcalf and wrinkle into high-cut boots. The inscription on the plaque reads Appalachian Trail/ Georgia to Maine/A Footpath for Those who seek Fellowship with the Wilderness—a novel concept in the early 1900s. Benton MacKaye is credited with originating the plans for the trail, but it took thousands of volunteers in the 1920s and 1930s to construct the trail, and it took many supporters to rally for the protection of a continuous footpath that spans most of the length of the United States. I wondered if the figure on the plaque was Benton himself or one of the thousands of nameless supporters who made the nation's first long trail a reality.

Hiking and exploring near his Massachusetts home was an integral part of MacKaye's childhood. He studied forestry at Harvard and graduated in 1905, the same year the U.S. Forest Service was established. Benton immediately went to work for the Forest Service, surveying land in the White Mountains. Although most commonly referred to as a regional planner, MacKaye took great interest in forestry, architecture, geology, flood control, and disarmament, among other things.

In 1921 he introduced the idea for a trail from Mount Washington, New Hampshire, to Mount Mitchell, North Carolina, which would be interspersed with recreation camps and farms where urbanites could come to escape. In his essay "The Appalachian Trail: A Project in Regional Planning," MacKaye wrote, "The project is one for a series of recreational communities throughout the Appalachian chain of mountains from New England to Georgia, these to be connected by a walking trail. Its purpose is to establish a base for a more extensive and systematic development of outdoor community life. It is a project in housing and community architecture." A few years later, Benton changed his tone, declaring that the intention of the AT was "to organize a barbarian invasion," presumably to counter the industrial invasion that was occurring in the cities and consuming vast amounts of countryside in its sprawl. He believed there was a pressing need for people to understand nature, and he believed that people would only be able to understand nature if they had the opportunity to experience it.

In addition to the trail, the project called for "shelter camps" which would be more developed than the three-sided structures we think of as AT shelters today. MacKaye's shelters would resemble the hut system in the White Mountains, fully enclosed cabins with bunks and cooking facilities. He also called for "community camps," nonindustrial communities that would provide opportunities for recuperation, scientific study, and field courses. The final part of the project included "food and farm camps" which would consist of larger communities developed for farming and sustainable forestry. He argued that such a project would provide opportunities for recreation, health, and recuperation. Further, the project would provide employment in rural areas, which would help redistribute the population.

He began to introduce his idea to legislators, city planners, trail clubs, and hiking groups. He wrote letters, gave speeches, attended banquets and conferences, and soon established a network of support along the East Coast. In 1925 the Appalachian Trail support clubs formed the Appalachian Trail Conference (ATC) to oversee management of the trail. At this point there was quite a bit of verbal support and a lot of ideas and encouragement, but little action. A few substantial stretches of trail had been completed, but by 1926 the momentum that had propelled the idea was nearly gone.

Fortunately, two prominent men rescued the idea and revived the project. Arthur Perkins, a judge from Connecticut, took an interest in the concept of a long-distance trail and eventually became chairman of the Appalachian Trail Conference. He led an ambitious campaign to form additional trail clubs, recruit workers, and plan routes. Myron Avery, a lawyer from Washington, D.C., proved to be an excellent organizer and motivated thousands of people in the Potomac Appalachian Trail Club. Avery eventually succeeded Perkins as chairman of the ATC. These two men were largely responsible for the Appalachian Trail becoming something more than an idea.

Perkins and Avery followed MacKaye's theory that the trail could be, and ought to be, built entirely by volunteers. MacKaye had written that the spare time of the American population was an "enormous undeveloped power." His rationale was not necessarily grounded in indisputable fact, but the point of his message was perfectly clear and his tone was powerful and inspiring: "Suppose just one percent of it [American's spare time] were focused upon one particular job, such as increasing the facilities for the outdoor community life. This would be more than a million people, representing over two million weeks a year. It would be equivalent to 40,000 persons steadily on the job."

Volunteers worked tirelessly, building trail and connecting trails that previously existed. By 1937, sixteen years after MacKaye's article appeared, the last segment of trail was constructed in Maine.

I thought about Benton and Arthur and Avery and wondered what made them think they could do it. What motivates a person to try something that no one else has, or to develop an idea that most people consider unthinkable? Thank goodness for dreamers, I thought, and gave silent thanks to those who had faith in their dreams.

§

"This is it," said Craig, gazing out into waves of forest, blued and blurred. I didn't expect to be so moved by Springer Mountain, but a year's worth of anticipation swelled in my eyes. I saw the first blaze. (Blazes are the two-by-six-inch white stripes painted on trees and rocks to mark the trail.) "Better get used to looking at these," Craig said. We had read an account of a woman who followed white markings for weeks after she returned from her thru-hike. When she saw two stripes on a telephone pole she instinctively made a sharp turn.

From the top of Springer Mountain we ambled two-tenths of a mile to the Springer Mountain Shelter, staked our hiking sticks in the mud, and took inventory of our recently acquired blisters and bruises. Everything we did that first night marked us as novices. In all of our efforts to plan the trip, we never thought about what we would add to the instant rice and instant mashed potatoes to make them edible. "Let's see," said Craig, unfolding the Camp Kitchen, "we have salt and pepper—that's about it." When he served me a plate of instant rice with pepper, I began to doubt the abilities of my mountain man. Our first dinner didn't matter all that much: we felt good; we were in Georgia on the AT. "I can't believe those first eight miles don't count," Craig said. For weeks, we still counted the eight-mile Approach Trail as part of our cumulative mileage.

The sun set as I washed our dishes. My fingers were numb by the time I began rinsing the first fork. I tucked my hands under my armpits and began jumping up and down. A little warmer. I gave the pot a quick rinse, not bothering to scrape off the rice that was glued to the bottom, and hurried up the hill. As the excitement of finding our first shelter wore off, the cold set in. The temperature fell to twenty degrees and continued to fall all evening. Our packs became icy and stiff and our hiking sticks froze into the ground. Fortunately we found some new friends to take our minds off the cold.

The mice themselves didn't bother me so much—it was the squeaking and shuffling and the sputtering of rodent feet by my head in the dark that made me edgy. Craig lit candles and suspended our food on a cord below an inverted tuna can. The mice must have been accustomed to this obstacle because they got into the food anyway. "Those bastards!" Craig shouted, as pieces of trail mix sprinkled onto his head. He said some other things about mice which I'd rather not repeat.

I honestly didn't think the mice would bother me; after all, I claim to be a biologist. I had used mice and rats in experiments. I had kept a stiff stomach while examining the insides of rabbits, rats, frogs, and squid. But this was different. There were no cages, no latex gloves. These critters had free rein.

And reign they did. For weeks we read shelter registers with similar messages: "Beware the mice!" Craig read accounts of hikers declaring war on mice and how the hikers were always defeated. The mice were always up for a fight, and they clearly had the home-field advantage.

Craig and I spent much of that first night filling pages of the register with poems of our own. "The mice are fuzzy, brown and cute/ but if I had a gun, a mouse I would shoot" and "The cover of my trail guide they chewed and flung/ and on the first page, they left some dung" and

"The mice are loud and very rude/ so light a candle and hang your food." The candles burnt to the floor and sleep finally overtook us.

After a couple weeks we grew accustomed to the mice, but we never truly felt comfortable sharing our home. I remember one shelter in particular, the Deep Gap Shelter, where the mice ran the show. The sun slipped behind the western ridge at about seven o'clock and the mice immediately emerged. From every crack and crevice they crept, searching for our food. They raced in and out of canvas bags, gnawed on wood and tin cans beneath the shelter, and let out an occasional ear-piercing squeal. They were doing gymnastics from the rafters, scaling the walls, and having races around the perimeter. Unfortunately, my sleeping bag sprawled over a crucial part of their race course. For the mice it was a bonus, another obstacle on the course. But for me, it was an uneasy, sleepless night. I kept imagining a mouse darting across the floor and ending up inside my sleeping bag. Every time I shifted positions I drew the collar of the bag as tight against my body as it would go. It was then that I began to rethink the passage engraved on that plaque. Does "Fellowship with Wilderness" have to include mice?

Indeed it did, whether I wanted it to or not. That was the thing about the wilderness—you never quite knew what you were getting yourself into. I imagine the pioneers felt a similar mix of emotions when they first explored these hills. They must have been awe-struck by the beauty of this land, but to them wilderness was an obstacle. It was a challenge to overcome, and it terrified them.

"Craig," I said, "do you know how silly we are?"

"What do you mean?"

"We lie here shelter after shelter trying to figure out how to deceive mice. I mean, we actually *have* a shelter. We have maps and guidebooks, and we have all this equipment. What do you think it was like for the first Europeans who came here? They had no idea what to expect. It must have looked like an endless sea of forest. And so dark and quiet and mysterious."

"That would be incredible," Craig said. "Can you imagine going to a place where no map exists? I would love to have lived back then."

"I'm pretty sure they didn't think it was that great," I said. "I'm pretty sure they were scared shitless. And I'm pretty sure they hated a lot of it."

It's hard for me to understand what the pioneers were feeling, because they forged their way through the Appalachians for survival; Craig and I forged our way for pleasure. Regardless, I felt certain that their fears of unmapped territory were more justified than our anxieties over a few mice. And I still thought we were being silly.

Since wilderness was a physical obstacle to westward expansion, it posed a serious threat to the settlers' survival. Religion and folklore instilled in American settlers the idea that wilderness harbored monsters and possessed supernatural powers, that it was dark, alien, uncomfortable, a moral and physical wasteland, godless, desolate, and to be feared until conquered. The earth was good only if it could be farmed or mined, and the forest was good only if the trees could be cut down for firewood or houses.

In contrast, Native Americans often have maintained a spiritual connection with the land, and their rituals and religious ceremonies have incorporated images of nature and female power. They have seen themselves as part of the cycles of nature and have viewed the land with reverence; it is not something that is wild and fearsome, as the settlers saw it. As Chief Luther Standing Bear stated, "The old people came literally to love the soil and they sat or reclined on the ground with a feeling of being close to a mothering power. . . .To us it was tame. Earth was bountiful and we were surrounded with the blessings of the Great Mystery. Not until the hairy man from the east came and with brutal frenzy heaped injustices upon us and the families we loved was it 'wild' for us." Although Native Americans considerably altered certain regions of the American landscape with fire, they did what they needed to do to survive. I believe they were driven by tradition and a desire to subsist on the land; they were not driven by greed and a desire to obtain dominion over the earth.

The region Craig and I were walking through was once the thriving empire of the Cherokee Nation. In 1885, James Mooney was hired as an ethnologist by John Wesley Powell, director of the Bureau of American Ethnology, to document Cherokee language and stories. During the late 1880s, Mooney met with Cherokee elders and shamans, who over time revealed to Mooney their sacred concepts of spirituality, hunting, and illness. Mooney discovered that the Cherokees felt connected to their surroundings in a way that the early Europeans could hardly comprehend. I found one excerpt in his essay "The Sacred Formulas of the Cherokees" particularly indicative of the respect for nature and interconnectedness of people and their surroundings that is common in most Native American cultures. It is the story that explains the origin of disease.

According to the myth, all things lived together in harmony until the human population began to increase very rapidly. Humans spread over the entire earth and began killing animals. The animals feared for their safety and met in council to find a solution. The bears met first and decided to make bows and arrows so they could fend off the humans, but their long claws got in the way when they tried to shoot the arrows. The deer met next. They were alarmed by the injustices to animals, but after witnessing the failed attempt of the bears to physically fight humans, they realized that disease was the only thing that could deter this rapidly proliferating species. They agreed to inflict rheumatism upon any human that killed a deer without asking pardon for the offense. Also alarmed, the fish and reptiles decided to make humans have frightening dreams about slimy snakes and decaying fish. Birds, insects, and small mammals were equally enraged by humans' cruelty toward animals so they began making lists of diseases that would afflict humans and decrease their numbers.

The plants eventually got word of the animals' deliberations and agreed to help humans. They decided that every tree, grass, shrub, moss, and herb would furnish a remedy for one of the diseases the animals created. When a doctor isn't sure which remedy to use, the doctor consults the plant spirits to guide him or her to the proper remedy.

In this way, Cherokees see themselves as vulnerable to natural forces. They are in no way superior to or dominant over animals and natural processes. Much of the folklore focuses on appropriate dealings with animals, especially animals that are hunted. Specific prayers and rituals must be performed when hunting various animals, and ignoring these rituals can bring negative energy and disease to the hunter and his community. A similar level of respect is given to plants. Mooney writes:

> In hunting it, the first three plants found are passed by. The fourth is taken, after a preliminary prayer, in which the doctor addresses it as the "Great Ada'wehi," and humbly asks permission to take a small piece of its flesh. On digging it from the ground, he drops into the hole a bead and covers it over, leaving it there, by way of payment to the plant spirit. After that he takes them as they come without further ceremony.

Cherokees seem to have a healthy respect and reverence for all components of the world. Even encounters with nonliving things like mountains, rocks, and rivers require similar ceremonies. In contrast with the settlers, Cherokees feel no need or desire to tame and conquer nature. As long as precautions are taken, there is no need to fear nature. Natural systems, of which they are a part, will maintain a comfortable level of balance and harmony. Christopher Camuto, in *Another Country*, writes, "The Puritans feared the pathless woods and imputed much evil into wild nature's instructive tendency to balk human progress. The Cherokee derived a religion from that fact." Unfortunately, the settlers lumped Indians with the myriad of other wild and natural things they feared. American settlers did their best to drive off Indians, convert them to Christianity, and reduce the Cherokee empire to a destitute and fragmented society.

In a few hundred years, how did Americans change their minds from wanting to tame and conquer all wild land to rallying for the protection of a corridor of land from Georgia to Maine, solely for the purpose of allowing man to immerse his collective self in wilderness?

The pioneers' terror of wild things and the need to conquer them, tame them, or use them lasted until the Romantic period of the eighteenth century, when writers, artists, scientists, and anyone else whose life did not depend on battling wilderness for survival began celebrating nature in their work. More and more, people began to see corruption, ill will, and stress pervading human society, and they began to seek refuge in wild country. Roderick Nash, writer and wilderness scholar, reports that the settlers eventually began to believe that "peace, love, and harmony (in wilderness). . .would replace the immorality, conflict, and materialism of the towns." The frontierspeople in America, still moving west, accepted this viewpoint to a degree, but these new ideas did not totally displace the fears and anxiety they felt about wilderness.

By the nineteenth century, American independence was secure. The nation was anxious to make a name for itself but had few historical monuments to serve as symbols of national identity; it didn't have famous cathedrals or museums or castles as the European countries did. It had nothing valuable to claim as its own except wilderness. When Americans began to realize that other countries did not have a Grand Canyon, a Yellowstone, California redwoods, a Niagara Falls, Great Smokies, the woods of New England, they began to take pride in the country's natural beauty. These natural wonders somehow validated the worthiness of the new country and compensated for America's lack of artistic and historical accomplishments.

In the nineteenth century science and art exploded, and wilderness was perceived as valuable and rich and not quite so frightening. Some Americans also began to find mental, emotional, and spiritual discomfort in society so they turned to wilderness for consolation, inspiration, and even mystical communion. Henry David Thoreau and the transcendentalists recognized a divine presence in nature, and the writings and energy of the transcendental movement influenced much of the country. By the mid-1800s, many Americans had developed a substantial appreciation for wilderness.

With the new appreciation for wilderness came a regret that so much of it had been destroyed. Nonetheless, the idea of actually setting land aside for the sake of preservation seemed downright absurd. Thankfully there were people who believed preservation was necessary. Environmentalist pioneers like John James Audubon, Horace Greeley, William Cullen Bryant, Washington Irving, John Muir, and Henry David Thoreau rallied for the preservation of wilderness. In 1872, the first official move toward preservation occurred when President Ulysses S. Grant signed an act to establish Yellowstone National Park. About a decade later, the Cinnabar and Clark's Fork Railroad Company sought to secure a right of way across the park to assist with their mining claims. After considerable debate, Congress voted to deny the railroad the right of way. As Nash puts it, "[N]ever before had wilderness values withstood such a direct confrontation with civilization."

The late nineteenth century saw the formation of organizations dedicated to the preservation and enjoyment of the outdoors, among them the Appalachian Mountain Club (1876), the Boone and Crockett Club (1888), the Sierra Club (1892), and the Campfire Club of America (1897). By the early twentieth century, wilderness appreciation had grown into a national cult. Hundreds of books and articles propounded the horrors of civilization and the value of wilderness. It was during this period that such time-honored works as *Alone in the Wilderness*, *The Wilderness City*, *The Jungle*, *White Fang*, *The Call of the Wild*, and *Tarzan of the Apes* were published. Americans also began to be aroused by the transcendentalist concept of wilderness as a spiritual realm. The works of Thoreau and Muir spearheaded this spiritual movement. Although Thoreau's writing was not widely recognized until nearly fifty years after it was published, by the early 1900s Americans finally recognized its value, and the works of both Thoreau and Muir were nationally acclaimed.

Of course, not everyone agreed, and many people couldn't understand what all the fuss was about. Beginning with the Hetch Hetchy controversy in the early 1900s over the damming of the Tuolomne River in Yosemite National Park to supply water to San Francisco, the American public began the battle of preservation versus exploitation of natural resources. That the battles were occurring at all is significant, because until a hundred years ago Americans would not have thought twice about damning a river or cutting down a forest. But something was beginning to change.

Aldo Leopold led the next generation of preservationists, urging Americans to develop an "ecological conscience." It was around this time that Benton MacKaye proposed his Appalachian Trail project, and it was met with widespread approval. Around the middle of the century others added their energy to the fight: Robert Marshall, Sigurd Olson, Rachel Carson, Howard Zahniser, and David Brower. Although most people still wanted to preserve wilderness for utilitarian or aesthetic reasons, others were rallying for the protection of wilderness areas on the basis of their inherent value. Logging and mining operations were halted, dams were stopped, parks and wildlife preserves were established. The Wilderness Act of 1964 designated 9 million acres of land as Wilderness and gave Congress the sole power to make future designations. In 1968 the Grand Canyon Dam Project was aborted; the National Wild and Scenic Rivers System Act was passed; and the National Trails System Act was passed, establishing the Appalachian and Pacific Crest Trails and opening the door for many other long trails. The environmental movement continued through the seventies with the passage of the Endangered Species Act, the Clean Water Act, the Clean Air Act, and, in 1980, a bill that tripled the National Wilderness Preservation System by establishing 56 million acres of Wilderness in Alaska.

It seems as if many Americans have begun to embrace the values and belief systems characteristic of many Native cultures. Native values are often reflected in the environmental movement and in "radical" movements like deep ecology, where *all* things (even plants, rocks, and rivers) have intrinsic value. It seems to me that if we return to this way of thinking, return to seeing ourselves as connected to nature, sharing with it a common destiny, this would force us to recognize that environmental issues are a high priority. We would recognize that our paradigm of humans versus nature is a naive one, for if we allow ecosystems to degrade and natural processes to fall apart, we are jeopardizing our own future and neglecting part of ourselves too.

I'm not a gambling woman, but I'd feel confident wagering a month's salary that Ronald Reagan never heard about Cherokee myths or deep ecology. Reagan clearly favored industry and economic growth over the environment. Of the California redwoods he was often quoted as saying, "If you've seen one, you've seen 'em all." And so it was during his administration: wilderness issues were buried. He took the controversial step of appointing an antienvironmental extremist, James Watt, as his secretary of the interior. Reagan even went so far as to veto a wilderness bill (that would have protected more than 2 million acres in Montana) that had taken nearly twenty years of compromise in Congress to be passed in both the House and Senate. Although Reagan quickly made enemies with environmentalists, he had a lot of support from the American public in general, and although many of his supporters didn't agree with his stance on the environment, they agreed with his other policies and remained staunch supporters. At this time there was also considerable backlash from the environmental movement of the 1960s and 1970s. It took awhile for opponents of wilderness protection to get organized, but by the 1980s coalitions had formed and the antiwilderness movement established itself as a large and powerful presence in the legislative arena. Antienvironmentalists had support from big business, the logging industry, the mining industry, the motorized-use industry, the president of the United States, and James Watt, the secretary of the interior.

The concept of wilderness is a source of ongoing debate and conflict in America. Legal and ideological battles over wilderness continue today, and there are hundreds of disputes and stewardship dilemmas along the Appalachian Trail, although most of the issues no longer focus on the *preservation* of land so much as how to *manage* it. There is not much disputed land left in the U.S. It is either privately owned or neatly packaged into one of a number of government designations: national park, national forest, Wilderness, national recreation area, national monument, or wildlife refuge. So the focus shifts to management. With the explosion of the outdoor recreation industry, and with advances in outdoor gear and technology, large numbers of people now penetrate the deepest forests, the highest mountains, the most desolate deserts. We have put considerable strain on the places we love the most. With a population that continues to grow rapidly, the question remains how to keep wild places wild.

I love wild places—even when they're cold and icy—and even if I have to share my bed with a few mice. Although I consider myself part of the solution, I can't help but feel that no matter what, even in the woods, as long as I am human, I am part of the problem, simply because there are too many of us to live in harmony with our surroundings. As I walked the AT, I thought about how much energy I was saving by not taking hot showers, not using electricity, not driving a car. But the rumors of dozens of thru-hikers vying for limited spaces at the shelters, hundreds of hikers pooping in the woods, hundreds of hikers trampling stream-side vegetation to get to water sources, and dozens of hikers discarding gear along the first few miles of trail because they realized they'd brought too much, made me realize that even out here I have an impact on the environment. I am part of the land-management problem. I am part of the group of people who love wilderness so much that we are loving it to death.

I have to admit, though, that all this selfless contemplation was a short-lived phenomenon on the trail and was better addressed in retrospection because the situation at hand was this: It was cold, my feet hurt, I was tired, I didn't give a damn about trampling the stream-side vegetation, and I knew that, unless I wanted to die young, I could not increase my daily mileage with forty-five pounds on my back.

$

Georgia was tough walking. If we were ever going to make it to Maine, we would have to lighten our loads. That my pack weighed forty-five pounds and Craig's weighed sixty-five was ludicrous. After three days of walking we diverted from the trail to mail some things home: snow-shoes, Gore-Tex glove liners, sunglasses, sandals, a compass, a T-shirt, deodorant, a spatula, and a fork.

"How far y'all going?" asked a postal worker in Suches, Georgia. Craig and I looked at each other, wondering how to reply. "Maine," said Craig after a moment, "we're going to Maine."

As we headed back to the trail, we spotted the general store and stopped for a drink. A wizened old man and his wife, with curlers in her hair, greeted us. They recognized us at once as thru-hikers.

"You're crazy," he said. "Why you wantin' to start the trail so early? Don't you know it's cold out there?" He turned to me and through a toothless smile said, "I bet he's making you carry everything too."

"So, where y'all from?" he continued.

"Colorado," said Craig.

"Where's that?" he chuckled. "Southern Georgia?"

Craig and I headed to the back of the store to treat ourselves to a bottle of orange juice. I whispered to Craig, "What a cute old man."

"Honey, first of all, I don't see why you have a thing for old men, and second, men don't like to be called cute."

"You're going to be cute when you're old," I said, ignoring him. "You're going to be just like that."

"And you can't wait, can you?" Craig shook his head.

The old couple gave us directions back to the trail and wished us well. "I think it's supposed to get a bit warmer out there," she said, and waved us on.

It did get a little warmer. Daytime highs rose into the forties and fifties, and then the Arctic wave washed in, postponing spring and all hopes of staying warm. My twenty-degree sleeping bag failed in the single digits. If I wasn't walking, I was usually cold. I began to realize that those were the cards I had been dealt. There was no reshuffling the deck: no house to come back to, no hot shower at night, no guarantee of dry clothes or comfortable walking. I began to realize that this was no vacation. I laughed at the people back home who thought I was taking time off to play in the woods. This was work, hard work.

Craig was taking it well. He is one of those men who is weatherproof, especially in the cold.

"I'm freezing!" I shrieked as I leapt from my sleeping bag in the morning and immediately began doing stiff-muscled jumping jacks on my back.

"Come here, Hun. I'll be your heater," he said as he pulled me into his arms.

"How can you possibly be this warm?" I said, "I don't get it."

Despite my constant proclamations that I was going to freeze to death, I could tell he was proud of me, although he never said it. He was impressed that he never had to wait for me. In fact, I was usually the one who waited for him. He didn't have to show me how to use the stove or set up the tent or wait for me to find the right clothes. I knew I was living up to his expectations, and I could tell he thought I was turning out to be a decent partner. But he never said so; that's just his way.

Craig is playful and vulnerable in private, confident and tough in public, but he's not overly talkative in either setting. He is exceedingly honest and emanates a good-ol'-boy wholesomeness and work ethic which I've seen in few other men. Craig is one of those men whose masculinity could never be questioned. He is six feet tall, broad shouldered and big boned. He cut his soft, curly brown hair for the trail, saying that it would just get in the way if it was longer than an inch. When we started dating he told me that seven years ago, when his little brother, Marc, died, he inherited Marc's curls. Before then his hair was straight.

After his brother's death he got a tattoo that wraps around his leg from his knee to his ankle. It's a picture of a chained eagle that's breaking the chains and soaring to the heavens. It's healthy for Craig to talk about his brother, but although he says he thinks about him often, he rarely feels like talking about his death. Craig's eyes are as blue as turquoise in sunlight and I saw them moisten for the first time when he told me about Marc. The trail, he said, would give him time to work through the emotions he hadn't allowed to surface.

After four days of hiking, our feet had taken quite a beating. I had blisters on both heels and I couldn't get moleskin or band-aids to stick to my skin. Every afternoon the moleskin balled up in my sock and, instead of protecting my blisters, chafed them even more. Duct tape was the only thing that wouldn't fall off, but once it was on, it stuck to my feet for days. There was no way to clean the blisters, and I prayed they wouldn't get infected.

I wanted to feel warm again, and Craig wanted a shower. On the fifth day, only forty miles into the trail (forty-eight if you count the Approach Trail), we descended from Blood Mountain into Neel's Gap and ran into a seventy-three-year-old veteran thru-hiker named Ned. Ned must have seen a look of desperation on our faces, our bodies begging for mercy. He gave us some words of encouragement and told us that "if you want to make it to Katahdin you have to take days off every now and then." He recommended that we start today; we weren't about to disagree. He blessed us with our first dose of trail magic. Ned drove us to the Goose Creek Cabins and left us in the hands of Keith, the benevolent and generous owner.

Keith checked us into a cabin beside the creek. The cabin had a small porch with two chairs, a bedroom that wasn't much wider than the bed, and a bathroom that had a maximum capacity of one. When Craig took a shower, the entire cabin filled with steam. It was rustic and charming and we happily called it home. That afternoon, we washed our clothes in the shower and dried our tent in the room. Nighttime temperatures fell close to zero. The creek froze. In the morning, Keith filled our fuel bottle and told us he had seen the Weather Channel. He seemed confident that warm weather was on its way.

I found an entry in my journal that I had written a week after our stay at the cabins. I wrote, "Craig and I frantically pitched the tent, cooked our pasta dinner and ate inside our sleeping bags. The wind-chill was 15 degrees below zero and I shook all night. Every breath froze, creating a glaze of ice on the inner wall of the tent. That was five days ago, and I haven't been warm since."

It was a bitter, gray winter—the most brutal winter the East Coast had seen in recent history. We were frequently caught in blizzards. One afternoon, quarter-sized snowflakes began speckling our jackets, and soon the entire left side of our bodies and faces were coated with snow. It was difficult to see where the trail went; it was difficult to see, period. Fortunately we stumbled upon a shelter and collected enough dry wood for a fire. I was chilled and still shaking. I volunteered to hike to the creek for water; I had to keep moving. There was a fifty-yard descent down "steps" from the shelter to the water. I began running sprints up the steps, up and down, five times. I thought, "My God, I'm exhausted and I'm doing sprints on the AT. Which am I going to die from—hypothermia or exhaustion?" Craig was mostly silent and tended to the fire. If he was uncertain about our condition, he never let on.

We figured the tent would shield us from the wind better than the three-sided shelter, so we pitched the tent and crawled in for the rest of the day. It was too cold to move, too cold to change clothes, too cold even to wash my hands in the stream.

In the late afternoon a father-and-son team, Tom and Tommy, arrived at the shelter. They were dressed in old army fatigues and carried a two-weeks' supply of Ramen noodles, metal canteens, a camouflage tarp, and rucksacks with no hip belts. Tom watched Craig hang his backpack out of the snow. "Them hip belts are a nice feature, hunh?" Tom said.

"Yeah," said Craig in disbelief. "They really make walking more comfortable." Tom and Tommy also chain-smoked. Instead of planning mileage to get to food drops, they planned their stops according to where they could buy cigarettes. I suspected they were in for a long, hard haul.

Still, Tom was good spirited and determined. "I heard it's supposed to get warmer," he said. This was a trend I was beginning to doubt. I could picture a man in town, telling Tom how he heard the weather was changing, how spring was around the corner, and what a beautiful day it would be tomorrow. I had heard that before, from the old woman in Suches and from Keith at the cabins. I was now fairly certain that neither of them had seen an actual forecast; they just wanted to see us smile. Our first lesson in southern hospitality.

§

My problem, I think, is that I'm in love with the West, with snow-covered Rocky Mountain peaks, remote alpine lakes, and meadows that make you wonder if any person ever stepped in the same spot as you. As Thoreau put it, "Eastward I go only by force; but westward I go free." But I would try to love the East. There were parts of the Appalachians I had never seen—the mountains of New Hampshire and Maine and the Southern Appalachians in Georgia, North Carolina, and Tennessee which boast more biological diversity than any other deciduous forest in the world. Their diversity is equaled only by a similar north-south range in eastern Asia. That should be enough to keep me going when things get tough. That and my desire to follow Craig anywhere.

The Southern Appalachians have more than 100 species of trees; more than 2,000 species of fungi; and 2,500 species of shrubs, mosses, and lichens. In the high-peak region between Knoxville and Asheville, 2,500 species of vascular plants flourish and 300 species of wildflowers bloom between March and May. The number of animal species is equally impressive. The Smoky Mountains alone support 27 species of salamanders, 40 species of fish, 50 species of native mammals, and 200 bird species. Both the Appalachians and the range in Asia are diverse because of glacial movements during the Ice Age. As the glaciers approached from the north, animals moved south to escape the ice. Seeds and spores from trees and plants drifted south too. The warmth of the south was their only escape route, and the continuous ridge of the Appalachians was their path to survival. The south became a refuge, and when the glaciers retreated, the refugees stayed. Some species had no choice; the cool climate on the mountaintops was ideal, but the warm lowlands presented a barrier to migration. Species like salamanders and fungi that can't fly or can't disperse seeds or spores by the wind became stranded on the mountaintops. That is why the Southern Appalachians have so many species that are found nowhere else. We call those species *endemic* to the Southern Appalachians. Two hundred species of plants, including 40 species of wildflowers, are found nowhere else in the world.

But when I arrived at the Southern Appalachians all I saw were brown, brittle limbs and barren earth. And when the snow came, even they were covered.

The weather had gone from cold to warm to bone-chilling, and I hugged Craig every chance I got. I'm not sure if it was because

I wanted to touch someone or if I wanted to make sure he didn't leave me out there. During the first couple weeks it was clear that each of us had to rely on our own strength and perseverance and sense of humor. We could support and encourage each other, but ultimately it was up to us as individuals to shoulder our own packs.

Although our success depended on both of us being individually strong, I could tell we were becoming a team, a helluva team, without realizing it. We began to accept each other and rely on each other, and shift from two individual hikers to a pair of hikers. That may have been our first obstacle, having to accept each other no matter what. "I love your ways," Craig finally said, "all your quirks—the way you brush your teeth while you go to the bathroom, the way your hat is always lop-sided, the way you're always cold, the way you always save a sip of water in your jug for emergencies—all of it."

Craig's beard was filling in all over his neck. It was reddish and squirrelly around his throat and barely covered his cheeks. I did not find this the least bit attractive. I told him he had a squirrel's nest growing on his neck and I cringed when he kissed me with sweat-soaked mustache hairs. When his mustache dripped with little icicles of snow and snot, I drew the line. He was disappointed when I didn't let him kiss me, but it really was gross.

I don't know, maybe I got used to it, or just didn't care anymore, or maybe it was love, but eventually I didn't mind the icicles and the red neck beard. A friend of mine once asked me when we knew we were in love, and the only thing I could think to tell her was that it was when we didn't mind the other's stink and general filth.

Our clothes were all synthetic because fleece and polypropylene form a good layering system and wick moisture away from your skin, but they absorb odor like a sponge. Unlike a sponge, you can't wring out the smell; it stays in the material no matter how many times you wash it. After a week of wearing the same clothes day and night, every day, you can imagine that there were some nights when we kept the tent flaps open for ventilation. Hair started to cover my legs and the hair on my head was matted and tangled under my fleece hat. Craig walked behind me and sang his own reggae tune, "Knotty dread man, dread lock rasta, oh, knotty dread lock," until I turned around and tried to push him off the trail. He was thoroughly amused at how easily annoyed I became, so he built a repertoire of sayings and sounds that grated my nerves and drove me half crazy.

Through all the body odor and toe cheese and greasy hair and hairy legs and farts and burps and filthy clothes, we managed to see a person whom we couldn't get enough of, whom we fell into at night, and whom we loved to wake up to in the morning. I saw eyes full of hope and hands so thick and tough I'd trust them to carry me anywhere.

Still, the walking was painful, and it would take more than giddy love to keep us going. Our bodies were breaking in to trail life and ached around the clock. My quads were stiff with cold and fatigue, and the deep ache in my hip joints often prevented me from finding a comfortable sleeping position. My upper back and neck felt permanently clenched, as if they were holding the shoulder straps of the pack in a death grip. Sometimes we talked to take our minds off the pain, sometimes we focused on the sound of boots breaking snow. Sometimes we'd stop to play tick-tack-toe in a snowdrift; other times we'd stop just to kiss.

A week into the trip we approached the Low Gap shelter. That day it was too cold and rainy and foggy, and the trail too steep and muddy and rocky, to think of much besides putting one foot in front of the other. That's when walking became timeless, the trail seemed endless, and I began to question my intentions. By afternoon, the fog lifted and revealed a glistening world. Rhododendron leaves, curled and closed like umbrellas, lined the trail. Fallen logs, dissolving into the earth, were carpeted with mats of glowing moss. Beneath my boots, wet leaves, like soggy cardboard, squished as I passed by.

During those times I tried to think about nothing, afraid of the thoughts I might have if I let my mind go. I asked Craig what he thought about during the hours and hours that we spent walking in silence. "I think about Marc a lot," he said. "Sometimes I feel like he's with us."

We arrived at the shelter as the rain picked up. We proceeded with our ritual of unpacking our sleeping gear, making hot tea, and crawling in our sleeping bags.

"I can't believe how much time we spend in bed," Craig said. It was a combination of cold and exhaustion that kept us bundled like Arctic explorers. After a day of grueling uphills and a night of shivering, it wasn't difficult to wake up feeling like we needed more sleep.

"I bet this place is beautiful in the spring," said Craig, "It's too bad we're so early."

I agreed. I wanted to enjoy the details of the walk. I didn't want our trip to become a do-whatever-it-takes mad rush to Katahdin.

"It's frustrating to not be able to enjoy the scenery, to have to keep moving to stay warm, then dive in our sleeping bags. We even eat in our bags. If we could figure out a way to pee in our sleeping bags," I said, "we would." We lay there writing in our journals, writing about the thoughts that drifted in and out of our minds as we walked for eight hours each day. We wrote about our pain and the insanity of it all, and we wrote about each other. I looked at Craig, content in our home, content to have tea and animal crackers, content to sit with me and stare at wet trees. There was a peace in him; it was as if he belonged to these woods. Despite the pain, I thought, it felt good to be here. It felt good to be with him.

Craig looked over, "I know, Honey," and he closed his eyes.

After a night of freezing rain, we woke to fog so thick we could barely see twenty feet in front of us. Craig and I are usually morning people; it's rare if we sleep past seven o'clock. But on damp, frigid mornings like this, it was difficult to leave the warmth of my sleeping bag and cram my raw and bloody feet into icy boots. We pulled each other out of bed; distributed the pop-tarts, and sorted and packed the tent, sleeping bags, and Therm-a-Rests. We continued walking, day after day, making progress through Georgia.

It occurred to me then that I couldn't feel sorry for myself. I had chosen to be there; I had chosen to start in February and bring a ton of gear. Any discomfort I experienced was my own damn fault, and as hard as it was to stop cursing the wind and the snow and the frozen earth, I had to remember to be thankful that at least it was there—at least it wasn't a cold cement floor and at least the air wasn't smoggy. I had to remember that in a time when wilderness is fragmented and exists as islands in our civilized world, a corridor of wilderness, however narrow, that spans the length of our country should be cherished as a valuable component to America's wilderness system.

For me, wilderness is important for the ecological functions it sustains and for its aesthetic, spiritual, and recreational values. For Americans as a group, wilderness is important to our national psyche. It has become important for our sanity and our identity. Something about freedom and inherent danger and the endless possibilities in wild places conjures the same feelings we get when we talk about the American Dream and Independence and Freedom.

It is important to have wilderness and it is important to have long trails, even if we never go there and even if we never plan on hiking beyond our mailbox. Wallace Stegner in *Wilderness and the Geography of Hope* writes:

> [I]f I had not been able to periodically renew myself in the mountains. . .I would be very nearly bughouse. Even when I can't go into the back country, the thought of the colored deserts of southern Utah, or the reassurance that there are still stretches of prairie. . .is a positive consolation. The idea alone sustains me. But as wilderness areas are progressively exploited or "improved," as the jeeps and bulldozers of uranium prospectors scar up the deserts and the roads are cut into the alpine timberlands, and as the remnants of the unspoiled and natural world are progressively eroded, every loss is a little death in me. In us.

Stegner continues: "We simply need that wild country available to us, even if we never do more than drive to its edge and look in. For it can be a means of reassuring ourselves of our sanity as creatures, a part of the geography of hope." The American public attested to this in the 1960s during the landmark wilderness battle surrounding the issue of damming the Colorado River in the Grand Canyon. During an aggressive preservationist campaign, hundreds of thousands of Americans wrote letters to Congress urging them to save the Grand

Canyon. Certainly not all of those people had visited the Grand Canyon, and many who wrote letters would probably never see it, but the idea of a river flowing freely through the majestic canyon was critically important to their sense of the American identity. In the end, only because of tremendous public outcry, the dam was stopped.

It is part of me, this need for wild places, and I am of the breed that is not satisfied with just knowing it is there. I need more; maybe that's what brought me to the Appalachian Trail. And being able to experience it, as Benton MacKaye had known all along, made me appreciate it even more.

The cold and my curiosity kept me moving. We climbed one more hill, then another, and before we knew it we were approaching the Georgia-North Carolina border. On a chilly afternoon, seventy-five miles into our hike, we passed a small wooden sign nailed to a tree. Painted on the sign was this: GA-NC. My lips broke into a smile and we gave each other a high five. One state down, thirteen to go.

## CHAPTER TWO

# BEARS, BOARS, AND OTHER REASONS TO SLEEP IN CAGES

Three-fourths of the population of the United States live within a day's drive of the Appalachian Trail. The AT bisects Great Smoky Mountains National Park in a southwest-northeast transect, giving tourists an excellent opportunity to sample the park on a two-to-seven-day backpacking trip along the trail. It is not surprising, then, that the Smokies receive more than 9 million visits each year. One hundred thousand of those visits are to the backcountry.

There are dozens of parks, national forests, and even designated Wilderness areas along the East Coast, most of which provide easy access to the requisite scenery and a network of trails. These places, however, receive only a fraction of the visits that the Smokies do. Why, then, are the Smokies seen as the crown jewel of eastern wilderness? The allure of the Smokies certainly has something to do with the park's size. It is difficult to find large tracts of wilderness in the East, and 800 square miles by anyone's standards is a respectable chunk of public land. It is also the place where the mountains reach higher than anywhere else in the Appalachian Range. They crease and fold in every direction until distant ripples of earth meet the horizon. It is the place where fog hangs like a skirt around the base of mountains. Turkey vultures break through the fog, teeter against the wind, arc and glide as they find the updraft, and circle the broad, forested summits. Sometimes I agree with the ornithologists that these raptors soar because they're looking for food, but sometimes I think they do it because they can't resist the thrill of shiny black wings pulling into sky. I know I couldn't.

It seems to me there is something beyond vastness that draws people to the Smokies. There is a tradition of wildness. When I think of this region, I imagine the Cherokee Indians growing beans and corn, hunting deer, building sweat lodges, and having team competitions with a ball and a stick in a sport that resembled present-day lacrosse.

My great-grandmother was a Cherokee. I didn't know this until a year ago when we discovered that my great-grandfather, a white man, had been buried on the reservation. I think of my great-grandmother in these mountains, living in the traditional drafty cabin with no windows, just an open door. I picture her inside the cabin, building a fire to take the chill out of a damp November night, and I wonder how she spent her days and what she thought of this great land.

Of all the things we know about the Cherokees, it is Native medicine that intrigues me the most. I think about a shaman combing the forest for the right herbal cure, mixing plants in odd combinations, calling upon the plant spirits to guide him, trying to find the right remedy. I picture a shaman singing the sacred song as he rubs tobacco juice on a snakebite.

Every illness was cured with a sacred song and a ritualistic application of the botanical cure. One deadly ailment that routinely plagued the tribe was called the Great Chill, which in today's medical terminology would be called fever and ague. The cure involved mixing the pulp of cherry tree bark with water. While the sick person faced the sunrise, the shaman sang the first verse of the sacred song, took a mouthful of the mixture, and spewed it over the sick person. They repeated the singing and spitting (or, as the Cherokees called it, blowing—although I'm not exactly sure how you'd *blow* a mouthful of cherry tree pulp) four times. The song went like this:

> Listen! O now you have drawn near to hearken, O Little Whirlwind, O ada'wehi, in the leafy shelter of the lower mountain, there you repose. O ada'wehi, you can never fail in anything. Ha! Now rise up. A very small portion [of the disease] remains. You have come to sweep it away into the swamp on the upland. You have laid down your paths near the swamp. It is ordained that you shall scatter it as in play, so that it shall utterly disappear. By you it must be scattered. So shall there be relief.

Their sacred herbal remedies and songs kept various illnesses in check, but all the plant spirits and animal gods they could call on were no match for the diseases the white man brought. Between 1794 and 1819 the U.S. government pressed the Cherokees into making twenty-four separate land cessions, yielding half of their original 40,000-square-mile domain. About 6,000 Cherokees fled the East in search of a new home in the West. In the 1830s Andrew Jackson intensified the campaign to remove Indians from the Southeast and forced the Cherokees to exchange their land for $5 million and a reservation in Oklahoma. U.S. soldiers made it clear that the deal was nonnegotiable. In 1835, 14,000 Cherokees were forced to walk 800 miles to their new reservation. A quarter of the Cherokees died along the way, a route that became known as the Trail of Tears. As the last Cherokees were herded to their desolate replacement homeland in Oklahoma, the singing that once echoed through the valleys of the Smokies had ceased. About this time, another song also was silenced. It was the song of the red wolf.

Wolves and Indians were inextricably linked in the minds of the settlers. Both were symbols of wilderness, both were feared, and both were targets of the settlers' effort to conquer and subdue all that was not civilized. They succeeded: By the turn of the century, the Cherokee Nation in the Southern Appalachians had been reduced to pockets of impoverished populations, and the red wolf had been successfully exterminated. A most respected hunter, the red wolf, which once roamed from Pennsylvania to Florida and as far west as central Oklahoma, had been reduced to less than 100 individuals that had managed to survive in isolated areas in Louisiana and Texas.

In the 1960s scientists from the U.S. Fish and Wildlife Service (USFWS) discovered that predator-control projects had successfully exterminated the red wolf from most of its range. They determined that the red wolf population would likely go extinct if left alone, so between 1973 and 1980 they captured all the remaining wild wolves. After biologists conducted breeding experiments with the captured animals, they discovered that only fourteen individuals were pure wolves. The wolf population had declined so significantly that coyotes had moved into the area. Apparently, wolves had trouble finding mates so they bred with coyotes. Most of the "wolves" were really coyote-wolf hybrids. A captive breeding program was immediately initiated to increase the number of true wolves. Those fourteen individuals not only became the foundation for the entire wolf reintroduction program; they are the ancestors of every red wolf alive today.

According to Cherokee lore, Kana'ti and his wife, Selu, lived at the edge of a clearing beside a forest. Selu was responsible for agriculture and Kana'ti, with the help of his hunting companion, the wolf, was responsible for the hunt. Hunting was a simple task because all the animals lived in a cave. The hunter called an animal out and shot it with a bow and arrow. The hunter never missed. Agriculture was equally effortless; growing crops was a matter of magic and ritual, not labor. In this way, hunting and agriculture were balanced, man and woman were equal, and humans and wolves were partners.

Because the wolf is the greatest hunter on earth, it is both wolf and man who initiate the history of the world as we know it today. The story continues as Kana'ti and Selu have a son who befriends the Wild Boy, a devious child of the river. The two boys are reckless. They release all the animals from the cave and they kill Selu for practicing magic. From then on, hunting and agriculture become challenging and unpredictable. Kana'ti retreats to the edge of the world and calls on the Wolf People to kill the Wild Boys. The Wolf People try to kill them, but the boys are prepared and drive them off. According to the Cherokees, it is the wolves who then teach man how to hunt game that can now flee him.

The passage of the Endangered Species Act in 1973 marked a change in the way American people think about wildlife by acknowledging that endangered species are of aesthetic, ecological, educational, historical, recreational, and scientific value to the nation and its people. We formally acknowledged that these animals are important—maybe, if it's not too late, they can teach *us* something too.

The song of the red wolf hadn't been heard in the Smokies for 100 years. It hadn't been heard until 1991 when USFWS, charged under the Endangered Species Act with the task of preventing the red wolf's total disappearance, attempted to bring the wolves back.

Gary Henry was appointed the coordinator for the red wolf reintroduction program for the U.S. Fish and Wildlife Service in March
1991. He has a booming voice and a home-grown, Garth Brooks sort
of friendliness about him. Although he's told the story hundreds of
times, his eyes light up when he recalls interacting with the reintroduced wolves.

In 1987, Warren Parker, who preceded Henry as red wolf coordinator, and his field team reintroduced the red wolf into the Alligator
River National Wildlife Refuge (ARNWR) in northeastern North
Carolina. The wolves seemed to flourish there. Gentle lowlands provided the wolves with a large prey base. Their territory was easy to
defend since there were no coyotes to contend with, and the wolves
were not tempted by large cattle operations or sprawling subdivisions.
Encouraged by the success in northeastern North Carolina, Parker's
team decided to reintroduce the wolves in a more challenging site, but
one that, if successful, would return the wolf to one of America's most
treasured places—the Great Smoky Mountains.

In November 1991, under Henry's direction, the Smokies got a bit
of their wildness back when one pair of wolves with two pups were fit-
ted with radio collars and released in Cades Cove. This was an exper-
iment, a test to see if a larger reintroduction would work. Biologists
Chris Lucash and Barron Crawford tracked the wolves' movements
and monitored their interactions with coyotes, livestock, and humans.
They collected wolf scat and analyzed its contents, finding that the
wolves ate deer, raccoon, and rabbit. The field team was interested in
determining if the wolves would be able to find prey, if they would
leave the park and wander into surrounding urban areas, if they would
either fight with or breed with coyotes, and if they would attack cattle
in the nearby Cades Cove cattle operation. After ten months, the
experimental reintroduction was judged successful in demonstrating
the possibility of reestablishing red wolves in the Southern
Appalachians. In 1992 two families totaling four adults and eight pups
were released into the wild, this time, Henry hoped, for good.

For hundreds of years before the Europeans extirpated Cherokees
and wolves, the Smoky Mountain ecosystem was intact, complete with

its top predator. Today, top predators—the grizzly bear, the mountain lion, the wolf—are missing from even the largest, most protected places. Without these animals, the ecosystem gets a little off-kilter, a little out of balance, a little less wild. Interestingly, it is now often the wildness of a place that draws people to it.

In the summer of 1999 I felt privileged to see two red wolves at the Western North Carolina Nature Center in Asheville. What impressed me most about these animals was their gait—swift, smooth, steady, as if they were floating over the ground. The pair moved with grace; their bushy, black-tipped tails floated behind them as they ran. When their eyes met mine I knew I was in the presence of wildness. What is conveyed in those eyes is something that may very well be present only in top predators. It is a look of confidence, of certainty, a look that commands respect. It might be a look we are unaccustomed to seeing because we are unaccustomed to having an animal look at us and see its dinner. To me, the eyes said, "I can kill you, easily, if I have to." I suppose the eyes reflect the fearlessness that comes with that knowledge.

§

As I walked along the Appalachian Trail, I longed to make contact with that wildness. Apparently, a lot of other people had heard about the wolves too, for as we approached the Smokies, our solitary walk gradually became a social experience. Warm days roused hikers from their groggy winter thoughts and lured them into the woods. The thought of witnessing the arrival of spring, and seeing an end to this endless winter, was reason enough to stir any sun-loving person from hibernation. And so a motley assortment of eclectic and eccentric sojourners flocked to the trail.

Every hiker brought a unique story to the trail, but they all had the same questions. I often thought about making a card to hand out to other hikers: I started February 14 at Springer Mountain in Georgia, I'm going all the way, I'm from Virginia/Pennsylvania, and my trail name is Raindrop. I was not annoyed by the questions; I was just learning how to share the trail. About five times a day, I recited my responses with enough enthusiasm to convince even the most skeptical inquirer. After walking in silence for hours, or days, even trivial talk defined a nice evening, and most encounters were welcome.

We spent roughly half the nights on the trail in our tent; the other half we spent in shelters that have been built every eight to twelve miles along the trail. We opted for shelters when they coincided with our mileage for the day. If the weather looked threatening, we increased or decreased our mileage to make sure that we spent a rainy or snowy night with a roof over our heads. Shelters made life at camp considerably easier since they offered ample room to organize and arrange our belongings, and they provided a level spot on which to sleep and cook. We found them especially useful for stringing clothes-lines to dry clothes and equipment.

Many hikers flocked to shelters not only for convenience but for companionship. As Craig and I approached one, we always wondered what quirky personality we would get to know. One evening in North Carolina, eighty miles south of the Smokies, we approached the Standing Indian shelter and saw the ubiquitous food bags hanging from the roof.

"Someone's in there," I whispered.

We had had a long day—twenty miles—and arrived at the shelter as darkness was beginning to transform the clear afternoon into a hazy evening. I entered the shelter and rested my pack on the wood floor. A lean woman with long brown hair sat at the edge of the shelter, whittling a stick. Her name was Michelle, she said, and she had been roaming the world for more than twenty years. She had gotten word when she was in Nepal—or was it Greece or Turkey?—that her mother had become ill, so she returned to America and somehow found herself wandering along the Appalachian Trail. She didn't know how far she intended to go.

As Craig and I settled in, she disappeared. A while later we heard the most beautiful music floating through the woods. It was neither bird song nor radio, and we couldn't place it until Michelle returned with a wooden flute. In the evening, she said, she plays for the Indian spirits on the mountain. The Cherokees call the mountain *yuhwi-tsu-lenuh-i*. It is a sacred place because a mysterious being was said to have been seen standing on the mountain. Maybe that's who she played for.

Michelle built a campfire and smoked Captain Black tobacco in a corncob pipe. I began to feel that my camping skills, which consisted of things like lighting a stove and pitching a tent, paled in comparison to someone who whittled wooden flutes and played to Indian spirits. We sat around the fire, listening to the resonating knocks of woodpeckers and the echoing hoots of owls. "I can feel the spirits here," she said, closing her eyes and raising her arms, palms up. "Can you feel them? They're so strong." I sort of nodded yes, afraid to say I couldn't.

We hiked at a good pace for a few days and for the first time I really felt that I was in a rhythm. Craig and I almost always hiked together, rarely getting more than fifty yards apart. The first two weeks of the trip we traveled about two miles per hour, but now, into our third week, our pace was up to three. After leaving Michelle and the spirits, we didn't see another person for three days, until we passed through the small community of Wesser.

Just outside Wesser (which consists of a whitewater slalom course, an outfitter that sells Ben & Jerry's, and a restaurant with a burger buffet that Craig insisted we hike thirteen miles by noon to get to), we met a man who was maintaining a section of trail. He warned us that a snowstorm was on its way and suggested we find a place called the Fontana Motel, just two days ahead and a couple miles off the trail. We consulted our guidebook and set out to find shelter.

We arrived in the town of Fontana Dam, North Carolina, just as the temperature began to plummet. Jeff and Nancy Hoch own the six-room Fontana Motel. Craig and I spent the first two days of March at the motel, waiting for a snowstorm to pass so we could begin the seventy-mile stretch through the Great Smoky Mountains. The *Farmer's Almanac* called for forty inches of snow, and people there seemed to respect that book as much as they did the Bible. So, we hunkered down with two other stranded hikers, EZDUZIT and Seldom Seen, and shared stories about small-town living and our recent adventures on the trail.

"This is a town where men are men," exclaimed Jeff in a thick southern drawl. "You look at someone wrong and they'll beat you to the ground. But come Sunday mornin'—lumberjacks, farmers, forest rescue squads—they are on their knees weepin' and hollerin' to the Lord."

Nancy interrupted. "The collection basket totals over $1,000 every single Sunday," she said. "That's from a congregation of seventy-three. The following Wednesday, every penny goes to the family who needs it the most."

Jeff continued, "People's lives are guided by three things: high morals, strong families, and the church, in whichever order suits you best."

Craig moved close to me and whispered, "I hope you're taking notes." EZDUZIT looked like he was in his late forties, but I heard that he was much older. He had a curt Brooklyn accent and abrupt movements, all of which seemed strikingly out of place in the slow pace of the South. "I been doin' sections of dis trail for years," he said. "I got one piece left, from here to Harpers Ferry." As his trail name suggested, he took it easy. Long days and a fast pace were out of the question. He was a seasoned hiker, even if he was from New York City, and I hoped he would make it.

Seldom Seen spoke with a deliberateness that is common in much of the South. Never short of a story, he vied for air time with Jeff. Seldom, from Tennessee, was an outdoors-lover by nature. At twenty-one, he had made up his mind about many things. One was the Appalachian Trail. Last year he hiked from Georgia to Pennsylvania, but he twisted his ankle in the Pennsylvania rock fields and had to abandon his trip. He returned to the trail in February to start over and do the whole thing. Seldom shared many stories with us at the motel. It was actually in Jeff's living room, which served as the motel office and lounge, that Seldom Seen told us how he wanted to die. "I've given this a lot of thought," he said, "and I think the best way to go would be to get eaten by a bear, by a griz up in Montana. I can see myself as an old man. I'd just walk around the mountains and run into one, and it'd just git me."

Craig and I talked about the past week on the trail, how we had slept on the brittle grasses of Siler's Bald. We dragged our sleeping bags to the top of the grassy summit and watched a fiery pink sunset ignite the mountains in every direction. We snuggled into our bags as the last molten drop of sun slipped behind the horizon. That was our first experience on a treeless peak below treeline. Grassy balds (as opposed to heath balds, which are dominated by rhododendrons) typically occur at high elevations (5,200-5,800 feet). People like the balds not only for the fabulous views they provide in an otherwise forested range, but because they harbor an exceptionally high number of plant species, including many rare plants. Many people also appreciate balds for their historic value; they view them as remnants of Native American culture. Jeff told us that the formation of balds is still a mystery. "They don't know if it was the weather, or Indians, or aliens that cleared them balds," he said.

An old Cherokee legend offers one explanation. According to the myth, children often spent their afternoons playing on the mountaintops. One day, when the children were called in for dinner, one boy was missing. The villagers searched for the boy but couldn't find any clues to his disappearance. A couple days later another boy didn't return from the mountaintop. Hunters and trackers from the village searched the mountains and found a set of large footprints that led to a cave. Here they found some hair and other signs of a struggle. The villagers resolved that the Little People—the mischievous, leprechaun-like spirits of the mountains—were eating the children, so they called upon the Great One for help. The Great One told the people to stay inside the next morning and he would take care of it. The next morning the villagers witnessed a violent and terrible thunderstorm. Lightning struck the mountaintop and set it aflame. It looked as though the entire mountain would burn, but the Great One sent rain to put out the fire after the top of the mountain was burnt. When the storm cleared, the people climbed to the cave and found the remains of the monster. Ever again, if a monster came to the mountains to eat children, the Great One would send a storm to burn the mountaintops to kill the monsters and give the children a lookout so they could see if a monster was approaching. Today we refer to those cleared mountaintops as balds.

Most scientists I talked to about the formation of balds had effectively ruled out precautions for children-eating monsters. They had also ruled out aliens, although something told me Jeff still maintained it as a possibility. The most widely held theory explains that balds were created from a combination of grazing by the elk and woodland bison that once inhabited the Southern Appalachians, by Native Americans and early European settlers who cleared land for agriculture and grazing pastures, and by past climate patterns that were conducive to fire at high elevations. Scientists who study grassy balds agree that there is not one theory that can answer all the questions. It seems likely we may never know for sure how balds were created, but the more pressing question today is not how they formed but what we should do with them.

The problem is that balds are succeeding to forest and shrub communities. Whatever forces created them are no longer present. If left untouched, it wouldn't take more than twenty years before balds would begin to turn into forests. Dr. Peter White, professor of biology at the University of North Carolina, says that it would take less than 100 years for Gregory Bald and Andrews Bald to be completely taken over by woody plants. Land managers are left with a big question: If balds were not really "natural" to begin with, should they be preserved? Would we essentially be preserving a human-caused disturbance, like a clearcut or a cornfield? Officials in the Great Smokies know that people like balds, however, so they have been actively managing Gregory Bald and Andrews Bald since the late 1980s. Rangers cut down woody plants that try to grow on the balds, they use herbicides on woody stumps to keep new shoots from growing, and they seed open areas with grasses. I enjoy the balds, but I couldn't help but wonder if, by preserving a piece of nature that is trying to change, we are trying to preserve an artifact. Are we putting nature in a museum, preserving balds the way we would preserve a suit of armor from medieval times? Should park officials stunt evolution so tourists can have a nice view? Shouldn't we be preserving ecological processes? There are no easy answers. I envy the majority of park visitors who don't know or care that balds today couldn't exist without people maintaining them. I envy people who are content believing that balds were created by aliens.

Jeff shuttled his four thru-hiking guests to the post office and the store to get food and supplies, and Craig and I organized ourselves for most of the day. For lunch, Jeff's daughter drove us all down the road to Tooties to get their acclaimed Master Burger, a half-pound of ground beef dripping with cheese and ketchup, covered in all the fixin's and topped with chili. Craig had two. That evening we gathered in Jeff's living room and talked about the people in his town. "If these folks have one apple left on their tree," he said, "they will give it to you even if they ain't never seen you before and ain't never going to see you again. But if they got 100 apples and they catch you tryin' to take one without askin', they will shoot you dead."

We hikers called it an early evening and returned to our rooms to plot the next few days through the Smokies. The Great Smoky Mountains are often described as the most rugged, most wild tract in the Southeast. We knew that the next seventy miles would be one of the most memorable weeks of the trip. The next morning, Craig and I entered the park with a week's supply of food and our warmest gear. We left foodless and freezing, but carried with us a rich collection of memories.

We were greeted with a 3,000-foot ascent up a steep, twisting trail. After a few miles, we caught up with Seldom Seen, crawling under a felled tree.

"It's slow walking today," he said, pulling himself to his feet.

"Yeah," said Craig, "it doesn't help having sixty pounds on my back."

"The maintenance crews won't clear the trail for another week," said Seldom. We meandered forty yards off the trail to get around tangled brush and downed trees.

"Have y'all smelled any bears yet?" Seldom asked.

"No," we replied, wondering what bears smell like.

Seldom informed us that their scent is a combination of wet dog and skunk. It occurred to me that we smelled like that too, but Seldom seemed serious so I didn't mention it. "If you smell one, you'll probably see it within a minute." Seldom told us about his numerous encounters with bears. "They're drawn to me," he said, then added something about his spirit being connected, but at that point I was no longer listening. I was planning what I would do if a black bear suddenly appeared ahead of me on the trail. The three of us, pausing every few minutes to sniff the air, slowly negotiated our way to Mollies Ridge shelter.

A shelter in the distance was always a welcome sight, but the refuges in the Smokies were a bit unnerving. The shelters are built of stone instead of the usual wood. They are situated on ridges windy enough to warrant stone walls. I felt like the third little pig who was smart enough to build a strong house to withstand the wolf's mighty blows. But these stone walls were erected not to withstand gusty winds, but bears. The fourth side, instead of remaining open, is a steel fence with a tiny, narrow door—too narrow to allow a bear comfortable entrance. Shelter use is mandatory, and park rules require all food and gear be kept inside the fence with the door bolted at all times. The three of us lay awake that night secretly wishing that a bear would visit. I figured we had a pretty good chance of seeing one since Seldom Seen felt so deeply connected to the spirit of the bears. It was a quiet night, though—no visitors.

Fifty years ago it may have been hard to believe that by the year 2000 there would be around 6,000 black bears in the Southern Appalachians and 1,700 black bears in the park. Thousands of bears were killed in the 1700s and 1800s, and those that weren't picked off by rifles died of starvation as settlers cleared nearly all of the old-growth forests. Without oak and chestnut trees there were no nuts, which meant there was little food for the bears. As the human population in the Southern Appalachians exploded in the twentieth century, bears retreated farther into patches of habitat and became isolated from bears who occupied other patches. Their food sources dwindled with their habitat, and people called the bears pests when they raided garbage dumps in urban areas.

The decline in bear numbers meant that it was novel to see one. In the 1970s, visitors ranked seeing a bear as the primary reason for visiting the Smokies. Land managers, encouraged by a new era of environmental protection, responded to the declining bear population by creating sanctuaries for the bears and making sure that oak forests were allowed to mature. The population rebounded, and it looks like the bears are here to stay. Dr. John Peine, former senior scientist for Great Smoky Mountains National Park, explains that when bear cub numbers are moderate and the mast, or acorn, crop is plentiful, there are virtually no problems. However, climate change, drought, gypsy moths, or a late frost can devastate the mast crop, which in turn causes bears to go hungry. "The conflict arises," Peine explains, "when bears wander onto private lands." Bears are smart animals; they teach each other how to get food. When wildlife officials find a bear that has learned how to get food from humans, they often shoot the bear before it can transfer the behavior to other bears. In 1997 there were a lot of young bears and a low mast crop, so bears came into boundary areas like Gatlinburg where they raided garbage cans and dumpsters. State officials reported that 440 bears were killed that year in Tennessee.

Most management efforts are directed at separating bears from people. The park has since worked with surrounding towns like Gatlinburg to install bear-proof garbage cans, and as Craig and I discovered in our fenced-in shelters, the park is determined to separate bears from hikers as well. Park officials recently installed pulley systems at shelters and campgrounds to help backcountry users store food safely. I once believed that the separation precautions were necessary for human safety, but I've learned that these measures are for the bears' safety as much as they are for ours.

As Craig and I walked along the trail, I began to notice a trend of exclusion and separation. We were here to absorb the wildness of the place, yet we would somehow degrade it if we got too close. I wasn't thinking about ripping the cages from the shelters, or for that matter tearing down the shelters altogether, but it was interesting to inventory the restrictions land managers put on us in order to uphold a certain degree of natural integrity in the park. Craig and I also discovered that, in addition to separating humans from bears, scientists and land managers had been separating animal species from plant species, and the zoolike resemblance of their efforts was a bit uncanny.

As we stumbled through the park, over tangles of roots and jagged rocks, we came upon a fenced-in area of, well, nothing that seemed worthy of fencing. Was some large mammal burrowed away and we just couldn't see it? We stood for a while but observed nothing but plants. I learned later that those fences were erected to protect plants from wild boars. Inside the little cages were the only places where park managers could be certain that native plants were safe.

In the 1930s, hunting clubs released the European wild boar into the Southern Appalachians, hoping it would provide the excitement of the sport they loved in their homeland. The boar did well in southern Appalachia. In fact, it did a little too well. It had no natural predators and it feasted on the abundant roots, leaves, and shoots of lush Appalachian vegetation. It also developed an appetite for animals like snakes, snails, frogs, voles, shrews, and the eggs and young of ground-nesting birds.

Since boars can start breeding when they're seven or eight months old, and since they tend to have litters of four or five, it wasn't long before biologists felt the boar's presence. Because 71 percent of their diet consists of things they have to dig up, the boars essentially rototill the forest floor. Their rooting destroys huge amounts of vegetation, and, because there are so many rare plants in the Smokies, this behavior poses a serious problem. It also poses a problem for animals like voles, shrews, the endemic red-cheeked salamander, and the Jones middle-tooth snail, whose habitat is essentially destroyed when a pack of boars travels through the area. The boars compete for food with native animals like black bears, wild turkeys, deer, squirrels, and chipmunks. In the 1970s, scientists set out to document the impact of the boars on native plants, so they constructed exclosures throughout the park. After a few years, the effects were obvious; the boars had devastated the unprotected areas.

There are currently 500-800 boars in the Smokies. A more precise estimate is difficult to come by since boars are the most prolific large mammal in North America. Eradication efforts in the park commenced in the 1960s but were met with protest when the park recruited hunters from out of state to kill the boars. The European sport of boar hunting had woven itself into the culture of southern Appalachia, and the people, it appeared, would have a hard time letting it go. The park also met opposition from groups who felt that hunting boars to extinction was unethical and inhumane. Realizing the need for compromise, the park agreed to capture boars from the park and move them to hunting preserves where the public could enjoy killing them at their leisure. "The Park agreed to export them in exchange for political acceptance of their control inside the Park," writes Dr. Peine. When I spoke with Dr. Peine about the management of the boars, he agreed that the Park Service has it under control. He admits, however, that it is a big financial responsibility over the long haul, since total eradication is not feasible. Park ranger Kim DeLozier told me that 50 percent of the hog population must be removed from the park each year to keep the population in check. Because hogs reproduce quickly, their populations can rebound over a very short period of time. Essentially the park will have to continue trapping and shooting them forever.

§

I expected to be awakened by the rattle of the metal door, by a snout—bear or boar, it didn't matter, I found them equally menacing—shoved through the chain links, sniffing for peanut butter and granola. Instead, I woke to a quiet, light snow. I left the cage and made my way to the designated toilet area, about fifty yards from the shelter on the slope opposite the water source. I stepped into the minefield. Toilet paper escaped from cat holes and flapped in the wind. The shelter came with a hole digger, but it was evident that few people dug a hole six inches deep. I stepped carefully. As I claimed my own patch of ground and squatted, I was struck with a revelation: We humans were being caged and herded through the Smokies.

It seemed like a good plan: move humans along a three-foot-wide path, make them all sleep together and relieve themselves in the same place, confine litter to fire pits, and in general keep them from messing up the rest of the park. Not a bad idea at all. Campers often don't realize the extent of their impact. They collect deadwood for a camp-fire, swiping the earth's natural fertilizer and habitat for insects and mammals. They burn all the wood in the vicinity for a night of fire and smoke, for browned marshmallows, for ambience. Once campers use all the deadwood they can find, they often collect live wood, dismember-ing trees and tearing apart their limbs. I have seen hikers leave candy wrappers and soup cans at campsites, and burn used band-aids and plastic packaging in fire pits.

I returned to the shelter and reported the filthy condition of the toilet area.

"Maybe we should set aside tracts of land that are totally off-limits to humans," said Seldom Seen.

"Actually," I said, "that might not be a bad idea." A few years ago I had seen plans developed by conservationists that would link most of Idaho to the Yellowstone area to the east, and to the Great Basin to the west. A few radical scientists proposed a core area that was essentially off-limits to visitors and a surrounding buffer zone that was protected but open to certain human uses.

"Wasn't there talk of something like that in Maine too?" Craig asked.

"Yeah," I answered, wondering if we could ever get Congress to support such a preserve.

"As it is now, even those of us who love these places aren't doing the land any good by hiking through it. Just look at those trenches we walked through yesterday," said Seldom, referring to the trail that had been worn three feet deep by millions of hiker's boots and thousands of rainy afternoons. "We are loving the wildlands to death," he said.

Seldom was right, and once again I couldn't help but feel like part of the problem. And the Appalachian Trail is only one example of overuse in the Smokies. The AT runs for 70 miles through the park but there are nearly 900 miles of trails, many of which are located in low areas where the soils are wet and erode easily. A 1998 study of trails in the park determined that 33 percent of water bars and 43 percent of drainage dips (structures that prevent water from eroding trails) were ineffective. Managers would need more than $1.5 million for repairs, but with insufficient funds available for trail reconstruction, few trails can be improved to accommodate the number of people who use them.

If Congress isn't willing to allocate money for trail maintenance, maybe the visitors should be charged. That was the rationale behind the Fee-Demonstration Program. Attached as a rider to the Interior appropriations bill in 1996, Fee-Demo authorized four agencies (National Park Service, U.S. Forest Service, Bureau of Land Management, Fish and Wildlife Service) to charge visitors who use public lands. The Forest Service claimed that the Fee-Demo program was designed to test the effectiveness of collecting fees to help maintain federal recreation facilities and enhance visitor services. Opponents of Fee-Demo fear that it's the beginning of the corporate takeover of nature, designed to turn nature into a highly developed, intensively motorized recreation product. In 2002, Congress will decide if the fee system will be permanent.

My first response to Fee-Demo was that it wasn't really a big deal. I could accept paying for my recreational experience if the money supported the otherwise poorly funded park or forest. My attitude changed after I had the chance to talk with Scott Silver, director of Wild Wilderness, a user group that supports undeveloped recreation. After Silver explained the genesis of the Fee-Demo program, I found good reason to be alarmed.

It is no secret that our land-management agencies are severely underfunded. Between 1983 and 1993, the number of people visiting national parks increased 30 percent, but the National Park Service budget stayed the same throughout the eighties. According to the General Accounting Office (GAO), the National Park Service needs $5.6 billion to maintain trails and basic facilities. The Forest Service's recreation budget and work force has been cut by a third since 1993; the agency presently needs nearly $1 billion for repairs and maintenance.

Silver explained that Senator Don Young (R-Alaska), backed by a powerful coalition of recreation and motorized-industry leaders, led an ambitious campaign to further cut funding to federal agencies. "They want to make agencies dependent on corporate sponsorship," said Silver. He informed me that the American Recreation Coalition

(ARC) formed a partnership with the Forest Service to develop, implement, and monitor Fee-Demo. This sounded somewhat legitimate until I inquired about the members of the ARC. Included among the 110 members are the Walt Disney Company; American Petroleum Institute; National Rifle Association; Kampground Owners Association (KOA); Chevron; Exxon; motorized-user groups; sports-equipment manufacturers; and motorboat, jet-ski, motorcycle, and RV organizations and manufacturers. Not one hiking or conservation group is represented.

What strikes me as inherently wrong about this setup is that the coalition views nature as a product and the public as a customer. I personally don't want to be a customer of nature, of the Great Smoky Mountains, of the Appalachian Trail. To me, wilderness ought to be the one thing that U.S. citizens should always have and that corporations should never be allowed to control or buy.

What I hadn't realized was that recreation has long since surpassed logging and mining as the major money-generator on public land. Jim Lyons, the undersecretary of agriculture, stated that by 2000, recreation will amount to $97.8 billion of the $130.7 billion generated by activities in national forests. The coalition is well aware of these numbers, so the profit-seeking recreation industry, conservative Congressmen, and cash-strapped land managers are out to turn nature into a commodity. Vicky Hoover at the Sierra Club national headquarters considers Fee-Demo a serious problem. "Fee-Demo is being deliberately used as a test program to see if people are prepared to purchase recreational products on public lands, to accustom people to viewing the provision of recreational 'services' as a commercial commodity," she says.

Silver explained how the partnership works: ARC helps foot the bill to implement the Fee-Demo program, and in return they get inside information about how the program is going and what the customers want and are willing to pay for. In this way, they get a little closer to "owning" public land. Vicky Hoover believes that ARC's goal is to expand the market for the recreational products, toys, and machines that members of the coalition sell or hope to sell in the future. It is the coalition that is responsible for evaluating Fee-Demo and informing Congress how much the public supports it. The corporations essentially want to provide wilderness, like a theme-park attraction, to a paying public.

Silver and Hoover agree that the next step will be the development of commercial resorts in wild places that are potential candidates for Wilderness designation. They referred me to a statement by the Army Corps of Engineers which declared that "the intent of the program is to encourage private development of public recreational facilities such as marinas, hotel/motel/restaurant complexes, conference centers, RV camping areas, golf courses, theme parks, and entertainment areas with shops, etc." Once a wild place is converted to a resort, it becomes nearly impossible to designate it as federally protected Wilderness.

Many wilderness supporters not only object to the privatization of our public lands for obvious ethical reasons, but we also feel that Americans already support the agencies with our taxes. It's like being asked to pay extra for public education, highways, and police and fire protection. "If we applied this pay-to-use concept in all aspects of our lives," Silver says, "only the very rich would be able to travel, get an education, have police protection, and be able to take a walk in the woods." The Sierra Club objects to the pay-to-play ethic and the privatization of public lands, but it is also concerned that because the ARC has an inherent interest in motorized use, ARC will promote these environmentally degrading activities on public lands.

The GAO, the investigatory arm of Congress, points to another problem with Fee-Demo. The office found that popular parks generate so much money they are forced to come up with innovative projects on which to spend the money, while less popular parks can't generate enough revenue to cover their costs. Fee-Demo rewards use and penalizes conservation and resource protection.

Great Smoky Mountains National Park is unique because, by law, there is no entrance fee. This was agreed upon in a unique compromise when the park was established. In an effort to help local economies, the park agreed to waive the entrance fee and keep the road through the park open year-round. Of course, the park came up with other ways to charge visitors: there are fees for campgrounds, the movie at the visitor center, and hayrides at Cades Cove. According to Bob Wightman, staff park ranger, special legislation in 1998 authorized the park to keep 100 percent of the collected fees while other parks keep only 80 percent (based on the fact that the Smokies can't charge an entrance fee). The Smokies anticipates collecting $1.3 million dollars from this program in 1999. I imagine they will be encouraged by these figures, and if Fee-Demo is allowed to continue they will find ways to charge fees in other areas and let private corporations help foot the bill that Congress refuses to acknowledge.

I can't imagine a trip to the Smokies where I'd pay a visitation fee, pay for a backcountry permit, walk past concessionaires, past the Great Smokies Theme Park, follow trail signs with corporate logos past the Great Smokies Golf Course to a grassy bald where a sign informs me that the bald was "improved" by the Canon corporation to more easily capture that Kodak moment. For me, the Smokies would lose the wildness that attracted me to it in the first place. The solution is to pressure Congress to give public lands the funding that will allow them to preserve and maintain the resource. I fear what will happen if they don't.

§

Although the trail through the west side of the park was icy and mostly uphill, the smell of the spruce-fir forests reminded me of the subalpine retreats in Colorado I had fallen in love with. Here, I got to fall in love all over again. We climbed higher each day, approaching Clingman's Dome at 6,643 feet, the highest point on the trail. For thirty-four continuous miles, the trail twists and turns above 5,000 feet. At this altitude, pine forests cling to steep valley walls and squeak into rock crevices. The narrow trail hovers on the edges of cliffs and dips into the woods. We stopped for lunch and bathed in sunshine on a granite slab. This was why we were out here, for these sweet moments: for the sun in my tangled hair, for the velvet pleated mountainsides, for this feeling of strong bodies, adventure, and freedom. Craig draped his arm around my shoulder. We were at home.

Craig and I joined Seldom Seen at Clingman's Dome. "Last year the observation tower was packed and the road was lined with cars," said Seldom. "Tourists everywhere were taking pictures and trying to find the best views." This year, the road to the Dome was covered in ice and we had the place to ourselves.

The eastern half of the park was nothing short of spectacular. We left the Dome and sniffed for bears. Still no sign. We also looked for red wolves, which now, four years after the two families were released, were estimated to include only a dozen individuals. During the past four years, Chris Lucash and Barron Crawford had worked tirelessly, monitoring, studying, and managing the wolves.

Cades Cove had been chosen as the main release site in the Smokies. Park managers maintain Cades Cove as a pastoral landscape, complete with 500 head of beef cattle that maintain the meadows in the park. The cattle belong to the Caughron family, who lease 900 acres of parkland for a minimal fee. Cades Cove was selected as the primary release site because it's one of very few low-elevation sites in the Smokies, and it has the best prey base in the park. Cades Cove was chosen also because it was a good place to study wolf behavior in the presence of human influence. "We chose the release site for a variety of reasons," explained Gary Henry. "There are people, livestock, and coyotes in the cove, and we wanted to look at interactions with all those things."

One obstacle the field team was able to hurdle successfully was the issue of public support. They spent much of their time conducting outreach programs all over Tennessee and North Carolina. They realized that even if the wolves thrived in the Smokies, the project would collapse if the public wasn't willing to welcome the wolves back home.

In addition to general wolf education, project personnel wanted the public to understand a few critical things about the program. Their first task was to persuade people that red wolves don't pose a threat to humans. Red wolves eat small to medium mammals such as rabbits, raccoons, rodents, and deer. They typically don't hunt in packs, because it takes only one or two animals to take down such prey. When wild prey are available, red wolves have demonstrated a selection for wild prey over domestic animals and livestock. In northeastern North Carolina from 1987 to 1999, only two cases of depredation were verified: one was an old lone wolf that killed an estimated thirty newborn goats, and the other was a hunting dog killed while illegally hunting on public lands.

It was also important for people to understand that wolves are important to the ecosystem. "Look at what happened when we lost top predators in terrestrial habitats," says Henry. "We have overpopulation of deer that cause huge financial losses from vehicle accidents, not to mention human deaths. We see periodic disease outbreaks in deer that we probably wouldn't see if we had a top predator that was taking the diseased animals." When a top predator is removed from the food chain, we tend to see a proliferation of midline predators like coyotes, skunks, raccoons, and opossum. "These animals are wreaking havoc on our ground-nesting species," says Henry. "They've caused huge problems for birds and sea turtles."

An environmental group became involved in rallying public support and sold as many Red Necks for Red Wolves T-shirts and bumper stickers as they could make. Mary Anne Peine, former director of the Southern Appalachian Biodiversity Project, was amazed by the overwhelming public support for the reintroduction efforts. "People liked the fact that their home was special enough to support the red wolf, and groups traveled to the park just to hear them howl." Henry and the field team, as well as Mary Anne's group, traveled throughout the region giving slide presentations at every opportunity.

The reintroduction team was especially concerned about relations with local ranchers. Livestock owners and hunting groups were afraid that they would mistakenly kill a wolf while shooting coyotes on their property. Under the Endangered Species Act, it is illegal to take an endangered species unless it is taken in defense of human life, by permit for scientific purposes, or to enhance survival of the species. An amendment to the act allowed the Fish and Wildlife Service to write prohibitions to address local situations. Livestock and hunting groups were thankful that the USFWS listed the red wolf population in the Smokies as "experimental-nonessential" and that they made it legal for private landowners to kill a wolf that was in the act of killing livestock or domestic pets. Henry explained that the "nonessential" listing was appropriate because the genetic lines were available in captivity to re-establish a wild population. If the Smokies population was lost, it could be replaced. "In my opinion," said Henry, "the experimental population provision in the Endangered Species Act is the one thing that allowed wolf reintroductions to proceed."

The USFWS established a fund to pay ranchers whose animals were taken by wolves, and they proved to be quite lenient in reimbursing ranchers for lost animals. Over the course of seven years, the agency paid cattle owners $7,200 for twenty-two dead calves.

After the first year of the reintroduction project, it was clear that newborn calves separated from the herd were most vulnerable to wolf predation, so Lucash, Crawford, and Henry helped the Caughrons build two protective corrals in which to hold calves and cows. During 1993, wolves killed calves only outside the corral. In one case, three newborns were killed when it snowed thirty-six inches in Cades Cove and no one was able to get to the calves to move them to the corral.

In March of 1994, the protective corral washed away in the spring floods, leaving the newborn calves unprotected from wolves. The herd was kept in an open pasture where the cows could more easily watch for predators. By early April, only one calf was reported missing and, although the Caughrons were reimbursed, there was no substantial evidence that the calf had been killed by a wolf.

The open pasture was becoming overgrazed, so the livestock owner moved the herd into more-secluded pastures. Lucash urged the Caughrons not to make the move because these pastures were located in wooded hills where wolves could easily hide. The field team offered to help move the calves back to the open pasture, but the Caughrons refused. Ten days later, seven calves were missing and the entire herd was returned to the open pasture. The Caughrons were reimbursed.

At this point, park and project officials sat down to think of a way to keep the wolves away from the cattle. They decided to build an electric fence around part of the pasture and create a new contract with the Caughrons. This time, the owner was required to move all expectant cows and cows with calves inside the fence until the calves were at least six weeks old. That technique proved to be quite effective in eliminating predation of calves.

It seems to me there is no reason why a responsible cattle operation cannot peacefully coexist with wolves. Henry describes the Caughron operation as "low management intensity" and acknowledges that there was often a lack of communication between project personnel and the cattlemen. Apparently, the cattle owners were not concerned with making the extra effort needed to protect cattle and deter wolves. In addition to not following Lucash's advice about where to keep the herd, they often let the bulls mix with the herd year-round, making it difficult to predict when the cows would calve.

More important than an occasional run-in with cattle was the wolf pup survival rate. Fourteen months after the 1992 release, the two breeding pairs had produced seven pups, five of which biologists Chris Lucash and Barron Crawford captured and surgically implanted with abdominal transmitters. Also during this time, seven wolves died. Four of the pups were believed to have died of parvovirus, one adult and one pup were killed by canids, and one adult ingested poison.

During the next couple years, the team realized there were additional problems. As can be expected with animals bred in captivity, the wolves were highly tolerant of people. Park visitors were often seen feeding the wolves. To park officials they responded that they were just trying to "help the wolves survive." Lucash and Crawford resorted to trapping wolves, removing food scraps from picnic areas, providing information to visitors, and igniting firecracker shells to scare the wolves away from human activity.

In 1994, adult male 451M was frequently seen following roads and acting confused. The team assumed that 451M was simply used to people from being in captivity for three years. The biologists realized a road-walking wolf was potentially injurious to the project, so they used automobile horns and noninjurious pyrotechnics to scare 451M from roads and human activity centers. Toward the end of the year, however,

451M was captured and diagnosed with a degenerative retinal disease, which causes total blindness. 451M was slowly losing his vision and was using roads to make travel easier.

A few wolves left the park to scavenge for food scraps in residential areas, but they were captured and released elsewhere. Wolves that continued to wander were removed from the Smokies program and exchanged for other wolves. There were always a couple breeding pairs in the wild throughout the project, but the pup survival rate was virtually zero. When I asked Henry why the pups were dying, he suggested that the adults could find enough food for themselves but perhaps couldn't give the pups the nourishment they needed to survive.

But the field team remained hopeful and kept trying. During the year before Craig and I set out on our hike, two wolves, 501M and 660F, were released in the Elkmont area of the park, a pack of eight wolves was released in Cades Cove, and a pack of five was released in the Tremont area. 501M and 660F separated immediately following their release, and 660F roamed north of the park and far away from any other red wolves. Project personnel realized that because she wandered so far, she would not be of use to the project. On a number of occasions, personnel tried to capture her, but each time she escaped. Her radio transmitter malfunctioned, making future capture efforts virtually impossible. Part of me was glad that she was free, even if she wasn't contributing to the project. Maybe she'd wander for the rest of her life and never come back to the other wolves. Maybe she'd get shot or breed with a coyote. But maybe she'd enjoy her wildness and freedom as much as a wolf can realize such things. Maybe she had a different agenda. I almost couldn't help but be happy for her.

I lay awake at night listening for her howl. I scanned the forest for wolf silhouettes, for a head peering behind a tree, for a tail disappearing in the brush. I knew that the red wolf is larger than a coyote and smaller than a gray wolf, but in my daydreams they were always much larger. I imagined 660F tracking the hot, musty scent of deer, her head hovering a few inches above the ground as if she were following a scent four inches in the air. She would pause momentarily to scan her surroundings. Her ears would perk and swivel, her nostrils would twitch and sniff the air. With a quick glance over her shoulder, she'd notice my trembling excitement. She'd turn to face me, and her enormous liquid eyes would meet mine. At that moment I wouldn't know what to do; I'd be frozen in a timeless lock of eyes.

When we left the park in March of 1996, we had no way of knowing that by October 1998 all the wolves we had hoped to hear, all the wolves that by their very existence made our experience a little more wild, every last one would be dead or returned to captivity.

Throughout the following two and half years more wolves were reintroduced, but none of the breeding pairs produced pups that survived to maturity in the wild. Too many individuals continually left the park boundary and tried to settle on private property. Wolves continued to die of unknown causes, a few wolves ingested poison, and most pups died before they were seven weeks old. In 1997, six wolves being held in captivity or acclimation pens were released, but there were no plans for bringing any new wolves into the project until scientists could better study what had been happening to the wolves already released. By April 1997 only ten collared adults were known to be alive in the park and twenty-eight pups were unaccounted for or dead. It was clear that the project had not taken off as the biologists had hoped.

In October of 1998 the project was officially terminated due to low pup survival and the wolf's inability to establish home ranges within the park. Of the thirty-seven wolves released during the course of the program, twenty-six were recaptured from or were killed outside the park. Biologists believe that wolves wandered because it was easier to survive in the lower-elevation agricultural habitat than in the steep, heavily forested, high-mountain areas inside the park. "Higher elevations may never have been good wolf habitat," says Henry. "They traveled through the mountains but I doubt they made a living there."

Henry told me that most people don't realize the tremendous obstacles involved with reintroducing a top predator in the eastern United States. "You've got the most people and the least public land," he says, "I mean, I wish I had a Yellowstone, millions of acres, nobody living there, no cattle there. Plus we're dealing with captive animals that have problems inherent with being raised in captivity. We can't go to Canada to get wild wolves." Henry explained that in some cases a red wolf may need 50-100 square miles to establish a home and hunt for food; however, the scarcity of large acreages resulted in originally considering 170,000 acres as a minimum size for reintroductions. Although they've had tremendous success with the wolves in north-eastern North Carolina, their success comes with a cap. "Presently there are somewhere between 44 and 101 wolves in northeastern North Carolina," said Henry. "If you have more than a hundred in there, you may be oversaturated. You can only have so many animals in a small space." Because there isn't enough space for large populations of wolves, the reintroduced populations may have to be managed forever.

They learned a lot from the Smokies project, and in 1999 the team was on the verge of selecting additional sites for future releases. This effort was put on hold when they realized the need to determine the extent of red wolf-coyote interactions in northeastern North Carolina and how to manage the situation. Barron Crawford had studied coyote populations for two years prior to the Smokies project. Some of the coyotes studied by Crawford were still present, and the field team found that wolves displace coyotes but coyotes are quick to move in once a wolf leaves its territory. At one point during the Smokies project, a male wolf was removed from the Cades Cove area, leaving a female to defend the territory. When biologists returned to the site, they found that the female was severely scarred from fighting with coyotes. In another instance, Crawford and Lucash captured a pair of adult wolves and two of their three pups to vaccinate them. Before the third pup could be captured, coyotes moved in and killed it. It appears that without a pair or without a large male, wolves are not able to exclude coyotes. An additionally dangerous situation occurs when coyote-wolf relations are friendly. Wolves that mate with coyotes become useless to the project, as they produce hybrid pups instead of propagating their own species.

The field team is dedicating the next three to five years to study-ing the problem. "We need to spend all our energy understanding how integration occurs and under what conditions; then we need to figure out how to manage coyotes," said Henry. "We can always have token island populations, but—let's face it—they'd be showcase populations, not an animal that is playing a significant role in Southeast ecosystems." In the summer of 1999 there were between 218 and 309 red wolves, 164 of which were in captive breeding programs across the country. The remaining wolves live in the wild in northeastern North Carolina and on three islands off the Atlantic and Gulf coasts. Biologists can only estimate the number of wolves in the wild because it's difficult to locate pups and fit them with radio collars, and it's difficult to keep track of births and deaths within the population. The team's goal is to have 330 wolves in captivity and 220 in the wild in at least three locations. Henry is hopeful that the project will succeed, and he's devoted to returning wolves to the region, but he made it clear that if they can't find a way to separate wolves from coyotes, the red wolf doesn't stand much of a chance.

Regardless of the red wolf's success or failure at the ARNWR or elsewhere, the red wolf reintroduction program should be viewed as a success because it was the front-runner in predator reintroductions worldwide. "We were the first ones to successfully do it and when you consider that we did it in the East with all the obstacles, it's a major achievement," says Henry. "We proved it could be done. After our success, the Yellowstone, Idaho, and New Mexico reintroductions got approved. It has been historically important because it set the tone for predator reintroductions throughout the world." One message Henry believes is important to get across is that it's important not to let animals get to the brink of extinction before we try to recover them. Henry and the field team faced tremendous obstacles because they had to build a population of hundreds of wolves from only fourteen individuals.

"I want to see the wolves back," Henry told me. "I'm a hunter, I've been all my life, but, God almighty, I'd be more than glad for a red wolf to take a deer and me not to get it. To see that animal out there in the wild and interact with it—oh God, tremendous. There's nothing like it." His gaze has shifted over my head and I sense that what he feels for this animal is something beyond what he can convey in words.

"You know," he says, "a lot of people consider the wolf the epitome of a wilderness experience. I tell you, to hear one howl is really something. They're a beautiful animal."

§

Weather became temperamental. Within a twenty-four-hour period we experienced every form of precipitation. Ice and snow melted into rain and washed in color like a watercolor paint book. Water transformed a dusty, dry landscape of grays and browns into red stems, golden straw, deep-green pines, lime-colored lichens, and chocolate mud. After two days of walking through pouring rain, Craig and I arrived at Newfound Gap. Here the trail bisects the park highway. There is a pull-off where tourists stop to eternalize themselves in Kodachrome. Craig and I crossed the road and headed into the public restroom. It was the most comfortable place I had been in a while, and I asked Craig if we could stay. I was ready to sprawl out on the bathroom floor. "After all," I said, "we have shelter, heat, and running water." He thought that was a bad idea. We walked on.

As we arrived at the shelter, I was thinking I should have been more adamant about staying in the restroom. It was almost dark but I counted twelve people already inside, all men, all on spring break. There was some shifting of sleeping pads to make room for us, and we claimed a spot and settled in. I ate peanut butter crackers in the dark and gulped down water that Craig had fetched from the spring. It wasn't until the light of the next morning that I saw that the water was brown and had chunks of leaves and bugs swirling in it. These are things you shouldn't dwell on for too long.

After another day of freezing rain, icy trails, drenched hiking boots, and dozens of college students on spring break, we were delighted to meet two other thru-hikers with whom we could bond over frozen water filters and wet socks. I can't remember the boy's real name, but I remember that night in the shelter we gave him his trail name. He was a gawky kid with curly red hair; he looked like a prepubescent David Letterman, a comment even he recognized as an insult. He was the kid that everybody loved to pick on in junior high school. But he's also the kid who took the abuse and survived. He wasn't sure college was right for him, so he set out with an enormous pack filled with all the wrong gear to hike the entire Appalachian Trail, and I respected him for trying. He carried two pounds of cheese and a three-foot-long pepperoni link. When he whipped it out of his pack and said he had been carrying it for days, Craig immediately thought of a trail name: Yard o' Beef.

It must have been close to 10:00 P.M., for it had been dark for some time. Craig and I, Yard o' Beef, and a handful of college students had long since settled into our sleeping bags and had called it a night. Suddenly there was a rattle at the metal door of the shelter. Someone was rustling with the chain and the lock, trying to get in. I felt Craig tense up. I had heard my share of stories about loonies in the woods, of convicts hiding out in the mountains, of people getting killed on this trail. What type of person would be wandering around in the freezing rain, in the dark?

A tall man, dripping wet, lumbered into our shelter. Even after he removed his hood, his face was hidden beneath a shaggy mat of black hair.

"Hello," he announced to a silent shelter, "I'm Nudeman." I was glad it was dark because the expression on my face couldn't have shown anything but disbelief. I slid a little farther away from where Nudeman stood and looked at Craig for assurance.

I was trying to make out his features for the police report I was sure I'd be filing the next morning, if I survived this night. I looked down for a second, and when I looked back up I was looking directly into Nudeman's eyes. He extended his hand for me to shake. "Hi," I said nervously, "I'm Raindrop. This is Hibird." He moved on to Yard o' Beef and I resumed breathing.

Nudeman chose a spot in the shelter and from the shifting and shuffling, I gathered he was organizing gear and making dinner. Although I was convinced that he was going to get naked and dance around the shelter (why else would he have a name like Nudeman?), he turned out to be a nurse practitioner from Washington State. "Last year I thru-hiked the 2,600-mile Pacific Crest Trail from Mexico to Canada," he told us. "I like to think I've got the hang of lightweight backpacking." We noticed that he hiked in tennis shoes instead of heavy boots, and he didn't carry a stove, pots and pans, a sleeping mattress, or a tent. Because he didn't have a tent, he had to hike twenty-four miles to get to the shelter and be out of the rain, which is why he was hiking at 10:00 at night.

The final day in the Smokies was one I will never forget; memory rarely releases the most uncomfortable experiences. We began the fifteen-mile descent to the park boundary in the rain. By noon it was snowing. Angry gusts spanked the pines and spat a mixture of snow and hail pellets at us, forcing us to retreat deep into our Gore-Tex hoods like turtles. All day it was only us in only white. The sky blended into the backdrop and that into the ground.

That evening we huddled in the Davenport Gap shelter with Yard o' Beef and Nudeman. Nudeman explained that he hydrates freeze-dried meals with cold water; his special concoction of brown rice, peas, and garlic is his favorite. "My loaded backpack," he informed us, "never weighs more than twenty-five pounds." Although I couldn't imagine never being able to eat a hot meal, I was impressed, and Craig immediately started making lists of things we could get rid of. We cooked dinner in our sleeping bags. Craig and I shared a heaping pot of pasta and had hot chocolate for dessert. Nudeman ate handfuls of granola.

Pasta and hot chocolate dulled the wind's icy bite, but nothing could block the night's damp chill. Seldom Seen's thermometer read negative nine, and I imagine the wind-chill was well below that. Bordering on hypothermia, I shook uncontrollably for fourteen hours, rocking back and forth in my twenty-degree sleeping bag. I tried to focus on one small part of my body that was warm, but sometimes I couldn't even convince myself that my belly button or a rib was warm. My hair was wet and cold with frozen tears, and it was matted to my face. My mummy bag felt more like a coffin than a source of warmth.

Around four in the morning I woke Craig. "I don't know if I can do this much longer," I said, "I'm really, really cold." My teeth were chattering uncontrollably and it scared me to see just how bad off I was. I could barely speak because I was shaking so much. "Craig, let's get out of here. I have to move. I can't sit here any longer."

Craig thought about it for a moment then said, "It's the middle of the night. Where are you going to go?"

"I don't know," I cried. "I don't care..." My voice trailed off as I put the hood back over my head.

Then I got an idea. "Can we switch bags?" I asked. He reluctantly agreed, so I slipped into his zero-degree down bag. He groaned as he pulled my cold bag over his head. Two hours later, the night was getting a shade lighter and we both agreed it was okay to get up. We were both numb and exhausted and eager to get to a warm building, only two miles away. I reached for my boots. "Oh, shit! Craig, they're blocks of ice." I made a frantic attempt to jam icy toes into the boot, but the leather had frozen solid. "We can't go anywhere without boots," said Craig. I knew he had to go to the bathroom but even that was out of the question.

We put emergency hot warmers in the boots and put the boots in our sleeping bags. After an hour, they were still frozen. Craig grabbed the stove. It wouldn't light—frozen. He warmed the stove in his bag and tried again. Finally, a spark. We held each boot over the flame until the leather softened. We jammed cold feet into stiff, damp boots before they refroze, stepped out into four inches of new snow, and headed to town.

We left the Smokies with the understanding that the mountains demand a lot from those who tread there. No wonder we didn't see a bear, or a boar, or a wolf—they were busy surviving.

## CHAPTER THREE

# THEN IT SNOWED SOME MORE

Georgia and North Carolina proved to be far more rugged than we had imagined, and the weather wasn't making the walking any easier. It seemed to me that it would be virtually impossible to have a bad backpacking trip if the weather was good, but now I was wondering if the reverse was true: that you couldn't have a good trip if the weather was bad. I decided it wasn't entirely true, although bad weather did add a certain level of discomfort that was difficult to ignore.

It wasn't until we traveled nearly 180 miles past the Smokies and spent two more weeks trying to ignore the brutally cold temperatures that we were able to bid farewell to Tennessee. A border crossing seemed like a good place to stop and evaluate how far we'd come and take inventory of how we were doing, physically and emotionally. It was important, every now and then, to study the situation, tally the miles we'd covered and the miles that lay ahead, and talk about our goals for the rest of the hike. But when I was cold and uncomfortable I didn't feel like reflecting; I felt only like getting to that night's destination as quickly as possible. If it hadn't been for the old man, we may not have taken the time to evaluate our situation.

Somewhere near the Tennessee-Virginia border we met an old man on top of a hill. His face was creased and weathered, his graying hair damp from the steep climb. From beneath a blue baseball cap, his eyes squinted up at us. He began a monologue describing the trail ahead, the terrain on every mountain, and every speck of civilization below. Then he described last week's weather and how he wouldn't leave the warmth of his house. He spoke in a squeaky southern twang. "T'ain't fit fer man or beast out there," he said. With that, he had summed up our time in Tennessee.

After a day of rest in Hot Springs, North Carolina, to recover from the Smokies, Craig and I gathered our strength and pressed on. We had been reading accounts of a handful of thru-hikers who were ahead of us, and we hoped to catch someone soon. As we approached the Jerry Cabin shelter, our destination for the night, we saw a lanky young man sprawled out in the corner, his head hovering over a tiny journal. His sandy-blond uncombed hair was bound by a bandanna, and he wore a tie-dyed Ben & Jerry's T-shirt. He looked up, "Hey, how's it goin'? I'm Otter."

"Otter!" Craig shouted, "Man, we've been reading your entries for weeks. I can't believe we finally caught up with you."

I looked around for his partner, the only other woman I had heard about on the trail. As if he read my mind, Otter said, "Did you hear about my partner?" We shook our heads no. "She left the trail yesterday, so this is my first day hiking solo. I'm glad to have some company."

I was immediately disappointed. I was anxious to meet another female thru-hiker, someone who might be feeling the same things I was, someone who might have the same concerns. There had been a number of times I wanted to complain to another woman about the tribulations of peeing while wearing a 40-pound backpack. I wanted to agonize with someone about having to leave the male-dominated shelters to change my clothes. I wanted to meet a woman who could show me that it was okay to slow down and that I didn't have to race the men to prove something to myself. But the trail wasn't what she had expected and she decided it wasn't quite the experience she was looking for, so she returned to Michigan to go back to school.

"Did you guys make it to town during the storm?" Otter asked. "I made it to the shelter just in time. I don't carry a tent so I have to plan these things."

"Raindrop and I froze our butts off with Nudeman and Seldom Seen," Craig recalled. "You'll probably meet those two soon."

We settled in beside Otter, who had peeled the sock off his right foot and was attempting to wriggle his mummified toes. Each toe was meticulously wrapped with medical tape. "These blisters are killing me," he said.

"No kidding," I said. "My heels are so raw I'm scared to look at them." We shared a bonding moment probing our raw and blistered feet.

Otter and I trudged into the night to the water source, a small creek, and filled our jugs.

"Is the trail what you expected?" I asked.

"In many ways, no. I sure didn't expect it to be so cold in Georgia. We started February first, which was a huge mistake."

Loaded with water, we ambled back toward the shelter. Otter continued, "It's been a lot harder than I thought, but in a way it's not about the details. It's about the overall journey and being able to do what we're doing. It's the lifestyle that's so great. You know what I mean?"

I did.

Talking with Otter was like visiting with an old friend. We had been walking for nearly a month, and although we had run across a number of day-hikers, we had met only a handful of other thru-hikers. We began to feel as if we were the only ones hiking the entire trail. There was comfort in meeting another person who had seen the same views, had shivered on the same nights, and had felt the same pain. Relationships came easy. There was a certain level of understanding, an immediate sense of trust and intimacy that could be achieved in society only after months of contact. On the trail, bonds were formed after a few hours. These shared experiences somehow built the foundation for a sense of community on the trail. Otter had a contagious laugh and an enormous smile, and I knew immediately that we would be friends.

My relationship with Craig had a similar smooth and easy feel to it. We settled into our daily routines and relied on each other to perform the tasks that would keep us going. We took turns cooking and making tea, we shared the responsibility of washing the pot, filtering water, and storing the food, and we affectionately fought over Big Red, which we decided must be the most enormous sleeping mattress ever carried on a thru-hike. Although I'm the one who had to explain that the big red stuff sack strapped to my backpack was not a tent but a sleeping pad, Craig was the one who tried to inch his way onto it in the middle of the night. But besides midnight mattress skirmishes, we hadn't had as much as a single argument.

Even though we started early to avoid the crowds and to have more of a wilderness experience, I was beginning to realize that there was no getting around the fact that the AT is very much a social trail.

I thought about Benton MacKaye's original plan for recreational communities and elaborate huts along the path; it seemed like the trail experience today had come pretty close to his Appalachian Trail vision. Even though farm camps were never constructed and the communities that now exist along the trail are more a product of urban sprawl than MacKaye's vision, I would argue that we have developed a trail and a hiking experience that is every bit as social as MacKaye intended. I suppose when you build a trail in such close proximity to so many urban areas, there is no way not to rub elbows with urban life.

Trail registers are notebooks located at trailheads, shelters, and hostels, and they provide hikers with a fairly elaborate communication network. Most hikers enter passages into these registers about where they've been, what they've seen, how they're holding up, and what they're looking forward to. Hikers leave notes for their friends and inspiring messages for those who will follow. The register was the first thing Craig and I sought when we arrived at a shelter. It made us feel connected to other hikers and part of a larger experience. It certainly added to the sense of community that MacKaye felt should exist on the trail.

Craig and I left a register (a spiral-bound notebook with vocabulary words printed on the cover) at the Brown Mountain shelter in Virginia. When it was full, a hiker mailed it back to us. In it were notes from our thru-hiking friends, entries from day-hikers, section-hikers, and thru-hikers with whom we never crossed paths. The register has become a treasured keepsake as it reminds us of the details of the thru-hiker lifestyle.

Ishmael began the register by challenging everyone to select a word of the day from the choices on the cover. He chose "prophecy" and prophesied that if you select a word, you'll be blessed with trail magic. It shouldn't be a surprise that the words that were used first were "restaurant," "achievement," "banana," "rhubarb," and "weather." They were really the only words that had any relevance to a thru-hiker's world.

The word game finally fizzled out and entries gave us glimpses into why people had taken to the trail. Linchen wrote: "Got here this evening after a hectic day. Just had to get out and away for one last solo overnighter before graduation from college. This girlfriend of mine dropped me off at the trailhead. Like a dumbass, I've fallen in love right before graduation and I don't know what this summer will bring. Thought maybe Brown Mountain and her tributaries could help me collect my thoughts. So good to see the rewards of the new spring in bloom. Happy hiking!"

Pariah, a section-hiker, philosophizes: "It was the best of times; it was the worst of times. It was the time we thought to do the unthinkable. When it is done, time will wash the memories clean, removing the stains and pains. And what is left will be the dream that we lived." He goes on to say that "if you face the rest of your life with the spirit you show on the trail, it will have no choice but to yield the same kinds of memories and dreams. I wish you all the very best."

Easy One (EZ1) left a note in our register explaining that this is his third end-to-end hike but his first thru-hike. "Say hello when you pass," he wrote. "I'm 73 years old and in no hurry to reach the end. Enjoy your hike because, believe it or not, life does not get much better than this." A previous entry by a thru-hiker had mentioned meeting EZ1 and had expressed bewilderment at EZ1's gear (which fit into an archaic canvas day pack with frayed shoulder straps and no hip belt). EZ1 responded succinctly: "If you don't ask, you won't learn. If you turkeys want to lug 60 pound packs, more power to you. I have my basic gear down to 16 pounds. It took 30 years of trying."

"Danger! Alert!" wrote the Cornell Crew. "The woods are no longer safe! Poison ivy spotted for the first time on our trip. I guess it gets leaves when everything else does. Hey you northbounders ahead: You always ask us to catch up, but you never slow down to give us a chance. I feel like we will perpetually be one week behind Otter and Gotta-Go. Maybe everyone ahead will get sucked into the vortex at Rusty's, so we may see you there. Lovely walk up the creek, and not bad swimming either!"

The culture of trail towns encouraged a similar feeling of community. In many small towns near the AT you can count on finding some sort of rustic lodging—whether it's a barn, a church, a hostel, or someone's garage—for a minimal fee. Hikers who are separated by many miles of trail funnel into certain towns, renew themselves, and connect with other hikers before they return to the woods and get scattered along the trail. Townspeople understand that thru-hikers are fairly easy to accommodate. We'll get giddy about even the crummiest showers, and we'll become nearly orgasmic at the site of pancakes. Most people in trail towns are fully aware of the thru-hiking phenomenon, and many people will give hikers a ride without thinking twice. As a hiker, you rely on these social aspects to keep you going. You count on the rides, the meals in town, the places to stay. You are delighted when a stranger picks you out of a crowd, asks if you are a thru-hiker, and encourages you to keep going.

You also relish meeting the person who's never heard of the AT and who looks at you like you've just descended from a distant galaxy. The people I found most amusing were the ones who made it impossible for me to define thru-hiking and subsequently insist that it was a rational endeavor. They gave me looks that almost made me admit, midexplanation, that it was a mistake.

"See, there's this path in the mountains that goes over 2,000 miles from Georgia to Maine," I would hear myself say.

No response, just a blank stare. They're pretty sure they've heard me correctly but don't want to be rude in case they misunderstood.

"It will take us six months to walk the whole thing," I'd say.

There's a long pause and I can tell they're exercising great restraint to keep from laughing. They can't, however, hide their bewildered expression. "You know, if you drove, it would only take a couple days," they'd say.

"Yeah, I know, but that's not the point of the trip," I'd say.

"What exactly is the point of the trip?" they'd ask.

Usually I would smile and mumble something about experiencing the landscape, a pathetic rebuttal, and one I immediately realize would have produced the same effect had I spoken Arabic. From there, one of us will politely change the subject, searching for a topic we both can manage, which is usually the weather. I'm left wondering why I chose six months instead of three days. Could I genuinely insist that I was having a good time? I was filthy, exhausted, and felt hungry all the time. I was usually freezing, dehydrated, and slept on the ground every night. Maybe I didn't understand why I was out there. Maybe I didn't have a good enough sense of what would be gained by walking. Maybe I had some things to think about.

$$\mathscr{s}$$

We stayed on the same schedule as Otter for a few days, losing him periodically throughout the day but always ending up in the same shelter by nightfall. One sleepy, rainy morning Otter took off early, but I insisted to Craig that we dawdle around the shelter. The trail just wasn't calling to me, I told him. Craig had learned when to let me call the shots, and he had realized early on that it was better to sacrifice an early start than witness one of my frustration breakdowns halfway to our destination. Once I had taken a couple hours to mentally prepare for a day in the rain, we packed our gear and headed out.

It wasn't that bad. After all, as Craig had pointed out, it was warm enough to get soaked and not mind. Or so we thought. After about an hour the rain turned to sleet, which turned to hail, which turned to snow. Three inches accumulated while we ate lunch. Our wet shirts froze on our backs and my bare legs turned red and wet and goose-bumped. We skirted waterfalls and balanced on slippery, snow-dusted rocks. Snow stuck to the trail and we crunched through a few soft inches for ten miles until we arrived in town. From the bunkhouse in Hampton, Tennessee, we watched it snow for three days and three nights. Temperatures were unbearably cold; we couldn't think of any reason to go outside or even to talk about going outside. Craig, Otter, and I huddled in front of the tiny heater, ate chips and salsa, and played Monopoly on the food-stained card table in the '70s-style kitchen.

It was right after the third time I landed on Park Place with three hotels that we heard someone enter the bunkhouse. Into the kitchen waltzed Yard o' Beef, a respectable coating of snow on his pack, but otherwise looking pretty good.

"Where did you come from?" we asked.

"I found a shortcut," he said, grinning.

A lot of people who consider themselves serious hikers frown on people who skip sections of trail or who stray from the white-blazed Appalachian Trail to take a shorter, more direct route. Side trails that lead to shelters, springs, vistas, or shortcuts are usually blazed in blue, so any hiker who follows these side trails is considered a "blue blazer." Taking this one step further, hikers who hitchhike to skip a section of trail are called "yellow-blazers," since they follow the yellow lines on the road. In this way trail language defines categories of hikers depending on the degree to which they follow the designated route.

Craig and I met hikers at the other end of the spectrum who called themselves purists; they literally touch every inch of trail, going to great lengths to make sure they begin each day exactly where they left off. If a shelter has side trails that approach from the north and the south, northbound purists go back down the south entrance instead of heading north to reconnect with the AT. Although I never tested my theory, it seemed to me that there were a disproportionately high number of Type A personalities in the purist category.

Yard o' Beef was no Type A. He was known as a blue and a yellow blazer and that was okay with him. There really is no correct way to hike the trail, and anyone who insists that there is ought not to worry so much about other people's experiences. Hikers need to hike the trail that's right for them and do what they feel they need to do to achieve their goals, whether that means touching every inch or bypassing a rugged section on a snowy day. I admit, though, that it was hard not to feel a twinge of frustration. After all, we cranked out long miles while Yard o' Beef took it easy and hitched the rest of the way, and we ended up at the same place. But we had to learn to focus on our own experience and appreciate the company, so I happily invited Yard o' Beef to take over my failing real estate enterprise, most of which was now mortgaged.

The bunkhouse also had a bathtub. I don't recall having any soap or shampoo, but the four of us took turns soaking in the steaming tub. Since hot water was scarce, we boiled water on the stove for each person. We each emerged pink and warm and sleepy. Craig and I lay down on one of the stained, tattered mattresses. Outside, the blizzard whirled snow in spirals. "I'm so glad we made it to town," Craig whispered, holding me with one hand and restuffing pieces of mattress foam with the other.

Maybe it was the cheap intimacy or maybe it was the excitement of dodging a tremendous snowstorm, but I felt like probing him about his past. I wanted to hear about every girlfriend he'd ever had and what his relationships were like. I wanted to know him in his younger years, the Craig I'll never get to know. Why is it that women want to pry? Is it a desire to understand, decipher, and control men? I wanted all the details and Craig wanted to put it all in the vault. He was reluctant but answered my questions. "Why do you want to know this?" he kept asking.

"I want to know your past," I said. "I think I have that right. I want to know what you used to be like." I didn't tell him that for some reason it turned me on to hear about his crazy younger years. I didn't tell him that it made me feel special to know that he had been in love only once before.

"But I don't want to hear about your old boyfriends," he said.

I know, I thought, and it drives me crazy.

When there was a lull in the conversation, Craig jumped at the chance to change the subject. "It doesn't take long to lose that feeling of thru-hiking, does it? It doesn't take long to forget the routine." Indeed it didn't. After three nights in the hostel it was almost hard to imagine what it was like to hike every day. It was difficult to imagine ever being cold or hungry. We felt ourselves getting soft, getting sucked into town. We were bored: there are only so many games of Monopoly you can play, and there are only so many ten-year-old *National Geographic* magazines you can read before you start to get a bit delirious. By the third day, the snow settled and we were anxious to return to the trail. In retrospect, we left prematurely.

During the ascent out of town, we realized the highlands had gotten hammered with snow. Drifts were two to five feet deep. Rhododendron leaves and pine limbs attracted snowflakes like magnets attract steel shavings. Branches heavy with wet snow drooped, sagged, and cracked. Instead of walking beneath a leafy canopy, we faced a snowy tangle of leaves and branches which hung to the ground. We beat the leaves with hiking sticks and shook the branches free of snow. The limbs rose high enough for us to crawl under, but not without dumping mounds of snow on our heads.

The blazes were hidden beneath snow and branches, and a clear path was difficult to find. We strayed a couple times but ended up guessing the general direction of the path. After eight miles of breaking trail, we reached the Vandeventer shelter and immediately began to freeze. We talked about turning back but didn't have the energy to fight the snow for another eight miles. We crawled inside our sleeping bags and remained there for a record time—eighteen mummified hours lying on the wood floor of the shelter. It was too cold to move. The water source was a long way down a ravine so we melted snow for cooking and ate granola in our sleeping bags. We purposely dehydrated ourselves so we wouldn't have to leave our sleeping bags to pee in the middle of the night. "There's no one I'd rather freeze to death with than you," Craig said, laughing.

"Thanks, I'm flattered."

He wrapped me in his arms and we slept holding onto each other, waking throughout the night to nudge our bodies a little closer.

We broke trail for three days. On the fourth day, temperatures rose enough to let it rain. There were times when I cursed the trail and the weather for hours. But after you sulk and consider your options, you eventually realize that you can sit there and cry, or you can walk. Likewise, you can take your frustrations out on your partner or you can take it out on a rock or keep it to yourself. It doesn't matter so much if you cry or walk—I did a lot of both—but if you turn on your partner, you'll never make it together. We learned to focus our attention outward, on our surroundings, instead of dwelling on discomfort. We learned that humor and encouragement went further than we thought.

With damp clothes and high spirits, we crossed the border into Virginia and descended into Damascus.

The old man told us he hikes up that hill often. "I come up here every week," he said, "jest to git away from it all." I know what he means. All those things spinning around down there can make a person dizzy. Sometimes it's hard to distill the meaning from anything when you don't take time to stop and look around. Life is littered with material things and societal stresses. Our minds become cluttered with extras—with meetings and deadlines, Serbian wars and presidential debates, scandals and shootings, alarm clocks and cell phones, latest fashions and lawsuits. Sometimes it takes a view from a hilltop to get a perspective and clear your mind. Backpacking has a way of reducing life to its most simple rituals, like eating and finding shelter. It strips away the distractions and lets you focus on the core of life itself.

I was finding that sometimes, even when you're in the mountains, it's hard to keep perspective if you don't stop for a moment and let the mountains fill you up. I had to remind myself what the mountains do for me, how they fill me with a pureness that I can't find in civilization, how they make my head stop spinning, how they ground me when I'm feeling lost and confused. Craig and I decided that we needed to make an effort to remember those things. We needed to remember that we were out here to enjoy the journey, not just the destination. I needed to let the trail get inside me and allow myself to learn from the challenges it threw my way. I sensed I had a lot to learn about life and relationships, and I believed I could if I allowed myself to absorb what the trail had to teach me. People often asked me why I was still out there battling the darkness and cold. I often asked myself that question. Then, I thought of the old man and remembered.

In Damascus, Virginia, I received a letter from a friend. She urged me to find the pleasure in pain and the beauty in darkness. That is the perspective we unveiled when we peaked each hill: that there is joy in sharing painful experiences, that we can do anything together. Our relationship became a little more clear with every snowy step and every beautifully bitter night.

## CHAPTER FOUR

# OATMEAL IS NOT FOOD

It was the first day of spring and the two highest peaks on the trail in Virginia, Whitetop Mountain and Mount Rogers, were literally dripping with ice. Every blade of grass, every stalk, twig, and branch wore a sheath of ice. A crystalline, crunchy, glassy world.

I didn't want to be on the trail. I was tired of hiking, tired of being cold, tired of all the East Coast grays and browns. I was thinking of people who were warm and satisfied and doing something, *anything* other than hiking. That's when I walked into a tree. I smashed my head on a low limb and started to cry. Then I began to laugh. I'm not sure why.

It was foggy and cold when we passed through Grayson Highlands, a state park thirty-five miles into Virginia where wild ponies graze protected pastures. I was certain that in the spring, when it really was spring, the pastures would be beautiful. We came within ten feet of two ponies, their silhouettes emerging from behind cool wisps of fog. They were still and unafraid and we walked slowly by. After crossing miles of soggy pastures, Craig and I arrived at the shelter. I arranged our sleeping pads in the corner and silently settled into my bag. Craig reassured me that the sun was still at the center of the solar system, although after seven straight days of rain I was sure that it had spun off into a different galaxy, leaving Earth in eternal darkness. Craig realized then that I am solar powered. He offered me treats from Damascus: dried pineapple, Celestial Seasonings peach tea, and a game of cribbage. The treasures improved my spirits. He kissed my bruised forehead.

"I know one thing you should be excited about," Craig said. "We get to see Kodiak in a few days."

"Yeah, I can't wait to see my boy."

"*Your* boy?" he said.

"Well, I *am* his mama," I said, and lay back on my sleeping pad.

"I just want you to be happy," he said. "The sun will come out again, I promise."

I tried my best to smile.

"There you go, Sunshine," he said. "There's that beautiful smile."

I had to laugh every time he thought of a new nickname for me. I laughed because I knew he was sincerely trying to be affectionate and because it was out of his character to give me names like "kitten" and "sugar pie" and "sunshine," and it was out of mine to accept them.

I began to notice movement, sound, and color more than I ever had, and I began to notice how my surroundings shaped my moods. The browns and beiges seemed benign at first, but winter's drab face often left me solemn. Every day we walked through tunnels of brittle brown trunks and stark charcoal limbs, hypnotized by our steps, brown on brown. Once I spotted a flower. It was just a tiny white one, suspended on a slender stem. I panned the forest for other colors: purple, green, red, yellow, white. There was nothing—just a solitary splash of white next to my brown boots.

I was waiting for the colors, movements, and sounds of spring to energize me and snap me out of my winter depression. Spring is skinning my knee as I climb a maple tree, feeling mud ooze between my toes when I walk barefoot in the rain, belting the lyrics to "You Are My Sunshine" in the shower, dancing in my bedroom. These are the details that get under my skin and make me think, So *this* is what it feels like to be alive. Eventually the sun made an appearance and I dreamt of bare legs, bathing in streams, and wringing out a bandanna drenched with sweat. My hopes for permanently warm weather soared. But night delivered rain and cooler temperatures. It snowed the next day. My high hopes crashed.

"It'll get warmer," Craig said, "I promise."

"You have been saying that for two months," I said.

"But this time I'm serious." He was laughing now and pulled me close.

I shot him a skeptical look and pulled away.

"Come on, Baby," he said. I shouldn't have turned around and smiled, but I love it when he calls me "baby."

One week later we found our way to a barn in southwestern Virginia. Members of the church across the lawn had turned the old barn into a hostel for hikers. The downstairs, which once housed tons of grain, was converted to rustic living quarters. Yellow foam pads covered most of the loft floor and various maps and sketches of the Appalachian Trail decorated the walls. In a tiny alcove beside the heavy wooden door sat a wood-burning stove. Three slanted shelves held rows of trashy romance novels and a collection of *National Geographic* magazines. Antique farm tools were tacked to the barn board walls. Craig and I sat on benches next to the stove, grinning into pints of Ben & Jerry's Cherry Garcia ice cream.

It was Easter Sunday and the townspeople of Pearisburg filed out of the church in all their pinks and pastels, all their bows and bonnets. It was thirty degrees and snowing.

Craig and I relaxed in the barn after a week of record mileage. "We hiked 161 miles in the last ten days," Craig calculated. Our bodies took quite a beating, especially during the final 24-mile stretch, which we completed in one day.

Rainy skies had cleared by the middle of that record week, and the fog had dissolved into blue sky. Gentle hills, dimpled with silver silos and red barns, stretched across the landscape. We sloshed through muddy cow pastures, staring down cows that stood on the trail. And then it got hot. For one sticky, sweaty day we saw spring take over. The air hummed with mosquitoes, gnats, and flies. I nearly stepped on two garter snakes.

Again the weather tempted us with warmth but left us in the cold. Gusts increased to forty miles per hour as we walked the exposed ridge for miles. Still a day's hike from town, we were out of food, fuel, and battery power. So we pushed for a long day, eventually dropped out of the wind into a low-elevation forest and landed in Pearisburg. We stashed our packs at the barn, bought two large pizzas, and headed to the post office, where we found our two friends rummaging through their supply boxes.

It was fun to be associated with such a motley bunch, with people who call themselves Nudeman and Otter. We staked our claim on the post office lawn and began the ritual of trading food. I felt tough with this group. I felt people stare. Townspeople hurried past, tossing us inquisitive looks. Some clutched their purses and grabbed their small children. Once I looked in a mirror I understood why. I looked like I'd been living in a corrugated box my whole life. I had dirt-stained cheeks and greasy hair that clumped around my head. Craig looked pretty sketchy himself, especially with that wild red beard around his neck. It had been ten days since our last shower and all of our clothes had essentially been on our bodies for the duration.

Some townspeople were not frightened, just curious. They were drawn to us, wondering what on earth we were doing that made us look so grungy, smell so earthy, and eat so much. They were curious because they had always thought about hiking the trail and still believe that someday they will. . .someday. There were also the ones whose fascination stopped long before a desire to begin planning their own hike. Instead, they wanted to arm themselves with stimulating dinner conversation. They would go home to their families and over a steaming pot of beef stew slip a line into the conversation about how they were talking to a couple who, can you believe it! is walking up the whole country. I enjoyed people who were amused by my ambitions. It kept me going.

Their questions generally followed the same format: How far have you come? Where are you going? How many miles do you walk each day? Have you seen any wildlife? Where do you sleep? How do you get food? We offered the answers to most of these questions with mild enthusiasm, but what hiker would not want to talk about food? After all, we spent hours on the trail every day fantasizing about all the food that was too heavy to carry or would spoil too quickly—the food that we craved but could never have.

"Craig," I said, "what would you do for a cheeseburger and a glass of milk?"

"How about pizza and a coke?" he replied.

"Ice cream," I said, "Breyer's vanilla with Hershey's chocolate syrup."

"Apple pie."

"Fresh apples and peaches, and green beans and carrots."

"Fresh bread, home-cooked lasagna."

"Stop! I can't take it," I shouted.

We often subjected ourselves to this torture. It was a strange, quiet feeling to be hungry all the time. It is a feeling that most of us in the West have never felt.

Responses to the food questions involved describing the procedure of boxing and shipping food to various post offices near the trail. "It was difficult to plan our menu for six months," Otter told one inquiring man. "Now that my partner quit, I have to go through each mail drop and send half of everything back home."

"After all the planning we still managed to get it wrong," said Craig. "In the beginning, we were planning on consuming 12,000 calories a day for me and 8,000 for Raindrop, but we couldn't possibly carry that much food and we didn't need to eat that much."

"It was fun buying all the food, though," I said. I explained how we bought all our food in bulk and spent three months prior to our departure dehydrating much of it. We reduced pounds of apples, bananas, pears, pineapples, broccoli, peppers, and mushrooms to ounces of fruits and vegetables that not only weighed a lot less but took up a fraction of the space of the original hydrated foods. We made beef jerky, dried black beans, and turned pasta sauce into powder. It was a monumental task assembling our dehydrated concoctions, staples of oatmeal, rice, and pasta, plus homemade trail mix and hundreds of power bars, Snickers, and granola bars. "Unfortunately," I added, "our calculations of days and miles and rations failed to consider the possibility of getting tired, disgusted, or repulsed by recurring meals of oatmeal and instant mashed potatoes."

The man in front of the post office was enthralled, so I continued with my oatmeal anecdote. I never liked oatmeal to begin with but I managed to eat it for thirty-three days. When we assembled the food for the trip, oatmeal seemed like the only logical winter-camping breakfast food. Food preparation was becoming a hassle and we wanted to avoid any complicated planning. Oatmeal is inexpensive and light, so we stocked up with a six-month supply.

I remember waking up to frigid Georgia mornings, stiff and hungry. Tea was the first priority and the only real chance of getting warm. Craig would pour boiling water into our plastic mugs and I'd pour icy spring water into the pot for oatmeal. After a few minutes, we'd pour in the oats until our pot was gurgling with lumpy bubbles. Breakfast was bland but edible. Every morning we added more brown sugar in a desperate attempt to alter the oaty flavor.

The first meal of the day soon became a chore. Eating oats became so painful I held my nose as I shoveled the lumpy paste down my throat. We tried the instant oatmeal packets flavored with apples and cinnamon, maple syrup, and brown sugar, and various berry flavors. Dehydrated blueberries and strawberries changed the color but my taste buds were not fooled.

I survived a breakfast of oatmeal for thirty-two days in a row, but on the thirty-third day I thought I was going to heave. I scooped a pile of oats onto my spoon and just sat there looking at it like a stubborn child refusing to finish her vegetables. The texture was like spackle; I felt like giving the shelter a good caulk. Blueberry juice bled purple streaks through the white paste. I stood up, still balancing the pile on my spoon, and walked around the shelter, trying to psyche myself up. Steam rose from the spoon; the oats were getting cold. I flung the food to the ground. (Note: You should NEVER get rid of food like that, especially near a shelter. Under the circumstances, though, I will have to plead temporary insanity from oats, an understandable plea.)

I gave it another try. I stuck a loaded spoon into my mouth and froze. "Swallow it," Craig said sternly, but I couldn't get it down. I leapt up, ran away from the shelter, and spat it out. That was it, I thought, I can never eat oatmeal again.

We ate Ramen noodles the next two mornings—of course, Ramen is only a half step above oatmeal—but it got us to town. We shuffled through our new food box at the post office and removed the oatmeal. One call to Craig's brother stopped the shipment of oats. We instructed his family to remove oatmeal from all the boxes and get rid of it. Trust us, we said, we will never touch that stuff again. The man at the post office offered his condolences. "Wow, I wish I had some food to give you," he said.

We assured him it was okay, that we had stocked up on pop-tarts and that they really were more nutritionally sound than most people think. We didn't actually believe that last part, but at the time we needed to convince ourselves that *something* we were eating was in some way contributing to good health. As our hike progressed we relied mostly on pop-tarts, Snickers, and pasta. I'm sure we didn't score too high on nutrition, but we did better than some. It was rumored that a man did the whole trail on Little Debbie Oatmeal Creme Pies, those preserve-saturated oatmeal cookies glued together with marshmallow cream. Another hiker with a suffering budget survived on peanuts, Gatorade powder, and Ramen.

Weight was a factor. After a few weeks we had eliminated all the extras—the spices, the bullion, the dried onion. Cookware was reduced to one pot and a spoon for each of us. We cooked as little as possible, eating pop-tarts for breakfast, peanut butter for lunch, and Lipton noodle packets supplemented with a pound of plain pasta for dinner.

Occasionally we found a hiker box (a collection of unwanted food donated by hikers—found at most hostels, some general stores, an occasional post office) with an unusual trail mix, cereal, or gourmet dehydrated meal of chicken cacciatore or beef stroganoff. There were usually Ramen packages that no one wanted, and always oatmeal. We would pick through the boxes and sometimes leave extra trail mix, turkey jerky, or pasta or rice that was too heavy to carry.

The man left and Craig and I divvied up our new supplies.

"You carry the pop-tarts," I said.

"I'm already carrying the tent and the stove," he said.

"But you should, you weigh a hundred pounds more than me."

"No, I don't, and besides, look how much room you have in your top pouch. You can take the peanut butter too," and he threw me the food.

I threw it back at him. "I'm not carrying all that," I said, waiting for Otter to interrupt our battle. Somehow Otter always happened to witness our "fights" over who was supposed to carry what.

"I have never heard two people bitch more about their loads in my entire life," said Otter, laughing and shaking his head. Deep down he knew our bickering was a unique way of expressing affection, but sometimes we needed him to tell us how ridiculous we were, before we made complete brats of ourselves.

§

We stopped in Pearisburg for another reason—to add a third member to our team. Craig's family drove down from Connecticut to spend Easter with us and to deliver our dog. Kodiak had grown up to be a 110-pound Alaskan malamute, although technically he was still a puppy. Everyone who meets him comments on how enormous his head is; we're still hoping that someday his body will grow to match his enormous cranium. We planned on having Kodiak join us for the remainder of the hike. He was able to comfortably carry a dog pack filled with twenty pounds of dog food. "We'll probably have to stuff the extra space in his pack with rocks just to slow him down," said Craig. We figured it would be quite an adjustment for us all. He seemed to like the barn, although he tried to run off with other dogs all afternoon. Luckily we restrained him from jumping on the pastor. His trail name was easy: He was clearly going to be Trouble.

We hit the trail once again, but this time as a family. There was something amusing about hiking with Trouble, watching him get used to his saddle bags, trying to anticipate when we needed to restrain him. We laughed a lot then, and somehow the walking seemed pleasant. I had always liked southern Virginia; the rolling hills and wide valleys were comforting. There was one particular spot, however, that stood out above the others.

I recall staring into a white curtain of falling snow for three days. The fourth day was seventy degrees. The snow melted that morning. The sun's glare was intense, reflecting a dizzying light off everything it touched. Although surprised by the drastic change, we welcomed the warmth. The following two days were hazy and hot, as baby flies, a million strong, entered the world. They swarmed around our heads, bit our legs and necks, and obstructed the views of hazy ridges and green checkerboard farmland.

*The Appalachian Trail, stretching some 2,159 miles from Georgia to Maine.*

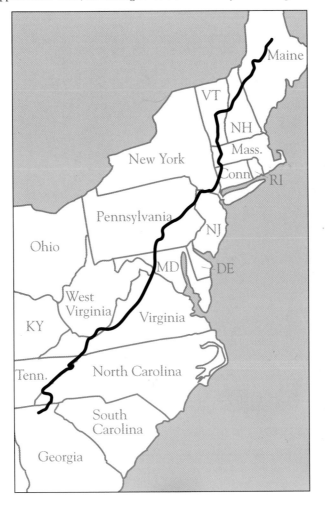

Craig and Adrienne.

*Tending to blisters in Georgia. Mt. Katahdin in Maine is about one million footsteps away.*

*Trying to stay warm on a frigid morning at an AT shelter in Georgia.*

*Breaking trail in Tennessee, where winter conditions still prevailed when Adrienne and Craig started their journey.*

*Caught in another snowstorm in Tennessee.*

*Craig and Adrienne admiring the view from Standing Indian Mountain, North Carolina.*

*Red wolves,* canis rufus, *were unsuccessfully re-introduced into the Smokies in the early 90s.* Photo and copyright, U.S. Fish and Wildlife Service.

*Craig hiking up a bald in North Carolina. Scientists still aren't sure what conditions created the balds but Cherokee stories provide one answer.*

*Craig and the two-pound teepee in Virginia. Though lightweight, the teepee would prove to be no match for the swarms of insects that lay ahead.*

*Today, old growth trees, such as this chestnut with a base circumference of 28.5 feet, are rarely found in the Appalachians.* Photo courtesy of Margaret A. Roth.

*Storms such as this deposit acidic pollutants—nitrates, sulfates, and ozone—on the entire Appalachian range.* Photo by Jim Renfro.

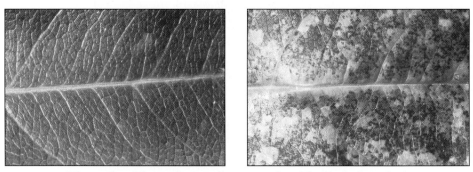

*The results of this acidic rain are catastrophic. The black cherry leaf on the left is healthy while the one on the right has ozone damage.*
Photo by Jim Renfro.

*Visibility of over 100 miles (above) is cut to 10 miles (below) when airborne pollutants settle over the Smokies.* Photos by Jim Renfro.

*Trout are among the animals susceptible to environmental damage in the Smokies.* Photo by Jim Renfro.

*Communication towers favor tall peaks. Along the AT grass-roots organizations are working to minimize the impact of such towers.* Photo by Jim Renfro.

*Negotiating the rugged terrain of the Southern Appalachians.*

*Craig, Adrienne, Rusty, and Otter at Rusty's place, where thru-hikers are welcome but televisions are not.*

*Hiking along the lowlands of the mid-Atlantic region.*

*The rocky paths of Pennsylvania, the author's homestate.*

*Kodiak, a.k.a. Trouble, takes to the trail.
Adding a dog to the adventure introduced
an entirely new level of joy and anxiety.*

*Adrienne and "Kodi" posing before a shelter. Along the trail, Kodi
would encounter serious trouble in the form of a gun.*

*Returning to the woods when the AT enters Connecticut. With the woods came swarms of hungry mosquitoes.*

*Craig working his way through Maine's infamous Mahoosuc Notch, where a huge jumble of boulders litters the trail.*

Mail drops such as this in Caratunk, Maine, provide fresh food and a respite from a diet of gorp (Good Old Raisins and Peanuts) and oatmeal.

Crossing the swollen streams in Maine, the final state for northbound AT hikers.

Craig proposing to Adrienne atop Saddleback Mountain, Maine.

*The triumphant duo atop Mt. Katahdin, Maine,*
*2,159 miles after their journey north began.*

The events of that week are slightly blurred. I remember only the tree.

On the edge of a pasture in Sinking Creek Valley stood a giant white oak. It was more than 300 years old and it was the biggest tree I had ever seen. Standing beside it I looked into a wall of bark. I pressed my body against its mass and felt the rough, corky bark against my cheek. I had to walk back forty to fifty yards to get the entire tree in my range of vision.

The trunk, eighteen feet around, rose fifteen feet before branching into enormous arms. Each branch was as thick as a common tree—horizontal and suspended. The branches were giant octopus arms frozen in midair.

Compared to the old oak, surrounding trees looked like toothpicks, like the shaky legs of a newborn fawn. They trembled in the wind while the old oak remained motionless, fixed, grounded.

The old tree had witnessed a lot of change in the past three centuries. Why had this tree been allowed to live while the surrounding forested mountains and valleys were cleared for farmland and grazing pastures? Its neighbors were cut and carted off, and cattle were carted in. Old growth was cut, then cut again, to make room for housing developments and cities and for roads and power lines that slice through the mountains for miles.

For the past 50 years the old oak has seen hikers pass by. Every thru-hiker climbs over the fence and stile attached to its trunk, walks across the pasture, and enters another patch of skinny trees. That day we did the same thing. I kept looking back, trying to envision what this area looked like, what the entire East Coast must have looked like dominated by 300-year-old trees.

Glenn Cardwell remembers. Glenn is what some people might call an old-timer. His family was living in the Smokies before the park was designated, and they were relocated once the park was established in 1940. Glenn spent most of his life leading natural history tours for the Smokies and is now the mayor of Pittman Center, a community located just outside the park's western boundary. Glenn can tell you about the old-growth chestnut forests he walked through as a boy, how

chestnut trees once accounted for one-quarter of all the standing timber in eastern forests, and how by the 1950s virtually all the chestnut
trees had died from a fungus called chestnut blight which was introduced from Asia. He can tell you about old-growth spruce-fir forests,
the way the ravens called to each other from their high perches, how
today entire mountaintops are covered with dead red spruces and
Fraser firs, and how hardly anyone sees ravens.

Glenn remembers spending many summer days in the 1930s and
1940s in the high-mountain region of the Southern Appalachians.
He and his friends used to spend most of August under the canopy of
300-year-old spruces and 150-year-old firs while he waited for the fall
harvest. "We'd go up there to escape the summer heat," he told me. "It
was mystical, like entering a different world." When he'd take people
there for the first time they were always astounded by how dark it was
and by the intoxicating smell of pines, as if an oily odor was oozing
from the trees. "It was like someone had sprayed perfume all through
the air," he said. Glenn's mother would send him to the high forests to
collect the resin that flowed from the smooth bark of the fir trees. He
collected the sweet-smelling sap, he says with a smile, in a Prince
Albert tobacco can.

The dense canopy trapped moisture and allowed a thick understory to grow on the dark, damp forest floor. Glenn recalls walking
through Rugel's ragwort, mountain oxalis, mountain cranberry, wood
ferns, and witch-hobble. The moss, he said, grew to be a foot deep.
Moss also covered the spruce trees, finding purchase in the frayed bark.
There were all kinds of spiders and salamanders, flying squirrels,
shrews, and golden-nosed voles. And there were birds: chestnut war-
blers, golden-crowned kingfishers, juncos, and ravens. "To some people a wolf or a grizzly bear is a symbol of wilderness," he said, "but to
me it's the raven. They lived up there when the forests were healthy.
Now, they're real hard to find."

It scares me how eager we are to accept that what we see today is as
wild as it gets. It's easy to be satisfied with young forests when we
haven't experienced anything different. I fear that in a hundred years
children may grow up not knowing what even a marginally healthy

forest feels like. I fear they'll be content with pavement, the way I've become content with forty-year-old trees, unable to grasp the dimensions of a larger nature. I wonder if I had grown up with old-growth forests if I'd fight harder to keep them around. It's important, I think, to keep a tradition alive of what once was. Only if we're able to compare the present condition to a benchmark can we see how far we've come or how much we've lost. I try to imagine ravens soaring above enormous old trees, circling the steaming canopy, their calls echoing through the hollow, getting lost in the valleys. I tell Glenn I'll try not to forget.

The discouraging part of the story is that even if we stop logging and let the trees live, most trees would die anyway, long before they get to be 300 years old. Eastern forests have been wiped out by a number of exotic insects and diseases with names like the hemlock wooly adelgid, gypsy moth, butternut canker, dogwood anthracnose, pear thrips, and beech bark disease. These insects and diseases hadn't significantly affected the forests until recently, for two reasons. The first is that these insects, which scientists often call exotic pests, weren't on this continent 200 years ago. They are called exotic pests because they were introduced from Europe or Asia or some other faraway place. Exotic species evolved in an ecosystem that kept them in check, but when they arrived in America there was nothing to kill them. They outcompeted native species and had free rein in eastern forests. Exotic species can be plants like kudzu, insects like the gypsy moth, mammals like the European wild boar, or fish like rainbow trout. Across the country, the control of exotic species is a top priority for land managers.

Our forests are dying for another reason. Over the last few decades many trees have become weaker; they have become more susceptible to diseases and inclement weather that, a hundred years ago, they would have been able to withstand. Air pollution has been cited as the culprit for human health problems, limited visibility, and economic loss, and it may very well be delivering the death blow to trees that blanket the Appalachian Range. In fact, the quality of air in the eastern United States may be the number one threat to ecosystems along the entire Appalachian Range. Harvard Ayers, author of *Air Pollution and Tree Death*, writes: "Century after century, these forests have survived the ravages of bugs, disease, harsh climate, and even rapacious human logging. Occasionally, single species have declined.... But never have we witnessed the decline and mass death of almost all the major tree species of entire ecosystems." Ayers believes that air pollution significantly contributes to the poor health of both terrestrial and aquatic ecosystems.

When you really begin to look into these issues you soon realize that it's tough to draw lines around causes and effects, and you realize that a variety of forces worked together to produce a number of harmful effects in ecosystems. As it is with just about everything in nature, it's tough to separate individual strands of fabric from the tapestry because everything, in one way or another, is woven together. Take the gypsy moth, for example. The moth was brought to New England in 1869, and within ten years it began defoliating every tree in sight. The moth prefers oak-hickory forests, and it just so happened that after the chestnut blight (another exotic species) killed virtually all the chestnut trees, oak-hickory forests filled in the gaps. The moths actually aren't that particular, so when oak trees aren't available, they'll settle for hemlocks, cottonwoods, pines, and spruces.

Even though it's common for the moths to eat more than half the leaves on a tree, a healthy tree can survive several years of attacks. A substantial die-off of trees due to gypsy moths wasn't seen until recently. In 1991, the moth had infested 125 million acres of forests around the nation, and entire mountainsides of trees in the Shenandoahs were stripped of leaves. Some scientists think the trees died because they were weak—weak from acid rain and air pollution that sucked the nutrients from the soil and inhibited the trees' ability to photosynthesize.

The fear of total gypsy moth takeover subsided when a virus was found that attacks the moths. On the prowl for other natural enemies to the moth, managers imported an exotic fungus in 1920 in hopes of killing the moths, but for some reason the fungus didn't kick in until the 1980s. Scientists aren't sure what long-term effects the exotic fungus will produce. Remember that childhood song? The one that ends like this: "I swallowed a spider to catch the fly. I don't know why I swallowed a fly. Perhaps I'll die."

The Cherokees have a story about why the Appalachians are hazy. Every year the Cherokee people held a hunting training camp in the forest to teach the younger tribe members how to hunt deer. When the training camp ended, the men set out to find meat for the village for the winter. One year, as the men set out, they came upon an attractive stranger whom they let join their hunt. They didn't realize the stranger was a mischievous Little Person in disguise. The stranger began to make the tribe careless. He told some of the boys that it would be fun to shoot arrows near their friends to scare them. No one was hurt and the men thought it was very funny, so practical jokes started throughout the tribe. The men spent more time harassing each other than seriously hunting, so it was no surprise when they returned to the village with little meat. During the winter, there was not enough food to go around and some of the old people and some of the very young people died.

During the next few hunting seasons the men were delinquent and were sometimes injured or killed in their pranks. The older men decided to call for a council to put an end to this foolishness. When the chiefs convened, they knew that they could smoke the peace pipe only after a peaceful solution had been agreed upon. But the Little Person had spread his ways throughout the tribe, and the chiefs soon became grumpy and impatient with the process. One of the chiefs took out the peace pipe and started smoking. Soon all the chiefs were smoking and laughing and had forgotten about the problem. This continued for several days until there was a billowing cloud of smoke rising from the mountains. The Great One looked upon the chiefs and decided to put an end to their behavior, so he turned the old chiefs into plants called Indian pipes. These flowers grow from the Southern Appalachians to New York and they remind Cherokees of places where friends and family quarreled. The Great One still needed to do something with all the smoke, so he left it hanging over the mountains to remind people of the time when chiefs and hunters were inflicted with selfishness. Even on the clearest days in the Southern Appalachians you can often find a wisp of smoke. That, according to the legend, is to remind us that people are never completely free of selfishness.

It is true that the Southern Appalachians are naturally hazy. Things like high relative humidity, warm summer temperatures, stagnant winds, and high amounts of precipitation predispose the Southern Appalachians to poor air quality. Gas emitted from the dense vegetation in the Appalachians create their own natural haze. These natural emissions, however, are overwhelmed by what is now being released into the atmosphere by power plants and automobiles.

It has been well documented that in the summer the Southern Appalachians is the haziest region in the United States. The average visibility in the Smokies should be sixty-five miles. Today it is twenty-five miles, and during severe haze episodes it has been reduced to less than one mile. Since 1948, average visibility in the Southern Appalachians has decreased 40 percent in the winter and 80 percent in the summer.

Jim Renfro, air quality specialist for Great Smoky Mountains National Park, explained to me that there are three major contributors to air pollution: nitrates, sulfates, and ozone. "The highest nitrogen deposition in the country is in the high elevations in the Smokies," said Renfro. "We're talking about an average of 100 pounds per acre per year of sulfate and 80 pounds per acre of nitrates. The soils can't buffer it anymore, so they release nitrates right into the streams. We get acidic pulses in the streams that can affect brook trout and aquatic insect populations."

Industries like paper mills, oil refineries, steel mills, power plants, and chemical plants that burn fossil fuels like coal, oil, and gas are responsible for 77 percent of the sulfates released into the air. It is the sulfate particles that create the haze hanging over the Appalachians. Sulfate concentrations increased in the Southern Appalachians by 23 percent from 1984 to 1998. In May of 1999, when I was visiting Dr. John Peine, research sociologist with the U.S. Geological Survey, on his porch overlooking the foothills of the Smokies, I could barely see the ridge line just five miles from his house. "Where is the threshold of tolerance?" he asked. "When will people say, 'No more loss, no more devastation'? It's a value-driven decision that everyone makes for themselves. The Smokies is the most highly protected landscape in the East and we still see all these problems. It's horrific when you look at other places, where man has a stronger presence. How much crap do you put into the air before you say you violated something sacred?"

Ground-level ozone is a colorless gas that is formed when nitrogen oxides from industry and automobile emissions combine with volatile organic compounds that are naturally emitted from forests. During the summer of 1998, eight-hour average ozone exposures taken from air-quality stations in the Great Smoky Mountains were the highest ever recorded. These levels have taken their toll on red oak, sassafras, black gum, tulip poplar, and sourwood trees. In the sun, the pores on leaves open to exchange oxygen for carbon dioxide but get deadly doses of ozone instead. Ninety percent of black cherry trees and milkweed plants in numerous park locations show symptoms of ozone damage.

These three pollutants—nitrates, sulfates, and ozone—return to the ground as acid rain, dry particles, and cloud water. Clouds laced with these pollutants have a pH of around 2.0 (similar to lemon juice and vinegar). The high-elevation spruce-fir forests are continuously soaked in these acidic clouds, so it only makes sense that they show the greatest effects. "The spruce-fir forest is the crown jewel of the crown jewel," says Peine, "and those trees can't be replaced." Dr. Peine leaned over the railing on the porch, gazing at the ripples of forest that were awash in haze. He told me that it's not only the trees that are affected but the hundreds of species that evolved in the forest and are dependent on the spruce-fir trees to create the right microclimate and soil conditions. "You're losing an entire system," he said. "Spruce-fir forests are endemic to the Southern Appalachians and are also endemic to a point in time that marks the change in vegetation patterns on the entire continent. From a biological perspective, you're losing the opportunity to understand how those systems functioned 10,000 years ago."

The air-quality problem is not isolated in the Smokies but continues north up the Appalachian Range. The hazy ridge lines that Craig and I gazed across the day we saw the old oak tree is evidence of the same pollution problem that plagues the Appalachian region from Alabama to Maine. As Craig and I walked up the spine of the Appalachians, we noticed patches of dead trees on many mountain-tops, and we noticed many trees uprooted. Dr. Peine told me that many of these trees were probably red spruces. "The acidic soils leach out nutrients that the trees need," he explained. "The pollutants also free up elements like aluminum that are toxic to the trees." If that weren't enough, acidic clouds hover over the spruces, causing damage to the needles. At the same time, Fraser firs are being killed by an exotic insect. This creates gaps in the forest. The red spruces are shallow rooted to begin with, are weakened from air pollution, and easily blow over since the Fraser firs aren't there to protect them from the wind. Once again, the interconnectedness of these systems is apparent.

"How can we let this happen?" I asked Peine and Renfro.

Apparently, the Park Service has been trying to work with the industries to set responsible emissions controls. The 1990 amendment to the Clean Air Act set emissions standards but allows companies to buy, sell, trade, or collect emissions allowances. Title IV of the 1990 Clean Air Act amendments outlines a market-based control strategy for sulfate emissions. In 1998, the National Acid Precipitation Assessment Program reported to Congress that "[t]he allowance market has given some sources the incentive to overcontrol their sulfate emissions and bank their allowances for use in future years. Other sources have deferred control by acquiring allowances from sources that have overcontrolled their emissions." The Smokies haven't seen a significant improvement because the companies are allowed to manipulate the system. For example, industries reduce emissions from coal plants in, let's say, Mississippi, where it is cheap to do so, and they actually increase emissions from power plants near the Smokies. The program, although well intended, allows companies to pollute certain areas as long as the company's overall emissions are in compliance with standards. The market approach was supposed to put pollution standards in business terms and provide a practical, workable strategy to give companies incentives to be better environmental stewards. Unfortunately, in many cases the system has been abused.

Although sulfur emissions have decreased due to tighter emissions standards in the 1995 amendment to the Clear Air Act, nitrate and ozone levels are still on the rise. "The South is growing," says Renfro. "Urban sprawl is increasing and there's a higher demand for electricity, especially in the summer." The industries keep expanding, keep asking for more power plants as more people demand more power. Peine recalls with frustration the permitting process: "The state of Tennessee only let the Park Service review proposals for new point-source emissions during a 30-day review period, so we'd have to drop everything and put together some response. It limited our options to respond, kept us off guard. Basically the industry and the state were not being up front with the Park Service when they were planning air quality regulations for the state."

In his book *Ecosystem Management for Sustainability*, Peine writes that since 1978 the National Park Service reviewed more than 500 major new-source permits for emissions within 100 miles of national parks. Thirty-two were for sources near the Smokies. In only twelve cases, Peine reports, the Park Service denied the permit. Three of those cases were in Tennessee and the state awarded the permits anyway. "The Eastman Chemical Company is one of the largest sources of toxic air pollution in the entire southern Appalachian region," he writes. The company emits more than 29 million pounds of toxic chemicals every year, a quarter of the toxic emissions in Tennessee. In 1990, Eastman proposed to add three gas-fired boilers; the Park Service objected. The state issued the permits anyway. The Park Service appealed, to no avail. "The state doesn't want to be thought of as impeding economic development," says Peine.

Craig and I gaze across the ridges of southern Virginia. The sky is light blue. There aren't many clouds and it seems the sky ought to be a shade richer. But we've tarnished the crown, let it corrode beyond what seems reasonable. The haze, as the Cherokee see it, should be a reminder of our selfishness and our collective unwillingness to be good stewards of the land.

Thankfully there are people who are trying to change the way we do business with the land. Many groups—outdoors clubs to agricultural organizations to historical societies—want to preserve the integrity of the place, and many people have been fighting to make it better. Federal legislation tightened standards for nitrates, and on a national level we've seen a decline in these pollutants. The Environmental Protection Agency (EPA) is currently working on strengthening emissions controls on vehicles, and in 1998 it announced its plan to reduce nitrogen oxide pollution by 30 percent by 2003 in twenty-two eastern states.

In the early 1990s the Southern Appalachian Mountains Initiative (SAMI) was created to identify and recommend emissions-management strategies to remedy existing and prevent future adverse air-quality effects in southern Appalachia. SAMI is made up of eight southern states, the EPA, the National Park Service, the Forest Service, industries, academics, environmental organizations, and the public. Since SAMI was formed, regional haze rules have been proposed, stricter emissions for industries have been developed, and tighter tailpipe standards for highway and off-road vehicles have been implemented.

Also encouraging was the April 1999 Governor's Summit on Mountain Air Quality in Asheville, North Carolina. Jim Renfro was very pleased with the turnout: 500 people attended—politicians, the media, government agencies, environmental groups, and the general public. "Air-quality issues are in the press and media every day," says Renfro. "People know that it's a big issue. Most people know we need to implement higher standards. But until that happens, I'm going to make sure people know that we are doing it or we're not doing it." He has recently set up an exhibit at Sugarlands Visitor Center in the Smokies which provides information about the cause and effect of air pollution. The exhibit is linked to monitors in the park which show real-time images of current visibility and ozone concentrations. Renfro also told me about the Great Smoky Mountains Parks as Classrooms project, where every year they bring 10,000 children to the Smokies to educate them about air quality and healthy ecosystems.

I asked Jim Renfro about future regulations and incentives for industries. "Sure, there are direct costs," he says, "but the socioeconomic benefits of clean air outweigh the direct costs of controlling pollutants. Human health, recreation, tourism, fishing, real estate, cultural resources, ecosystem health, a sense of place—it's hard to quantify the values but they are far greater than direct costs." Renfro also hopes the park will be allowed to be a more active participant in the permitting process. Tennessee and North Carolina recently signed an agreement that clarifies everybody's roles and responsibilities; the polluter must provide timely and complete information to the park and vice versa, so there are no surprises. Encouraged, but realistic, he adds, "We'll see if the agreement works."

As Craig, Trouble, and I made our way through southern Virginia, it wasn't difficult to feel overwhelmed when we passed entire mountain slopes that were forested in sick trees. It was equally depressing searching hazy views for blurred ridge lines for days at a time. We became well aware that air quality knows no boundaries, but this can also work to our advantage when we decide to clean things up. Just as poor air quality can degrade entire regions, once cleaned up, it can affect areas just as large. We need to start somewhere, somewhere local. For many, a park or a forest is a good place to start, and it seems that once we work on protecting a small tract, the rest of the region will follow. Of the Smokies, Jim Renfro says, "If you protect the park, you'll probably protect the region, and if you protect sensitive resources, you'll protect 99 percent of everything else." I like to think we are making progress.

## Chapter Five

# TROUBLE HITS THE TRAIL

My journal entry for May 1 begins, "If it snows this month, I'm giving up." Winter stalked us up the Appalachians through the beginning of April, and we continued to heat rocks in a campfire to give to Pariah, a physicist with a Ph.D. who figured the weather would be warm enough for only a fifty-degree sleeping bag. He wrapped the hot rocks in clothes and slept with them in his thin slumberjack bag. Our section-hiker friend spent many cold nights praying for spring. Fortunately, we saw the last snowflake of the trip in mid-April and sent home the extra thermals shortly thereafter. By April 20, a month after the calendar's declaration of spring, when we were 700 miles into our trip and halfway through Virginia, warmth was finally here to stay.

The concept of seasons fascinates me. We have divided the year into quarters of distinct trends in weather and astrological positions. We measure to the second the transition. After walking through the seasons, I discovered that the change is indeed that fast, but the timing is certainly unpredictable. April 19 the same scraps of leaves littered the ground—bare, brown, bland. Naked trees, hollow forest. On April 20 Craig and I woke to a strange buzzing outside the tent. "Do you hear that?" he asked. "The bugs are out." Flies, bees, butterflies, and gnats laced the air with a hum. All around us green tips parted soil and squirmed through the surface. That day life emerged on cue. The earth declared that it was time, and everything began sprouting, popping, flying, buzzing—all at once, an epic birth. The earth darkened and softened as we walked.

Two days after the greening of the earth began, the leaves and flowers were large enough to resemble their adult forms but still young enough to dot the forest in a panoramic smudge of green, purple, pink, red, and white. The forest looked like a painting by Monet, everything in dots and specks, blending together in a web of color and texture. Day after day we watched the forests fill in until the process was complete and insects and weather began to damage the perfect, virgin leaves.

"I think if we stand here long enough we'd actually be able to see a flower grow," I said. Nature approached life with purpose. Sucking nectar, bees moved steadily from flower to flower. Their movements were focused, patterned, fixed. Plants pushing their way through dry, rocky soil seemed to shout, "I'm dividing, elongating, photosynthesizing, respiring, reproducing!" I saw something in the arrival of spring that I, myself, had been striving for. Nature had intensity, direction, confidence, an elegant sureness of procedure, a sensibility to life.

Watching spring made me think about people I have known who lost their life-guiding set of rules and sense of purpose. I thought mostly about people who wear suits and drink martinis and play golf on Sundays, but we all may get lost from time to time. It seems like people often become obsessed with financial and secular security and lose sight of what they are surviving for. Some blame it on adolescence or midlife crisis, but I think we humanoids get confused now and then as to why we are here and what our lives mean. Some people go to churches or temples or to the woods to try and make sense of it all.

The root of our confusion, I gather, comes from disassociating ourselves from the guiding life force, the earth. Concrete and skyscrapers physically block our connection to Nature, and they spiritually inhibit us from identifying our purpose. We have become a society that relies on computers and cell phones and copy machines (things with which we cannot spiritually relate, not to mention things that break down a lot), instead of turning to the natural world for guidance. I have a fear that in twenty years every person is going to walk around with a computer monitor attached to his or her head, experiencing nature through virtual vacations and never leaving home.

Other species focus on survival and fitness, but to many of us in the West, survival is not a concern, and our fitness (ability to reproduce to pass on our genes) is limitless. If we get hungry we go to the store. If it rains we go inside. We crank the heat or the AC. Travel is no problem—jump in a car or hop on a plane. Drinkable water comes from a faucet, and lights turn on when we flip a switch. Do we appreciate these luxuries anymore? What *do* we care about? Money, sex, the NBA championship, promotions, what's on TV Thursday nights. These things are not evil, but they lead to a sense of purposelessness.

The trail stripped away most of those distractions and made survival something we actually had to work at. Thru-hikers often feel more connected to the natural world and reflect the drive and purpose they see in nature. They often leave the woods with an enlightened, relaxed feeling, like they have a big secret which no one else would understand.

That is the way I felt as spring arrived. I appreciated warmth and life and color more than I ever had, but as we approached boundless civilization, I knew that it may have been a temporary discovery. We were approaching the 500-mile stretch of trail that is considered the mid-Atlantic region. It is characterized by low elevations and heavily populated areas. Before entering this region, we stopped at a very special place, one that enhanced the enlightened feeling that had begun to grow inside us.

§

In a hollow on Virginia's Blue Ridge sits a homestead littered with sheds, barns, wood piles, and farm equipment. There is no plumbing, no electricity, no telephone. Instead there is an outhouse, a wood-burning stove and grill, a battery radio, gas lanterns. Blue barrels collect rainwater from the roof for cooking and washing. Drinking water flows from a natural spring. You collect the water yourself from the source.

Rusty is the definition of down-home. He is big boned, fair skinned and freckled, and speaks in simple, honest language. Rusty lives here year-round with his three goats and forty chickens (all of which he claims to know by name), and he opens his home to 1,000 thru-hikers every year. He shuttles hikers in a maroon Ford van that has white footprints painted all over it. Polaroid photos of each visiting hiker are posted on the walls and ceilings of the front and back porches. The porches are additionally decorated with random paraphernalia: an abandoned wasp nest, crutches, a few pairs of old sneakers, a badminton racket, miniature American flags. Take your pick of seats; there are metal folding chairs, a wooden rocking chair, a bright orange vinyl couch. I chose the porch swing. It creaked as I rocked.

Signs everywhere explain the rules of the Hollow. One sign warns that any electronic device—video camera, computer, cell phone—will be shot on sight. After a few conversations with Rusty, we learned that the sign is no joke. Craig and I came to Rusty's for a dose of thru-hiker culture. By this time we had discovered that off-trail experiences were as memorable as the actual hiking. We spent the afternoon washing our clothes with a plunger in a five-gallon bucket, lounging in the hammock, and playing horseshoes. "Help yourselves to food in the kitchen," said Rusty, "and there's sodas in the stream." Rusty has dedicated his life to helping hikers and requests only a minimal monetary donation or a helping hand around the farm.

As the sun set, Craig and I eyed the hot tub. Rusty agreed to fire it up for us, and as we walked out to the tub we realized that he was literally going to fire it up. Down in the valley, we came upon a metal rectangular tub that sat on stilts. Rusty piled wood under the tub, drenched the sticks in lighter fluid, and tossed in a match. "Don't mess with the fire," he said. "If you put one more scrap of wood under there you'll cook for sure." Craig and I stripped and climbed in the human cook pot as flames crackled under the tub. "This is unbelievable," Craig said, staring up at the stars and melting into the water, "unbelievable." When we finished soaking, we lay on the wooden platform beside the tub and dried almost instantly. Numb with comfort, I lay on my back and let the boards absorb all of my weight. Craig and I lay side by side and waited until our eyes adjusted to darkness and we could see a blanket of stars across the sky. After a while we reluctantly dressed and returned to the house to let other hikers have a turn.

The break was welcome after a strenuous couple weeks that included a number of twenty-something-mile days. We hiked past Catawba, over McAfee Knob, along the Tinker Cliffs. It had been a long trek through Virginia; the trail runs for nearly 500 miles through this state and hikers often feel they're not making any progress—

a condition known as the Virginia Blues. Despite the challenges it was a good walk, and now, nine weeks into the trip, we had traveled more than 800 miles from Springer Mountain.

The challenges we faced in Virginia were largely a result of our tent. The problem was that we traded the tent for a blue-and-turquoise-striped teepee. Imagine a swath of cheap material, like a windbreaker from Kmart. Now imagine the material draped around a center pole and staked to the ground. That was what was supposed to shelter us from snow. Shall I be kind and say it was less than optimal? The teepee was a floorless summer number, not a sturdy structure made of canvas or hide like those you see in pictures of Native American villages. Not even close. Our teepee was deficient in any sort of rain-deflecting capabilities and was certainly no snow shield. When it did warm up, there was no relief from the black flies since the teepee walls didn't touch the ground. Trouble didn't like the teepee either. He would begin the night inside it and in the middle of the night push his way under the fabric wall, nearly taking out the entire shelter each time. I can honestly say I thought it was a bad idea from the start, but I let Craig have his way and figured that at least we'd suffer together. Craig was right about one thing: it was certainly lighter, and he was proud of reducing his pack weight by five pounds.

Trouble required some additional energy during the day as well. He had a way of pretending to be content with following the trail, but the instant we turned away he'd dash into the woods after a scent or sound that only a dog can perceive. One day we searched for a good half-hour for him. We had planned to make many miles that day and didn't have the time or energy to wander through the forest looking for a dog. "I'm going to beat the shit out of that dog," Craig sputtered. A while later, and certainly on his own agenda, Trouble found Craig on a ridge. When the two of them returned, I asked Craig if he disciplined Trouble. "All I could do was laugh at him when I saw that big head of his," he said. "He had his ears back and that goofy expression on his face. He was wagging his tail like he was so happy to see me. I couldn't do anything." Somehow people have a way of falling in love with that dog.

During his second week, Trouble pounced on a skunk. For the next couple days, when the smell was most pungent, we didn't mind so much when he strayed from the trail. I'm sure he had no idea why I stopped petting him and why Craig and I would inch away when he came close. Fastening Trouble's saddlebags was instantly elevated to Worst Camp Chore. The bags were secured by a belt that fastened under his belly, and securing them required one of us to straddle the dog and wrap our arms around the dog's belly to clasp the buckle. It was nearly impossible to fasten the buckle without touching the skunk-dog, and our arms and hands soon smelled like skunk.

Trouble was physically challenged by two things: stiles and heat. A stile is a wooden ladder over a barbed-wire fence which allows hikers access to private lands while securing livestock in the pastures. Since Trouble is not designed to climb ladders, we had to lift his 110 pounds up and over each stile. By the third one, he was having second thoughts about being a trail dog.

Heat will undoubtedly be a problem for a dog that is made to pull sleds in Alaska. When the mercury rose, Trouble simply lay down in the middle of the trail and refused to move. It took a few bribes and a lot of encouragement to get him to continue. Even in the heat, however, he kept us entertained. For some reason, he thought that rocks were much cooler than the ground and often ran forty yards off the trail to find the perfect slab. He would perch on a distant rock for all of ten seconds before he had to move on. Once, we watched him scale a near-vertical rock outcropping and perch on the jagged ledge fifteen feet off the ground.

The sounds of spring helped his situation. As the forests filled in and the earth began to crawl, Trouble was all senses. The sight of a deer or mole, and the new smells and sounds, caused him temporarily to abandon his heat concerns.

"Why didn't y'all bring him along during the beginning of the trip, when it was cold and snowy?" Rusty asked.

"Dogs aren't allowed in the Smokies," Craig explained, "and we weren't sure how we would get him around the park. Besides, we needed to get used to the trail and to each other before we could worry about a dog." It was true. Having him in the beginning would have made the hard times even harder. We had to learn to trust each other and feel confident in our ability to survive before we could expand our hiking party. "It's too bad," said Craig, " 'cause he would've loved it."

It was a different hike with a dog. We were constantly monitoring his location, calling for him, and praying that he wouldn't get into trouble.

"The first week, he must have covered three times the miles that we did," Craig told Rusty.

"No kiddin'," said Rusty.

"He'd run way ahead, come back to check on us, then take off again," Craig added. "It took him a while to realize that he would be walking all day every day. Eventually he learned to pace himself and lie down when we take breaks."

I continued, "There's definitely a downside to hiking with a dog. He scares wild turkeys and grouse before we can get close, and it's more difficult to get rides to town. We're limited to pickup trucks."

The following week in the Shenandoahs, Trouble became infested with ticks and acquired tapeworms. I put Craig on tick duty and, to my tremendous relief, they both were good sports about it. A visit to the vet was an ordeal, but the tapeworms were flushed out with no further complications. Trouble was far from easy to manage as a trail dog, but Craig and I felt that he completed our trail family, and we never regretted bringing him along. Trouble was our boy, and he had a way of making us smile together or play together or worry together.

With all the farm animals at Rusty's, we were a little concerned about Trouble's behavior. Rusty must have sensed this because he locked him in a pen upon arrival. Rusty certainly had his own way of dealing with animals. "A while back I had this goat that wouldn't shut up," he said. "So I go out there and yell at it and come back in and it's still making a hell of a ruckus. So I'm getting mad, 'cause there's other people here and no one can sleep with that damn goat, so I get an idea. I take this bottle of vodka and a big bucket of corn out to the goat and I mix it up. The goat just loved it and after a few minutes that goat was falling all over the place and his eyes were all looking different directions. I tell you what, that goat shut up, all right."

Rusty seemed to deal with people in an equally unique way. My favorite story was about people who, over the past few years, thought it would be nice to give Rusty a television. "They thought I'd be lonely up here all winter by myself," he said. On three different occasions, Rusty asked his neighbors, "You are giving this to me? It's mine? You don't want it back?" With that confirmation, he pulled out his shotgun and blasted the television to pieces. The people stared dumbfounded at Rusty, who exclaimed, "You like to watch your television; well, I like to shoot mine."

"Thank goodness for people like Rusty," I told Craig. I couldn't explain why his mere existence was so important, but I was certain my life was richer because of him. Rusty made me think about my own life choices, made me open my mind to alternative perceptions of the world, and made me recognize the need for cultural diversity.

From a biological standpoint, an ecosystem that supports the greatest number of different species is considered more balanced, stable, and healthy than an ecosystem with many of the same kinds of things. We ought to extend this concept to our own culture. We should insist that diversity within human culture be allowed to flourish. Diversity of philosophies, perceptions, and lifestyles makes our own lives that much more significant. Just knowing there is a person, in the height of the Information Age, who will never touch a computer makes me smile. To maintain a traditional lifestyle and resist technology is not a cop-out; it requires far more effort to preserve his way of life than it does to assimilate. It would be physically easy for Rusty to get a computer, connect to the mainstream, start acting and thinking like everyone else; but to Rusty that would conflict with everything he stands for. As it is with preserving biological diversity, all that is required of the rest of us is acceptance and a willingness to leave well enough alone.

§

A couple days before we landed at Rusty's, we climbed to the Punchbowl shelter and ate lunch in a small clearing. It was a sunny afternoon and we decided to stop for the day because we couldn't pull ourselves away from that slice of mountain and we thought it would be enchanting to sleep beside a pond. The pond was thick with algae and teeming with life: tadpoles, frogs, salamanders. I used to play with tadpoles every day when I was a child in Pennsylvania, but I hadn't seen a tadpole in years. I remembered reading something in college about the worldwide decline of amphibians, about a deformed frog with legs growing out of its head, about amphibians being sensitive to pollution.

Dr. Joseph Mitchell is my friend and former mentor and happens to be the leading expert on reptiles and amphibians in the state of Virginia. Officially he is a research biologist at the University of Richmond and president of the Herpetologists' League, a scientific organization devoted to studying reptiles and amphibians. I remember one particular afternoon I spent with him when I was living in Virginia. We threw our backpacks in the bed of his pickup, letting them fall over piles of buckets, wire flagging, measuring tape, a headlamp, and rubber boots that he uses for studying salamanders, and we drove to the river for lunch. Sitting on a boulder in the James River, he told me that in the '60s, before he joined the marines, he was a tree-hugging hippie. I figured hippie-turned-marine was a rather drastic life change, but I see now how both lifestyles shaped the person he is today. Dr. Mitchell is short and stocky and marches from the classroom to the lab to the field to his office like he's on a mission. He wears his hair a little too long to go unnoticed at the conservative Richmond university, and he was the only professor I ever had who told me my research on beetles was "very cool," and meant it. Dr. Mitchell has a playful twinkle in his eyes and a fierce love for science and conservation. He approaches his work with the intensity and drive of a marine and with the passion of a tree-hugger.

When I spoke with Dr. Mitchell about the current status of amphibians, he told me that biologists have noticed dramatic declines in reptiles and amphibians across the country. In fact, some biologists believe the number of salamanders has declined 30 percent in the last thirty years. Several of the nation's frog species are endangered, and deformities in frogs and toads have been seen in at least eight states. The once common occurrence of seeing tadpoles and salamanders has become a novelty in many places, and I felt privileged to see so many in this high-mountain pond. That night at the Punchbowl shelter I lay awake listening to splashes and rustling grass. Curled in my sleeping bag on the wooden platform, listening to the shrill chirping and croaking resonating from the pond, I could only imagine what wet and wild nocturnal thrills I must be missing.

Years ago I had learned from Dr. Mitchell why salamanders in this region are so special. "The salamanders that are here now are basically the same as they were 10,000 to 12,000 years ago," he said. "Pockets of habitat that supported these animals persisted during global changes, and now local microhabitats maintain the different species." Richard Highton, professor at the University of Maryland, says that because salamanders have been around for so long and because populations are easily isolated from one another, many different types of salamanders evolved in the Appalachians. In fact, Dr. Mitchell notes, the Appalachians have more genetic diversity of salamanders than anyplace else on earth.

Scientists like Mitchell and Highton are worried about the vanishing salamanders because this group of animals is often thought of as being analogous to the canary in the coal mine. Salamanders are believed to be good indicators of what is to come; if they go, other species will soon follow. Mitchell and Highton are most interested in plethodontids, the largest group of salamanders. There are more than 220 species of plethodontid salamanders and none of them has lungs. Highton speculates that plethodontids lost their lungs as they evolved over thousands of years in the Appalachians and adapted to fast-moving streams. Since the salamanders search for food by walking along stream bottoms, it would be disadvantageous to be buoyant with air-filled lungs. Biologists hypothesize that there is enough oxygen in fast-moving streams that they simply don't need lungs. Plethodontids get all the oxygen they need by breathing through their skin, an adaptation that may provide an efficient way to exchange gas and forage but one that makes them especially sensitive to pollution. Chemicals and pollutants from the air or the ground dissolve in water and soak through the salamanders' skin.

Salamanders also don't move around much. They often spend all ten to twelve years of their lives in an area the size of a kitchen. This has some pretty serious implications if those few square yards get disturbed. Imagine standing at an intersection waiting to cross a street. A bus revs up and puffs a big black cloud of exhaust in your face. Naturally, you hold your breath until it passes. Now imagine how you'd respond if you went home and smelled gas in your house. You would leave the premises and not return until the leak was fixed. Salamanders can't do that. They can't escape pollution because they can't run away from it, and they can't hold their breath because they breathe through their skin.

Salamanders are also sensitive to environmental disturbance because many of them have complex life cycles that expose them to both terrestrial and aquatic habitats. For example, many species have an aquatic larval stage and a terrestrial adult stage, so if either place is polluted they will feel the effects.

Biologists attribute the decline of amphibians to a number of causes. Virtually everyone, including Mitchell and Highton, identifies habitat loss as the biggest threat. They tell me that most prime salamander habitat is lost to logging. In addition to the devastation that comes from removing trees, logging roads can fragment populations and create deadly barriers between salamanders' woodland homes and the pools they need to reproduce. Things like timber harvesting and gypsy moth devastation that reduce the forest canopy are bad for salamanders because they expose the forest floor to sun and wind, which dry the soils and leaf litter. Salamanders can't survive in these dry areas and, as I mentioned, they can't travel far enough to escape inhospitable conditions.

In addition to logging, there are a variety of other threats to amphibians. Across the country, wetlands are being drained for development at an alarming rate. Without these moist areas, amphibians can't reproduce. Eggs deposited in underground burrows, rotten logs, crevices, bogs, ponds, or stream-side debris require water to develop. Most salamanders live on the land as adults but even then they must remain in a moist environment to prevent desiccation.

Excessive ultraviolet radiation as a result of ozone depletion may have caused the deformities in frogs in the Midwest, as some amphibian eggs are quite sensitive to UV rays. Pesticides, herbicides, and fertilizers seep into ponds and wetlands and poison the animals. Others are killed by vehicles, acid rain, introduced species like trout and zebra mussels, and people who collect the animals for pets, bait, food, and research.

During our hike through Virginia I was on the prowl for salamanders that were somehow surviving all these threats. A few days before and after our stay at Rusty's, Craig and I passed the homes of the two species of salamanders that, outside of the Shenandoahs, are found nowhere else in the world.

The Peaks of Otter salamander has a dark body with brassy-to-greenish flecks on its back and grows to be about four inches long. The entire range of the Peaks of Otter salamander is a twelve-mile stretch of deciduous forest in the Blue Ridge Mountains. Because it has one of the most limited distributions of all plethodontids and because much of its range lies within a highly productive timber area managed by the Forest Service, it is listed as a sensitive species by the Forest Service and a species of special concern by Virginia.

In his research, Dr. Mitchell found that clearcutting reduces Peaks of Otter populations by almost 50 percent, and clearcutting with burning and disking of the soil kills virtually all salamanders and makes the habitat sterile. Mitchell and other biologists found that clearcutting forces the salamanders to eat a lower-quality diet. Soft-bodied prey like springtails and termites are a higher-quality meal because they are more readily digested by the Peaks of Otter salamander. After clearcutting, many of those critters are killed or flee the area, leaving hard-bodied prey like ants and beetles that are more difficult for the salamanders to digest.

Heavy equipment used to build roads and cut trees kills many individuals, and the roads act as barriers, fragmenting populations. Dr. Tom Pauley, author of *Amphibians and Reptiles in West Virginia*, told me his research shows that salamanders have so much trouble crossing logging roads and ski trails that just about any slice in the forest instantly fragments populations. Dr. Pauley found that even a well-used hiking trail can be an impassable barrier. The Peaks of Otter salamander is functionally divided into two populations by the Blue Ridge Parkway, a road it just can't cross.

Craig and I continued through the Shenandoahs, enjoying the gentle grade and relatively smooth trail. The trail crosses Skyline Drive twenty-three times, a constant reminder that we were never far from civilization. Anxious to get to Front Royal, Virginia, we pressed on, passing the side trails to the summits of Hawksbill Mountain and Stony Man Mountain.

When the trail crossed the Pinnacle, I remembered that Dr. Mitchell had told me to look for the Shenandoah salamander up there. The Shenandoah salamander is about four inches long, is dark brown with tiny white or yellow spots along its side, and at times has a reddish yellow stripe from its nose to its tail. Its range is even more narrow than the Peaks of Otter salamanders; it lives only on north and northwest talus slopes on three mountaintops in Shenandoah National Park: the Pinnacle, Stony Man Mountain, and Hawksbill Mountain. If this salamander had its way, it wouldn't be living in patches of soil on rock-covered slopes; it would be squirming through the rich soils and wet leaves in the forests that surround the talus. But the Shenandoah salamander learned that the red-backed salamander lives in the forest and will outcompete it there. Red-backed salamanders are bullies; they'll bite other salamanders on the snout if they get too close. For the Shenandoah salamander, the talus has become a refuge.

Although the Shenandoah salamander's range is restricted because of another salamander, human activity affects it too. Studies have shown that very few individuals are found in soils that have a pH of 3.7 or less. Because high elevations are most exposed to acid rain, the soils near the talus summits tend to be highly acidic, which is bad news for this species. The Shenandoah salamander was federally listed as endangered in 1989. Dr. Mitchell gets excited when I ask him about salamanders, and I hear a hint of urgency when we talk about their protection. "Landscape planning," he says, "That's what it will take to keep these critters around. We have to maintain natural habitat in the right places. We must educate land managers, planners, and developers. Economic pressure is incredibly intense, but we need to control growth and really think about where we are building."

Fortunately, people with power are beginning to recognize the importance of amphibians and are starting to think about ways to counter their recent declines. In 1998, Bruce Babbitt, secretary of the interior, formed the Task Force on Amphibian Declines and Deformities (TADD). Members of this group represented fifteen federal agencies and offices and they convened to investigate the recent reports of frog malformations across the country. The following year, Babbitt announced that he would allocate $5.6 million to monitor amphibian populations in America's parks, refuges, and Bureau of Land Management lands. The government wants to get a handle on what's out there and assess the extent of malformations of certain species. As of this writing, however, the House had reduced the figure to $2 million and the Senate had given it no funding at all.

Private interests also have begun to form coalitions to study the problem. In 1999, a network of scientists, managers, donors, and citizens formed Partners in Amphibian and Reptile Conservation (PARC). Their mission is to conserve amphibians, reptiles, and their habitats through public/private partnerships. In June 1999, PARC began to develop a strategy to guide continent-wide conservation efforts.

Formed in 1991 under the umbrella of the IUCN (the World Conservation Union), the Declining Amphibian Populations Task Force (DAPTF) was created when a network of more than 3,000 scientists and conservationists from more than ninety countries came together to determine the extent and causes of amphibian declines and promote ways to reverse those declines. PARC and DAPTF are just two of a number of groups working around the globe to prevent future losses of these animals. Although they understand the urgency of the situation, most of these groups are in their infant stages. They are going to have to mature quickly if they're going to make an impact before it's too late.

§

As we headed through the Shenandoahs I began to draw some comparisons between these slippery little critters and one big critter named Rusty. What at first felt like a stretch now seems obvious. Both Rusty and the salamanders are endangered species, and neither will survive if they're not left alone. Rusty is fighting to maintain a way of life that defines his very existence. He is fighting the poisons of television and technology as the salamanders are fighting dry soils and UV radiation. Both are threatened by development—development in its subtle form (which creates an increasingly homogenized culture and reinforces values based on money and power that don't figure into Rusty's world), and development in its muscular form as it knocks down trees and squishes little salamanders.

Neither Rusty nor the salamanders can make a decent life outside their home. The Shenandoah salamander is tied to the talus, and the Peaks of Otter salamander, trapped by trails and roads and its own limited locomotion, travels less than a yard or two. Rusty is clinging to a hollow beside the Blue Ridge Parkway the way the Shenandoah salamander is holding on to pockets of soil on a talus slope. Rusty's title to his tract of land can keep out development, and his signs can keep out technology, but his microhabitat is threatened all the same. It's a precarious situation when there is only one place you can go, when development is pressing in from all angles, when you're relying on a square meter or two to provide everything you need for twelve years of living, when you're counting on a few pinches of soil not to dry out.

§

We heard stories of hikers who loved Rusty's microhabitat so much they moved in for a month or more. Craig and I could see how easy it would be to get sucked in, so we pulled ourselves away and headed toward West Virginia. We didn't know that after leaving Rusty's we wouldn't see our thru-hiking friends again. We heard later that Seldom Seen hurt his ankle in Pennsylvania and abandoned the trip. Nudeman got injured as well, took a month or two off, and began walking south from Maine. I'm not sure how far he got. Otter wrote us later in the summer and explained his disappearance. A postcard told us that he got a case of the Virginia Blues that was too much to shake, and by the time he got through Pennsylvania it just wasn't fun anymore. He left the trail for good. I admire him for recognizing that, and I often wonder if his experience wasn't more pleasant than ours. Sometimes I wish I wasn't so stubborn and could recognize that it's okay to stop. Sometimes I think the only reason Craig and I were able to continue was because we had each other. There were times when, had either of us been hiking alone, we would have given up the dream. But we were at each other's side when one of us was having doubts, and we were always able to convince the other that there were things worth staying for.

Once we left the Shenandoahs it became evident that our corridor of wilderness was beginning to narrow. We could hear traffic in the distance even if we couldn't see the roads, and sometimes we could see houses through the thinning forest. At times we could hear children laughing in their backyards. It was also turkey-hunting season, and the number of people roaming the woods with weapons seemed to be increasing as fast as the wilderness corridor was narrowing. It was a dangerous situation.

Craig, Trouble, and I were excited to enter a new state after hiking 500 miles in Virginia. There was a light drizzle that day and the woods were thick and misty. One mile into West Virginia we heard an all-too-familiar gunshot, but this time it was frightfully close. "Kodiak!" Craig shouted (we call him Trouble only behind his back). A second shot. "Stop shooting!" we shouted. We dropped our packs and sprinted toward the bang. Craig raced in. My heart pounded. Not Kodi, I thought, please not Kodi. There were not more than 100 yards of woods between the trail and the houses to our left. Somewhere in the middle, a person heavy on aggression and light on brains shot our dog, twice.

We waited. Silence. Craig and I exchanged glances and I wasn't sure if he would go nuts or cry in my arms. A moment later, Trouble emerged, stunned and confused. "Thank God, he's alive," I said. We raced to his side. "Poor boy, it'll be okay," I said, stroking his bloody head. He sat there in the rain looking innocent and pathetic. Blood was dripping from his ear, and his black-and-white coat was splattered with blood from his tail to his chest. We discovered later that more than twenty BB-sized holes had pierced his skin.

Craig charged into the woods in a rage, but he never found the person who shot our dog. I was silently thankful that he didn't. "What were you going to do anyway?" I asked him later, "wave your hiking stick at a crazy man with a gun?"

With blood soaking the fur on his hindquarters and on his head, Trouble began the six-mile hike to town—the historic town of Harpers Ferry. Carrying a now wet and bloody hundred-plus-pound dog was obviously out of the question, so we coaxed him on, hoping he could continue on his own. Within a mile of town, Trouble was dragging. His joints stiffened and he could barely step over fallen logs. It was slow going but somewhere along the way, our anger turned slightly toward humor and we resumed talking for Kodiak, "Now I bin to jail *and* I bin shot."

The three of us arrived in Harpers Ferry and headed to the Appalachian Trail Conference where we had our picture taken and told them our story. Trouble was lethargic and limping when an older man named Papa Joe offered us a ride to the vet. It must have been a sight to see Papa Joe walk into the vet's office with two haggard hikers and their bloody dog. The office was closing for the day but they agreed to look at Trouble anyway. After we relayed our story to the veterinarian, he looked at us with an apologetic smile and said, "Welcome to West Virginia."

As the vet examined Trouble, Craig and I used his phone to price motels; we wanted to wash our boy's wounds and sleep in a dry room. Most places were too expensive for our budget, and I'm sure the vet overheard our conversations. Even if he couldn't hear us, I'm certain he could smell us. We hadn't showered in a week, my hands were sticky with drying blood, and we were drenched and muddy from hiking all day in the rain. The vet must have thought we looked pretty desperate because he came back with Trouble, a bottle of antibiotics, a bottle of painkillers, and dog shampoo, and charged us only twelve dollars. Trouble would be fine, he said.

Fortunately, Buckshot, as we now call him, is a tough dog. With painkillers and antibiotics, he was hiking the next day. Still, it was too dangerous for him and too stressful for us. The trail ahead promised abundant road crossings and many more people. We heard that glass and sharp rocks in Pennsylvania might wear down his pads. So, as we approached Maryland, Craig and I discussed the toll he was taking on us. We knew that two trips to the vet in the last week was not a good record, and that keeping him out of trouble in the mid-Atlantic region would be virtually impossible. As we headed across Maryland, Buckshot hiked his final mile of the Appalachian Trail. My parents met us near the Mason-Dixon line and took him home with them to Pennsylvania.

It broke my heart to see his nose pressed against the window of my parents' jeep as they drove away. He jumped up when he heard the click of our hip belts and he wanted to come. "It's the right thing to do," Craig said. I knew it was; we had been over it a hundred times, but I already missed him. We were parents saying goodbye to our child. Walking that day didn't seem as much fun without him.

The rest of our time near West Virginia was equally eventful, although less horrific. We had the unique experience of walking through a smoldering forest fire. For two days, twenty acres of forest were aflame. The morning's rain finally smothered the fire and allowed us to pass safely. The ground was as black as coal. Dangling from blackened petioles, charred leaves flopped and curled in the wind. A steady breeze held the scent of burning earth, and smoke thickened the air. We carefully stepped over burnt trees and glowing embers.

As Craig and I headed out of the smoldering fire and out of West Virginia, we passed a long-awaited mile marker—the one that tells you that you have hiked 1,000 miles.

That evening we got a terrific boost. A half-mile before the Pine Knob shelter, the trail crosses Interstate 70 via a footbridge. As we proceeded along the concrete walkway, about seven different truckers honked and waved at us, cheering us on. For a few moments we were celebrities, waving and smiling down at the people smiling up at us. It seemed like they were saying, "You can go another 1,000 miles. You can do it!" And at that moment, we felt we could.

## CHAPTER SIX

# WEEKEND WARRIORS
# AND THE AT FREEWAY

Craig and I had been hiking through a section of trail known as the mid-Atlantic lowlands when we realized that this area was not only low in elevation but low on wilderness. We had a better chance of being hit by a car or shot by a hunter than seeing any wildlife, except for Pennsylvania's millions of emaciated deer. But that's another story.

Readers may detect a hint of sarcasm in my writing about Pennsylvania. Since I claim this state as my homeland, I feel the slandering is somehow justified. Actually, at this point in the hike, my positive state of mind was deteriorating and sarcasm was often the only means by which I could convey my thoughts. We had been pushing long days. We didn't really have a choice since it was either raining or we were being eaten by black flies—it was not practical just to sit around.

My feet stung and I actually lost feeling in my toes and the balls of my feet for about three months. My hairy legs were red and swollen with sweat rashes and bug bites. Mom sent Bag Balm to soothe the rashes and I promptly sent it back. "Mom," I said, "The label says Bag Balm is for chapped teats. As far as I know, my teats aren't the problem." Besides, I told her, using Bag Balm was like glazing my legs with Vaseline. After a few hours of walking with a coating of Bag Balm, my legs became covered with dirt and bugs that stuck in the goo. I felt like a walking fly strip. About that time, I began carrying anti-inch ointment in my shorts pocket and began hoarding Advil from Craig. I realized that was a bad sign. I started to think I could really use some time off the trail, but we didn't plan on taking a break until Connecticut.

Road crossings were frequent, which meant that towns, motels, and hostels were easily accessible. Craig was tempted by the idea of a hot shower and a bed, and we stopped more often than I liked. "I just want to be clean and naked and lie on white sheets with you and eat pizza and Coke," he'd say. Sure, I wanted that too, but we were spending money we didn't have on something I felt was severing our connection with the trail, not rejuvenating our spirits. We had some comfortable nights, but it made the next days even harder.

People always ask if we got into fights often, and surprisingly, for the amount of time we spent together, our fights were minimal. One night, however, I got out of the shower, still steaming over what a waste of money the motel was, and Craig had a western on TV.

"Will you turn that damn thing off," I said.

"Come on," he said.

"You know I hate television and I hate this stupid western. Now turn it off!"

"Look, I paid money to stay here—I'm gonna enjoy it."

We went back and forth like that for a while, screaming and cursing, and I'm not sure how it ended except that I pulled the sheets over my head and wouldn't talk to him all night or the next day. Eventually we got over it. The absurdity of that fight was a good indication that the trail was beginning to break us. Our minds and emotions were surrendering to the monotony of routine and the terrors of urbanization.

§

We sloshed through the cow pastures and muddy fields of the Cumberland Valley in southern Pennsylvania. Rich topsoil supported a lush understory and made the tread soft and dark beneath my boots. Forests trimmed farmland and creeks, and we meandered through sweeping green pastures, the smell of cattle and tilled soil wafting up from the earth. This is a beautiful area, but, as I said, I was feeling a bit ornery at the time and couldn't appreciate any more rolling hills. Then came a series of road crossings: the Pennsylvania Turnpike, Interstate 81, U.S. 11, U.S. 22, U.S. 322, and at least fifty state roads. We were constantly serenaded by the roar of engines. Traffic wasn't the only form of noise pollution. One afternoon we heard a series of explosions, and the earth beneath our boots began to shake. I looked up at the ridge, expecting it to break away and crumble into the valley. Every hour or so, a violent explosion ripped through the rolling hills. That night we learned that was the usual behavior of the nearby military base. Are these people used to the explosions? "Maybe it's like living next to railroad tracks," Craig suggested.

After three months on the Appalachian Trail, our senses were fine-tuned. I learned to hear a single leaf twist and rustle its neighbor, I felt the subtle difference of pine needles rather than earth beneath my boots, and I snapped my gaze into focus when a squirrel twitched its tail. I learned to hear stillness and tried to find that stillness in myself. Tenderly I nurtured it, hoping that the peace and calm of the woods would grow inside me too. But it was a difficult sensation to maintain. A few miles south of Duncannon, Pennsylvania, when the distant rumble of civilization shattered the silence in the forest, it somehow shattered the stillness that for the past few months I had been carefully trying to cultivate.

The rumbling grew louder as Craig and I traversed down the face of a forested slope that rolled into the valley floor. As we rounded each switchback, we could see a few houses, a few manicured lawns, a few roads stretching away from the town center. I was tempted to head straight to the heart of it; make a beeline to concrete; leave behind the dusty, rocky trail; and trade trickling springs and muddy creeks for a faucet and a bathtub.

Craig and I developed a love/hate relationship with towns. We knew the holdings of civilization could satisfy our most recent cravings and provide some temporary comfort—a bench, a soda, a sandwich, maybe a lawn, a pay phone, occasionally a shower. As we approached town we dreamed of things that could make us happy: pillows, cotton T-shirts, a bed with clean sheets, and food—chocolate milkshakes, fresh bread, a big salad. But every town taught us the same thing: The appearance of pavement doesn't extinguish the fire in our burning feet or make the upcoming miles any flatter or fewer. Town was a distraction, a temporary reprieve from physical exertion, but it presented its own arsenal of stresses.

Unlike most towns, which require the hiker to leave the trail and make a special trip to resupply, Duncannon was one of the unavoidable towns; the Appalachian Trail is blazed down the main thruway and continues over the bridge to the other side of the Susquehanna River.

The trail spat us out onto a street that reminded me of the cul-de-sac in suburban Philadelphia where I grew up. I felt like I had been dropped off in somebody's backyard, and I couldn't help but hope we'd see someone barbecuing and they'd invite us over. To our dismay, it was a quiet street and we didn't see a single person. I focused my attention on the grinding of gravel between boots and blacktop.

"It's so much easier walking on pavement," I said, delirious from walking eighteen miles. For a reason I can attribute only to stubbornness, we felt compelled to push long days and arrive in town out of energy, out of food, and out of good humor. Had we arrived fresh, we would have had the energy and good spirits to deal more gracefully with noise and motion, but two stubborn hikers don't easily change their habits. This time was no exception. We arrived in Duncannon with little tolerance and a long list of needs.

As we shuffled along, side by side, Craig looked over with a sympathetic smile. We both knew we were not fooling anyone. Downtown was still a half-hour away and although there were no rocks to trip over, a surface as unforgiving as pavement meant a further flattening of the feet. Craig had told me that there are more bones in your feet than in any other part of your body. During the past few days I had sworn I could feel each tiny bone breaking.

We eventually entered the heart of town, where for a few blocks the main drag is lined with small eateries, bars, gift shops, a laundromat, and a gas station, all of which could use a fresh paint job and some renovations. We dropped our packs at the first major intersection. Mine fell limp on the ground like an understuffed pillow, full of bulges, or tumors, as Craig liked to call them. I didn't care. I took a seat on top of it. Craig's pack was always packed perfectly, every item balanced and snug. His pack stood erect while he removed the guidebook from the top pouch. He studied the map of town and spanned our current position and a possible destination between his thumb and forefinger.

"Couple more blocks and it's on the left," he said. I could have sat there a few more minutes but Craig was already cinching down his pack. I moaned and rose. The one or two tiny foot bones that were still intact cracked as I mounted my pack. Of this I was certain.

Craig guided me to the Doyle, a bar whose owners let hikers sleep in the basement. We had heard this was a legendary place to stay, and although the dilapidated entrance didn't give me a warm and fuzzy feeling, I was certainly up for anyplace that had running water and a roof. I slumped onto the sidewalk, still connected to my pack, and leaned against the sooty concrete wall of the tavern. Home, I thought, Thank goodness, just let me rest. Craig went in to sign us up. A minute later, two drunks stumbled out the door, laughing and yelling into the street. Craig followed them out shaking his head. "We're not staying here," he said.

"This is not the time to be picky," I said.

"Honey, it smells like urine."

"I'm sure it's not that bad," I said, "Really, I can do urine. We can handle it; it's just one night." But as I was protesting, Craig was picking up his pack and I had few reserves left for a fight.

We continued down the road until we spotted a sign for pizza and smelled the heavenly aroma of bread and tomato sauce. Dinner: two large pizzas, two beers, and a chance to sit. We slid into an orange booth and devoured the first couple slices without really tasting them. After a while, we sat satisfied with greasy lips and fingers and a pile of empty plates and napkins pushed to the far side of the table. It was time to take another look at the guidebook and find a cheap place to spend the night.

"We could camp next to the railroad tracks," I said. "No, never mind. It says trains go by regularly. Besides, with that damn tent of yours, we'll get eaten alive." Craig's ingenious idea of trading our tent for the two-pound floorless teepee continued to be the focus of a number of "discussions." Yes, it worked well under perfect conditions. But how often do you get a bugless, windless, rainless night on the Appalachian Trail? In our case, not very often.

There was one night in particular that the teepee was beyond dysfunctional; it was unbearable. It was the day the baby black flies hatched by the millions. It was the day we tried to erect the teepee in our matching red and blue Gore-Tex rainsuits because the flies were nibbling our arms and legs into bloody welts. It was also the night it poured for five hours, sagged the sides of the teepee into my sleeping space, and funneled a stream of water onto my head.

"Okay," he said, "maybe it wasn't such a good idea. Maybe we can ask your dad to send our tent back." Finally, I thought, an admission. That's all I wanted.

We left the pizza joint, walked for another mile, bought pop-tarts, bread, and peanut butter from a gas station, and headed out of town. Craig spotted a truck stop down an intersecting highway, so we headed toward it. Traffic roared by, slinging dirt and blowing exhaust in my eyes and hair. Looking down, I traced the white line on the side of the highway and tried to think about something besides pollution and the little fractured bones in my feet. The commotion clogged my mind and I all I could do was study my steps.

This town made me nervous. Everything was in motion. Before I could focus on something, it was on its way out of view—rushing past, zooming by, whirling across. After growing accustomed to a world where nothing moved faster than my own two-mile-per-hour pace, a string of traffic cruising at forty was enough to send my head into an unstoppable spin. The traffic, aggressive and angry, screeching and churning, made me want to run for my life.

A half-mile down the highway we arrived at a combination gas station, store, diner, and motel. Craig went inside while I stood at the window and guarded the packs. I tied my bandanna around my head to keep my three-day-old braids from unraveling. Reaching into my top pouch, I found a bag of granola and shoveled a handful into my mouth. It felt dirty here, I thought. I stopped eating and looked through the window of the diner. Two obese women with hair teased, gelled, and sprayed into tiny, spiky bangs, had squeezed themselves into the booth and were devouring hamburgers and French fries. Perched on a stool at the counter, a woman was studying a crossword puzzle while trying not to let each forkful of chicken-fried steak smear her bright red lipstick. Truckers sat in silence, drinking coffee and gazing at newspapers. Their trucks idled in the parking lot to my right.

"Howdy," offered a trucker returning to his rig. "Hey," I replied and provided the required nod which I learned in Trucker World should accompany all one-syllable greetings. Somehow even the nod didn't suit me, and I could tell the trucker thought so too. I don't belong here,

I thought, and I certainly have no chance of blending.

Craig returned. "Don't get upset," he told me.

"Why," I said, already knowing the answer, but wanting to buy another minute of rest.

"They're full," he said, "We're going to have to keep going." I didn't know how he thought I was going to take one more step. At that point I doubted my ability to stand. I arched my eyebrows and even got a tear or two to swell in my eyes; I was going for a helpless, pathetic look, which at that point seemed to come rather naturally. "I know," he said, "but it's getting late and we can't sleep on the side of the highway. We have to make it to the woods. Then we'll stop, I promise."

I lifted my pack, contorted my face into the best snarl I could manage, and began walking toward the bridge that led to the woods. Cars, vans, and tractor-trailers flipped on their headlights and sped by. Rush-hour traffic was thick at the edge of town, where a number of roads converged to cross the Susquehanna River. Route 11 spans the river for nearly a mile, and the shoulder of Route 11 is called the Appalachian Trail. Following Craig's steps, I walked as fast as I could. I wanted to run to the woods but I was exhausted. I squinted in case a fleck of road was suddenly thrown up from a whirling tire. My breaths were deliberate and careful as I tried not to inhale a lethal dose of fumes. Street lamps quivered on the river's dark surface, and I stared into the murky water. The noise was making me dizzy.

I worked in a cheese factory once. Although it was so awful that I refused to go back the second day, I took a lot from that experience. I was stationed in a cold, damp, cement room crowded with conveyor belts and loud, metal machines. There were no windows; bare bulbs lit the room. Workers were committed to a ten-hour shift with two ten-minute breaks and a half-hour for lunch. Management discouraged us from going outside and forbade us to sit outside or touch anything outside for fear of returning to the factory "contaminated."

The process of packaging cheese began as forty-pound blocks were chopped into smaller bricks. The bricks rolled down the conveyor belt and were snatched up by two frantic women who sorted them onto their respective packaging trays. The cheese bricks were subsequently sent through a loud machine that wrapped each one in plastic packaging. Cheese bricks sped down the line, were inspected for dirt inside or holes in the plastic, were automatically labeled, and were sent to me. I stood on the damp concrete floor at the end of the conveyor belt. If I didn't box the cheese bricks fast enough, they would pile up and spill. There was no stopping the process. I worked fast, but the cheese kept coming and coming and coming. It's a humbling experience to realize you failed at a cheese factory.

The shift eventually ended and I left my hairnet and white apron with all the women who would be returning the next day, probably the next day for the rest of their lives. Even at home I couldn't erase the sense of urgency, the rush to sort the cheese. I couldn't forget the clanging of the cheese-cutter or the rattle and hum of the conveyor belt. The feeling of factory life lingered for days. My ears rang all night. I'll never forget my uncontrollable desire to take a breath of fresh air and exhale the stagnant, cheese-flavored air. I needed to feel sunlight penetrate my skin. I needed silence.

I have always had a low tolerance for crowded, noisy places. The absence of green and the glaze of pollution that coats a big city make me edgy. I had gotten that cheese-factory feeling in Washington, D.C., New York, and Philadelphia. I never knew smaller towns could make me feel that way too. But as I headed over the Susquehanna on the side of the highway, I saw the Cheddar piling up and Monterey Jack was starting to fly.

$

Relief at this point did not come from the number of miles we covered or the places we saw. Relief came from people. Herbert, or Duffel Bag Dave, as he was called by other hikers, had become something of a legend on the trail. He was not a legend in a good way; he became a legend because most of us found him utterly deranged. The night Craig and I spent with him, he talked nonstop for four hours. Although he sat in the dark corner of the shelter, every so often the trees in front of the shelter would get blown out of position and a ray of light would find Dave's face. He had a long, narrow face, unkempt gray hair, and a crazed look in his eyes. Every time I asked him a question, he redirected the conversation to something entirely unrelated. He told us (although his rambling was certainly directed at the forest, the world, and any creature in the vicinity as much as it was directed toward Craig and me) that he had been living on the trail until he went to Florida to take care of his father.

"Then I went all over this damned country, everywhere, I tell ya, out to New Mexico and up to Wisconsin, and I'd get rides wherever anybody'd take me." He stayed with this listing of places he'd been for a good half-hour.

"I've seen a lot of messed-up people, drunks and thieves and beggars, and sometimes it's the government's fault and sometimes it's their own fault, but you know what we need to do about it?"

No response.

"Well, I'll tell ya."

And he did. For two hours. He listed all the problems with America and the world, and, of course, he had solutions for them all. By the time he started on the Gulf War, I had put my headphones on and was concentrating on blocking him out.

Eventually Craig and I slid out of the shelter to brush our teeth. When we had put some distance between us and Duffel Bag Dave, I turned to Craig and shrieked, "Oh, my God! Who is this guy?"

Craig said, "Did you see what he ate for dinner?"

"Yeah, cold Ramen noodles with ketchup," I said.

"I don't think he has a backpack," said Craig, "just those duffel bags."

Sure enough, the next morning Duffel Bag Dave headed down the trail in flimsy Converse sneakers and cotton knee-high socks, carrying two duffel bags. He used both arms to awkwardly balance his belongings on his head and shoulder. Two one-gallon Clorox jugs dangled from the bags. I wasn't sure what purpose they served.

Despite the rain, a surprising number of people flocked to the trail. Hunters paced the trail, shotguns slung over their shoulders, searching the fog for turkeys. When a hunter carries his gun like that and is approached from behind, the approaching hiker ends up staring down the barrel of the shotgun until the hunter steps aside. I got used to dodging shotgun barrels.

There was one hunter, a big guy dressed in camouflage from head to toe, who was particularly frightening. When I passed him, I said hello and he swung around and grunted. It took me a second to figure out what was different about him, and then I realized he was cross-eyed. When I expressed my concern to a fellow hiker about walking in close proximity to so many guns carried by people of such questionable ability, his reply was terse. "If you hear a gobbler gobbling, duck!"

That evening, Craig and I claimed some floor space at the shelter, kicked back, and watched the procession of weekend warriors. Some people seemed to be enjoying themselves. Many were not. Hikers were uncomfortable in their rain-soaked cotton T-shirts and dreaded the cold nights in drenched sleeping bags. Craig and I relegated ourselves to the corner while a hiking club took over the rest of the shelter. A father-daughter team joined us, apparently unfazed that the shelter had reached maximum capacity. Within minutes of their arrival, the man whipped out his cell phone and began what turned into a forty-five minute phone call to his wife, followed by a series of calls to business associates. The daughter, fortunately, had packed in her Diskman and a sizable collection of compact disks, so she was set for the night.

Craig and I exchanged looks of disapproval. We had had a number of conversations about cell phones in the backcountry. We knew that backpackers carried phones for safety, for business, and, as one man said, "to be able to share a sunset with my wife," but Craig and I viewed phones in wilderness as an inherent conflict of interest.

"It's just not compatible with the very reason we go there," Craig had said. "There has to be someplace a person can go to get away from technology and civilization."

I agreed. In 1999 there were more than 80 million wireless subscribers in the U.S. As more people bring technology into the woods, I have felt my experience becoming more and more diluted. Sometimes wilderness feels like a watered-down version of civilization.

"I think land should be managed to allow different degrees of urban intrusions," I said. I told Craig there ought to be some place that resists merging with civilization. Land managers should ban technology from designated Wilderness or from the core areas of certain wild places. People who want to maintain a sense of connection with society on their trips are looking for an experience that cannot or should not be found in that sort of wilderness. True wilderness should be reserved for those who are willing to take risks and deal with the consequences. It ought to be reserved for people who are willing to take responsibility for themselves.

In the case of the man at the shelter, I probably wouldn't have cared if he had left the vicinity to make his call. But he had little regard for our experience, and he greatly affected our visit. Maybe a place like the Appalachian Trail in New York shouldn't fall into the wilderness category. Maybe it should be one of the many places reserved for people who want to get out of town but also want to bring technology with them. Still, at the very least, guidelines should be developed to control the use of technology in these places. If it were up to me, I'd develop Leave No Trace guidelines for technology, a sort of Cell Phone Etiquette. I began listing the guidelines for Craig: no incoming calls; no making calls from peaks or shelters where other hikers are likely to congregate; leave the phone in the pack when you're not using it. Craig suggested we develop a punishment system as well. By the end of the evening we agreed that it would be fair to throw the person and their cell phone into the nearest lake if they make a call in the presence of other hikers.

Some land managers I spoke with felt technology like cell phones, laptop computers, and GPS units degraded the wildness of a place by taming and domesticating it, but most managers, even if they personally opposed the merging of wilderness and technology, felt that little would be done to restrict use. Some managers in the Forest Service actually considered creating No Phone zones or No Rescue zones, but the likeliness of implementing such a policy seems remote. "There are issues of safety and liability that managers are afraid of tackling," said one manager. "You also have to think about creating too many regulations for people. If the public's desires are changing, and if the visitors want to bring phones, it may not be worth the battle to tell them they can't."

Cell phone use usually brings up the issue of safety and backcountry rescues, an issue that has even search-and-rescue crews divided. Some rescuers like the idea of visitors carrying phones because it helps them more quickly locate the victims. They say it takes a lot of the guesswork out of rescue missions. However, many people who work for search and rescue would like to see a ban on cell phones because they get so many false alarms—the guy who gets cold and tired and wants a helicopter to come and get him, for example. In a number of cases in New Hampshire's White Mountains, hikers have called to ask for directions or to tell rangers they are cold and hungry. "People think of cell phones as a lifeline," says one New Hampshire rescuer. "They feel more secure in wilderness and they go farther and deeper into places they wouldn't have gone if they didn't have a phone."

Rescues are enormously expensive, and the number of rescues has increased dramatically. In national parks, the number of rescues increased from 3,000 to 5,000 in six years. To offset some of the costs, parks like Yosemite and Denali have decided to let climbers and hikers pay for their own rescues. In 1992, New Hampshire enacted a statute making it legal for the state to fine a rescued individual up to $10,000 if the person "recklessly or intentionally creates a situation requiring an emergency response." Rescuers agree, however, that most people don't intentionally create hazardous situations; they are just forgoing common sense and making stupid decisions. The law has been used only once: in 1993, a hiker on the Appalachian Trail in the White Mountains consumed a bottle of vodka and was rescued while crawling around in the snow. Rescues are not only extremely costly, but they often put rescue teams in danger. It must be difficult for rescuers not to resent many of the people who rely on technology instead of common sense and backcountry skills to get them out of trouble. Says one rescuer, "There may come a time when rescue teams may just have to say no."

The man finally put his phone away and reclined with a John Grisham book and a Snickers bar. At least he had good taste in chocolate. Later that evening a large group made camp just below the shelter. Even from a distance I could tell something wasn't altogether right with them. Maybe it was the way they threw tent poles at each other, or the way they paced instead of taking a seat on the ground. My suspicions were confirmed when a sixteen-year-old boy wearing those somehow fashionable oversized clothes wandered past our shelter looking for "that outhouse thing."

"Are you with a club?" I asked.

"Not really. We're kind of in trouble," then he added quickly, "but we're not too bad."

The boy was in prison. The group of juvenile delinquents was out for a month of reformation: backpacking, rappelling, and whitewater rafting. Their lives, apparently, could not be worse.

I talked with three of the kids, listening to them complain about their eight-mile day, their lack of showers, and their longing to get back to a city. A few of them strayed from the group and refused to follow instructions in hopes of getting sent back to jail. It didn't work. Their jaws dropped as they listened to my story. They could not understand why anyone would willfully subject herself to such a hike. At this point I was questioning my own sanity, so I didn't push it. They probably found me as amusing as Duffel Bag Dave was to us. They were nice kids, but the woods had a lot to teach them.

The weekend warriors were amusing, but Craig and I were entertained only for so long. The people and the landscape wore at my patience and sent Craig on a get-through-this-as-quickly-as-possible rampage. I was having trouble keeping up with him and lost motivation to try harder. And then it got worse. Partway through Pennsylvania, the terrain changed from fields of corn to fields of rocks. We had heard about the infamous rocks of Pennsylvania long before we started the trail. We heard the trail clubs joke about spending their time sharpening stones and placing them along the trail. For more than 100 miles, the rocky terrain bruised our feet and weakened our ankles.

Hour after hour I dragged farther and farther behind. I repeated over and over, "I hate this trail, I hate this trail." There was no scenery to look forward to; nothing I wanted to see for weeks. The scenery and mystery of what lay ahead had kept me going through the Southern Appalachians, but now even that was gone. Craig was angry at the trail too, but he was strong enough to move quickly and balance from rock to rock. I thought, Why am I out here if I'm so miserable? I must be in awful shape since I can't keep up and I keep tripping over everything. I couldn't stand it. I walked and cried for days.

"All we can do is keep going and get through this," Craig told me.

I believed him for a while. But one night we sat in the shelter, the heaping bowl of pasta positioned between us. I looked at it and started to bawl. "I can't go on," I said, "I just can't do this anymore. I hate the trail, and I'm beginning to hate myself."

Craig looked at me, waiting for a sign of what I would say next.

"I need to get off for a while," I said, "Tomorrow I'll find a road and go home."

After a minute of silence Craig asked softly, "Are you sure?" and I nodded. Then he said, "Would you mind if I kept going?"

I told him that was fine, that he should keep going and that I'd meet him in a week up the trail. I told him I'd just skip this section, that at this point I really didn't care.

The next morning when we came to a road, I was questioning my decision to leave. Craig and I had been together, side by side, every minute of every day for three months. I couldn't imagine a day without him. But I also knew I'd curse myself if I stayed.

"Well," I said, "this is it. Are you sure you have everything?" I could feel the tears coming. "Be careful, Honey, and . . ."

"You know," he said, "I can't do this. I'm not going to split up the team. We started this together and we're going to do it all together. If you're leaving, then I'm going with you."

I suppose I was relieved and grateful, but I couldn't help feeling guilty for pulling us off the trail. We hiked to a gas station and called my dad, who rescued us in about two hours. At my parents' house in Pennsylvania we indulged in urban luxuries. We rented movies, ate constantly, slept in a bed, took showers, and wore cotton T-shirts and tennis shoes. For the ultimate culture shock, we went to South Street in Philadelphia. Hare Krishnas paraded down the road, dancing and chanting through streams of people. I nearly tripped over a man's legs, his body slumped against a building, brown bag and empty bottle rested beside him. Taxis swerved around cyclists, bums rattled change in tin cans, and the flashing neon was hypnotic. It was a world that had become utterly foreign to us and one we had forgotten existed. So many people, so much concrete, so much noise and confusion. But it was the distraction we needed. In four days we returned to the trail.

I convinced myself that I would keep walking and I stored up some positive energy for emergencies. Rocks, I thought—wonderful. Housing developments and highways—lovely. Rain and black flies—that's perfect.

§

I had sense enough to recognize that rocks, rain, and black flies couldn't be avoided, so I accepted them for what they're worth. But Craig noticed that I was deeply aggravated by something else. Once we talked about it, we discovered that I was angry at how the land surrounding the trail was being used. During the times when the trail traced farm boundaries for miles, crossed a road every hour, and was in earshot of civilization from dusk till dawn, I thought, Is this the best we can do? Is this wilderness—where cows pass as wildlife, irrigation ditches pass as streams, and pastures pass as natural landscapes? Should I be satisfied with this? Maybe I was wrong to expect to find a wilderness experience on the Appalachian Trail. I was encouraged in the South when solitude and wilderness were easier to come by, and wrong or not, I expected to find an undeveloped corridor along the entire trail.

The encroaching development came in many forms: roads, houses, grazing pastures, telephone lines, radio towers. I later learned that

I was not alone. Throughout the mid-Atlantic region, trail-maintaining clubs identify encroaching human presence as the biggest threat to the Appalachian Trail and to the experience hikers ought to have when they walk it. It seems to me that a narrowing corridor of wilderness, or viewshed, has implications beyond aesthetics; it has something to do with my becoming frustrated with the trail, and it has a lot to do with destroying the last pieces of something sacred. The precious few tracts of wildland in the eastern U.S. ought to be cherished at least as refuges from the urban sprawl that keeps nipping away at the forests, reducing them to smaller and smaller islands. The Appalachian Trail corridor has the potential to link tracts of wildlands and provide a linear wilderness experience if we are wise enough to set it aside from development.

After sharing some otherwise decent views with antennas and satellite dishes suspended on metal scaffolding, Craig and I decided the most offensive threat to the viewshed is telecommunications towers. When we climbed a ridge, emerged from the woods into a clearing, and saw an enormous tower, we lost in that instant whatever sense of remoteness, independence, and separation from civilization we had achieved. What a terrific irony, to lose yourself in mountains, to sever contact with the outside world, only to come across a system that every second is making it possible for thousands of people to communicate all over the globe. Craig and I cringed as we passed the humming towers, their maintenance sheds, and utility roads. It was a good way to spoil an afternoon.

Not only are the towers an eyesore, but studies have determined that they are responsible for the deaths of 4 million birds every year. Many birds collide with towers when they're flying at night or under foggy or overcast conditions. Lighted towers have been shown to interfere with birds' navigation systems, as they tend to congregate at the lighted area around towers. Here they crash into each other or collide with the towers themselves. The birds that survive are often too confused by the light to continue their normal migration patterns.

About the time Craig and I began hiking in Georgia, a federal law was passed that changed the way telecommunications companies do business with mountains. The Telecommunications Act of 1996 was celebrated in many circles for reforming the telecommunications industry and giving American companies a competitive edge in the global communications market. The act also paved the way for the mass construction of towers by lifting restrictions on where companies can build them. As more people demanded better range and reception for their cellular phones, pagers, and digital televisions, communication was made a priority and we, as a country, agreed to sacrifice a clear view for a clear connection. As it is now, no mountaintop is safe.

Prior to the 1996 act, local governments could reject tower applications for any reason related to the welfare of the public, says Andrew Hyman, telecommunications coordinator for the Appalachian Trail Conference (ATC). That means that if a company wanted to build a tower on top of a pristine mountain, the township could tell them that the unobstructed skyline is more important to the town than cell phone reception. Local governments could, and did, tell communications companies to hit the road. Now, says Hyman, local governments cannot reject towers without risking federal lawsuits.

The shift in technology from traditional cellular analog to cellular digital and personal communications services (PCS) requires towers that are closer together. Instead of a network of towers a few miles apart, we are now seeing a network of towers a few acres apart. The act essentially gave companies the go-ahead to commence construction of a grid of towers across the landscape. Already there are more than 80,000 towers in the United States and about 5,000 new ones are constructed every year. Presently an estimated 100,000 towers, including digital television towers, ranging from 30 to 2,000 feet high, are slated for construction. (For comparison, the Sears Tower in Chicago is 1,300 feet high.) The impacts of many of the smaller rigs can be mitigated by mounting antennas to the tops of buildings, a strategy that ought not to cause anyone too much grief, but a 2,000-foot tower suddenly becomes a big deal when someone proposes that it go in your backyard.

As it happens, companies want to build towers on the highest points on the landscape to get the best reception. Likewise, the AT follows the highest points on the land to provide the best views and to avoid the towns in the valleys. This has caused a major problem for

those of us who love the Appalachian Trail and cherish an unobstructed skyline. In 1998, when Nextel proposed to erect a 200-foot
tower in Cumberland County, Pennsylvania, just 200 feet from the AT
corridor and in full view of the trail, it was more than the ATC who
challenged the construction. Local residents who didn't want to look
at such an obtrusive structure and who didn't want their property value
to decrease argued at the town hearing. Environmentalists put pressure
on the town to reject the tower. Farmers who feared the rural character of the landscape would be affected shared their thoughts at the
hearing. The county commissioners were afraid they would get sued
if they rejected the tower, but the ATC provided evidence showing
that, despite the rights given to companies in the telecommunications
act, townships still had the right to reject wireless facilities as long as
they could be constructed elsewhere. In the end, Nextel agreed to
attach its antennas to the Cellular One tower in the neighboring
township. A small victory for the landscape.

In many cases, local governments have worked with communications companies to select sites that will work for both the industry and
the local community. The ATC and the trail clubs pressure the industry
into making their mark on the land as unobtrusive as possible. They
encourage companies to build on pre-existing structures, erect towers on
downslopes instead of on peaks, build smaller towers that don't rise above
the forest canopy, disguise towers, and paint utility sheds to blend into
the landscape. Despite the ATC's efforts, many companies haven't been
eager to accept their recommendations. "It has been difficult to change
the company's plans when they're that far along in the process," says
Andrew Hyman. "By the time we find out about the proposals, the companies have already made the financial investment," he says. Recently
the ATC has gotten companies to agree to notify them early on so the
ATC can provide input and recommendations before it's too late.

I am hopeful that companies will be willing to listen to the ATC, but
relations with the industry are not always genial. Many companies are
outright uncooperative, and the ATC must put up a strong legal fight to
get them to change their plans. Dennis Shaffer, chair of the American
Hiking Society board of directors, butted heads with the industry over a

proposed tower on Mount Mansfield in Vermont's Green Mountains. Shaffer asked TV companies to remove the towers once they are no longer needed, and the companies refused. This is alarming, for it typifies communications companies' generally uncaring attitude and lack of responsibility for the mass construction of towers and the permanent scarring of an already narrow corridor of wilderness. What will happen when communications technology changes again, maybe this time to a satellite system that would render towers useless? Will the companies attack the removal of towers with the same zeal they brought to their construction? What about the roads that were built to gain access to the towers and the utility sheds? Will companies pay to restore the roads to their natural condition? Who pays for the damage? We all pay, and the price tag cannot be measured in dollars; it's far more valuable than that.

⚜

Craig and I kept walking, day after day, and we slowly made our way through Pennsylvania and into New Jersey and New York. Physically we were solid, but mentally it was difficult to stay focused. All I could think about were the things I didn't have; I couldn't have cared less about the things I did have or the good aspects of the journey—that I was healthy and physically strong, that there were small beauties along the trail, that I was spending time with someone I loved. When Craig and I both realized this, we knew it was time to make some adjustments. We were beginning to accept that taking breaks was okay and that it was a normal and necessary part of most journeys. After all, most thru-hikers awake one morning with a case of mental fatigue too heavy to carry. For many, the burning desire to hike the Appalachian Trail gets snuffed out in a heavy rain. The monotony of walking, the fixed routine, and the physical pain drive 90 percent of all thru-hikers off the trail for good. Craig and I were too stubborn to consider quitting, but we did realize we needed another break. As the ninety-seven-degree air boiled in 100 percent humidity in Unionville, New York, we decided now would be a good time to leave.

We had fallen into a rather pathetic state. The flies, the rocks, and the urban sprawl had once again reduced my optimistic outlook to a skeptical wince. Our food situation had completely deteriorated. Oatmeal, instant mashed potatoes, and minute rice had long since been abandoned. We were convinced that Snickers and Little Debbie Moon Pies were nutritionally sound.

This time, sarcasm wasn't enough to pull me through. The walk was wearing us down. It was time for a huddle. Time to regroup.

We retreated to the green hills of Connecticut and spent a week at Craig's family's house indulging in off-trail luxuries like fresh bagels, milk, tennis shoes, movie rentals, and couches. Craig got tired of his overgrown hair so together we shaved his head, bald and shiny like Mr. Clean. "Great," I told him, "now we'll never get a ride to town. You're now a big bald man with a squirrely red beard."

Craig and I amused our families with stories from our hike through New Jersey and New York. During that time on the trail, our sanity had escaped and we were thoroughly entertained by the comedy of the weekend warriors.

One Saturday morning in northern Jersey we had stopped for a break at the Gren Anderson shelter. To our surprise, a Boy Scout troop had already claimed it for the night. We were puzzled by their early arrival. Then we saw the cars. The Scouts hauled coolers, bags of groceries, and jugs of milk from the road fifty yards behind the shelter. We expected someone to break out a boombox and lawn chairs. "A hike around the shelter is optional," declared the Scout leader. "You can explore on your own." A real wilderness experience for these Scouts.

The afternoon progressed on the AT Freeway. We must have passed sixty people. At another shelter, a group of Scouts listened to their leader give instructions about the proper use of an ax. The Scoutmaster barked orders at four uninspired faces. They all seemed genuinely to dislike one another. They were sweaty and tired and looked like they would rather be in an air-conditioned house watching cartoons. We left before the axes started to fly.

Since camping in New Jersey is permitted only at shelters, we stopped early to secure a spot for the night. The peaceful afternoon ended abruptly as a stream of twenty-five Girl Scouts filtered in. Dave, their leader, was breathless despite the fact that he was wearing one of those band-aid things football players wear on their noses to open their airway. Dave was awkward and agitated. The girls began to erect a city of twelve tents, fumbling with tent poles and rainflies. I saw one teddy bear tossed into a tent, but most of their gear was legitimate. Dave marched around. "Don't just leave your food lying around, Elizabeth. Hey, girls . . . girls . . . okay, everyone listen up. Put all your food in the bear box. There are definitely bears around here." The girls paid him little attention.

Moments later, a group of three city slickers arrived. The gel in their hair was still glistening. They wore combat boots, leather gloves, and thick gold chains. I got the feeling they hadn't been here before. They huddled around the picnic table plotting their next move.

Craig and I sat in the shelter with Stan and the Happy Hillbilly. We had front-row seats and we people-watched all afternoon. Stan, a local resident, talked nonstop in a Brooklyn accent about corporate downsizing and job security. The Happy Hillbilly, a section-hiker from southern Virginia, explained that he has no use for a water filter. He stroked his red chest-length beard. "My mustache hair and stomach acid do an adequate job of filtering water," he said.

Then a Boy Scout troop arrived. The count at the shelter was pushing forty-five. The Scout leader quickly scanned the city of Girl Scout tents and searched the premises for a smooth, level spot. He returned and mumbled, "This is definitely not going to work."

He attempted to motivate the troop to move on, but the boys protested and dropped their packs. They were hot. There were twenty girls there. There was a quick shuffling of maps. They decided to stay. I hoped they wouldn't mind camping next to the privy.

§

There is no question that the Appalachian Trail has a social component; it is often the social aspect that compels people to go there, and it is also this component that makes experiences on this particular trail unique. The people who run the Appalachian Trail Conference (ATC) recognize the social aspect as valuable, but they also understand that certain uses and certain urban influences adversely affect the very purpose of the trail. Telecommunications towers and urban sprawl affect the viewshed, and illegal motorized use and overpopulation can have profound negative effects on people's experiences. In order to provide direction to trail managers who are responsible for maintaining the delicate balance between a wilderness experience and a social experience, in 1997 the ATC set out to define the "Appalachian Trail Experience." They concluded that the experience should involve the following: "opportunities for observation, contemplation, enjoyment and exploration of the natural world; a sense of remoteness and detachment from civilization; opportunities to experience solitude, freedom, personal accomplishment, self-reliance, and self-discovery; a sense of being on the height of the land; opportunities to experience the cultural, historical, and pastoral elements of the surrounding countryside; a feeling of being part of the natural environment; and opportunities for travel on foot, including opportunities for long-distance hiking."

I wondered, though, at what point does the social experience overwhelm the wilderness experience? How many hunters, hiking clubs, weekenders with cell phones, Girl Scouts and Boy Scouts, and juvenile delinquents will prevent me from achieving fellowship with wilderness? At what point does my experience more resemble a tent party in a friend's backyard than a backcountry journey? I suppose it's different for each person. For me, as long as I couldn't hear traffic or see a radio tower, as long as I felt isolated, I was having the AT experience. But here and there I found gaps in this experience, places where there was too much urban encroachment, too many people to have any feelings of detachment from civilization.

As entertaining as our tromp through the mid-Atlantic region was, at times it felt like an ominous foreshadowing of what wilderness experiences may be in the future, all over the country. I wondered if anyone else felt that way, so I began asking trail clubs about the number of people who use the AT and what that means for wilderness.

The first thing I discovered is that an extraordinary number of people are dedicated to preserving and managing the Appalachian Trail and the AT experience. Based in Harpers Ferry, West Virginia, the ATC has fifty-two employees and five field offices. They coordinate the AT maintaining clubs, distribute information, and manage and protect the trail corridor along its entire length. The ATC has around 29,000 members, and the thirty-one AT maintaining clubs boast a combined membership of more than 100,000. Hundreds of volunteers from the Appalachian Trail clubs put in more than 174,000 hours of trail work in 1998, and countless unrecorded hours were spent attending meetings, traveling, and taking care of paperwork. It seemed to me that the volunteers are probably the people most in touch with the trail. They are the ones who live near it and who interact with the surrounding communities on a daily basis. Many of the volunteers are veteran thru-hikers or section-hikers themselves. They are people who have been touched by the trail and who want to provide a high-quality outdoor experience for other people. "I get so much pleasure from my hiking," says Doug Nelson of the Old Dominion AT Club, "I want to give something back." For some volunteers, like seventy-four-year-old Gene McCarney of the Blue Mountain Eagle Climbing Club, after decades of trail use "it is payback time." Ed Kenna, chair of the Philadelphia Trail Club, believes in a "personal commitment to community" and hopes to leave a legacy for the future.

I learned that although these trail clubs are fighting hard to maintain a high-quality trail experience for future generations, they are losing ground. And overpopulation is the biggest threat. "Trails and facilities get a tremendous amount of use when they are not 'hardened' enough to support it," says Ned Kuhns of the Tidewater Appalachian Trail Club. He recommends that high-use areas be "hardened," that is, developed with things like outhouses, tent platforms, and water pumps so a large number of people won't destroy the resource. M. C. White, a volunteer for the Appalachian Mountain Club for thirty-five years, would like to see clubs and organizations stop promoting and advertising the Appalachian Trail. "The trail experience and the trail itself suffer greatly from overuse, and increasing publicity is worsening the situation," says White. As Doug Nelson of the Old Dominion AT Club notes, "I think the trail can absorb some overuse, but ruts cut by mountain bikes and ATVs, vandalism at our shelter, careless trashing, and cutting across switchbacks by large groups are big problems." Nelson also finds that people are increasingly attracted to the shelters, and shelters have become destinations in themselves. "We overbuilt, so now we're hosting drinking parties and groups who otherwise wouldn't be there," he says.

Most volunteers seemed to feel that if we don't protect as much land as we can from development and urban encroachment, and if we don't manage people who use wild places, we will be well on our way to losing a true sense of the word "wild." I don't believe you can sincerely love wilderness and not recognize that we need to limit the number of people who use it. We must do this to preserve both the resource and our experiences there. How to do this fairly is an enormously complicated issue for land managers. All over the country different strategies have been implemented, from charging fees to requiring permits and reservations. Each strategy comes with its own costs.

Permits certainly guarantee fewer people, but how should we go about issuing permits? Some areas use a lottery system, others have waiting lists. Some people feel that locals should get first priority, other people think that outfitters and guides should be exempt from the system. Already, in many of the more popular national parks, visitors must obtain a backcountry permit months in advance.

Scott Silver, director of Wild Wilderness, a user group that promotes undeveloped recreation, says that these regulations are severely changing the wilderness experience. Silver believes that we do need to limit the number of people who visit wilderness, but he feels that users shouldn't have to pay for a permit. "I can't afford to spend $15 a night to camp," he says. "A trip to the backcountry will be something only the rich can afford to do." Silver laments the fact that the wilderness experience is changing from a spontaneous challenge to something that is regimented and guaranteed. "It's like going to a hooker," Silver says of the new system. "There's no getting lucky anymore. When you pay for it, you're going to get it."

Of course, many people are against the idea of restricting use. Some see it as an infringement on their rights to public land. For others, the idea of registering an itinerary with a governing agency seems to defeat the very purpose of a wilderness experience. Some environmentalists fear that restricting people's experiences with nature will reduce support for trails and the great outdoors. Environmental groups like Wild Wilderness and Wilderness Watch disagree. They believe that support for wild places will come only if the resource is worthy of support. Think about this: If thousands of people vacation at a pristine lake, who will want to protect it once the shoreline is devastated, Coke cans are floating in it, and the surrounding land is smeared with human feces and toilet paper? Sometimes, I think, we need to have a little self-restraint, take responsibility for our actions, and consider how our actions affect the resource. If the only way to preserve the integrity of a place is not to go there, then that is a sacrifice we ought to be willing to make for certain areas.

One of the most vocal opponents to use restrictions is the American Recreation Coalition (ARC), the conglomeration of companies that are trying to privatize nature for a profit and increase access for motorized recreation. They'd like to sell as many dirt bikes, hiking boots, and rain jackets as they can, so why not pack people in and let them recreate? The coalition has led an aggressive campaign to fight restrictions, and they tried to get rid of "solitude" as something land managers should strive to manage for. Why? Because solitude puts a cap on the number of dirt bikes and jet skis they can sell. I see their stance as threatening to designated Wilderness, for solitude ought not to be compromised, not for a jet ski, not for anything.

What restrictions will be implemented on the Appalachian Trail? Will I have to wait twenty years for a thru-hiking permit? Will I have to pay per mile? per diem? Will I have to camp only at designated sites, next to a numbered pole?

Many of these strategies are being discussed right now, but many trail club volunteers feel that limiting the number of visitors, charging fees, and requiring permits is impractical on the Appalachian Trail because there is no way to enforce such regulations. There are too many roads and access points. "The Park Service and Forest Service can't be trail cops; they have enough to do," says Ron Rosen, volunteer for the New York-New Jersey Trail Conference for twenty-two years. So far, his club has done what it can, hoping people follow the guidelines on their own. In New York and New Jersey, all campers must stay at designated overnight-use areas. Groups are now limited to ten for overnight stays and twenty-five for day hikes. Rosen's club is trying to separate group camping areas from individuals and smaller hiking parties. But as Jill Arbuckle of the NY-NJ Trail Conference explains, "the states refuse to enforce the limits and respond to complaints of ATVs and irresponsible groups." Arbuckle, like most other club members I talked with, believes that educating the public should be a top priority.

Many trail clubs support the Ridgerunner program. Ridgerunners are paid individuals who essentially patrol the trail. They educate visitors about minimum-impact techniques, answer questions about natural history, and encourage people to respect the land and other visitors. Unfortunately, they don't have the authority to issue tickets or press charges for violations of trail guidelines. Nelson believes that education should extend beyond the trail and into local communities. He recommends that trail associations work with towns to "change their master plans, adopt Critical Environmental Areas, and make the residents more aware of the AT as a resource to treasure."

As much as I dislike the idea of restrictions, it seems that we must in some way limit ourselves, because as it is now, we are infringing on the resource, tearing it up and matting it down. Each tract of public land ought to be evaluated on a case-by-case basis. Each agency ought to consider its land-management goals, the use and abuse specific to that region, and the feasibility of different strategies to limit use. In some areas where recreation is a land-use priority, it may be okay to let people go virtually unrestricted, but in other special places where nature and a high-quality experience are important, I would rather preserve solitude and wait my turn than have my backcountry experience turn into an overrun tent party.

Eventually, the Girl Scouts stopped singing. Stan stopped his Brooklyn babbling and Dave lost interest in warning us about the bears. We finally got to sleep.

Craig and I told story after story, and our families listened and laughed and humored us. "You really just had to be there," we'd say as we doubled over in laughter at all of our own stories. After a week, we collected our thoughts, gathered our gear, and returned to the trail. No matter how awful the conditions were, the trail had gotten inside us and we just had to keep going. We figured the most heavily populated areas were behind us and we were excited to be back in the woods. We had come some 1,300 miles and had about 800 to go. By now I thought of Craig as a best friend. The strength of our friendship gave me hope for the remainder of the trip. Together, I thought, we can do this.

It was the end of May. The weather was still hot, but the terrain changed dramatically during the week. Wooden boards suspended our steps over soggy swamps. We jumped quickly from board to board before our temporary platforms sank into the muck. Wet flatlands soon gave way to farmland. The water collected in ponds and creeks. Within a day, the flatland buckled into lumps and we climbed straight up Wawayanda Mountain. The woods returned, thick and green, spilling into the trail.

The next day the woods thinned and enormous rock outcroppings extended from the ridge's backbone. We used both hands to heave ourselves over ledges and shimmy down vertical faces. Although our mileage decreased, it was a fun change of pace. From the eastern Pinnacles we peered down at Greenwood Lake, then passed through Harriman State Park. We climbed hill after hill, fleeing from swarms of vicious mosquitoes and biting flies.

And then, a few miles south of Bear Mountain, just as we were feeling that the woods had returned for good, we climbed to a view and there it was. Etched into the horizon was the skyline of New York City. We approached the Hudson River thinking about all the wildlife in the concrete jungle just over the hills.

We descended into the town of Bear Mountain and down to 124 feet above sea level, the lowest elevation on the trail. Before crossing the Hudson River via the Bear Mountain Bridge, the trail meanders through the Trailside Museum and Zoo, a stretch of sidewalk that passes caged bears, bobcats, red-tailed hawks, a bald eagle, and a coyote, as well as a geology exhibit and history museum. The zoo is visited by more than a half-million people each year. It was a high-heel, purse, and miniskirt sort of nature experience. Craig and I had trouble blending with the urbanites, but we enjoyed the close-up wildlife encounters all the same. While examining the caged bears and bobcats, the tourists from the Big Apple gave us some terrific stares. We then understood why the zoo path was blazed for thru-hikers: we were clearly part of the exhibit.

## CHAPTER SEVEN

# AMBASSADOR TO
# THE WORLD OF MEN

I've always tried to respect every creature, even the pesty ones, believing they fill some critical niche. During that midsummer week in Massachusetts, however, one species dammed the outpouring of my seemingly endless love. If I were given the powers of creation, there would be no place in my world for mosquitoes.

Here is the scene: eighty-five miles of Massachusetts swamps and mosquitoes by the millions. The trail circled, skirted, and plunged directly through nearly every swamp in the state. Craig and I sank and sucked and slogged in the mud. We jumped over small creeks and balanced on slippery rocks and wooden planks that bridged drier ground. Nearing 100 degrees, the stagnant air was itself a chore to walk through. After two days of steady rain, the drops disappeared but the air remained just as wet. For six days, I don't believe I was dry for a minute.

The wetlands had slurped down the fresh rain and belched out swarms of bloodthirsty mosquitoes. They attacked with gusto. Our tent became our only refuge, and erecting the tent was a battle of sheer numbers versus creative, but limited, strategies. Despite the heat, we armored ourselves in gaiters, pants, and hooded jackets. I once read that mosquitoes can pierce the scales of snakes—I figured if they tried hard enough they could probably work their way through Gore-Tex too. But Gore-Tex would be more difficult than cotton, so we layered up, determined to make them work for our blood.

Craig and I added Gatorade powder to our water and refilled our jugs nearly every hour. While not overjoyed about our new set of challenges, I was not overly distressed either. This was new territory for me, my pack weight hovered around a manageable thirty pounds, and although my sleeping bag was always damp, I wasn't the one who was responsible for lugging the soaking tent through Massachusetts. Craig, on the other hand, was quick to realize his intolerance of heat and humidity, and he developed what soon became an irrational animosity towards mosquitoes. To this day, the ambush of Massachusetts mosquitoes is something he hasn't recovered from.

Each day began with a battle. We had only seconds to leap out of the tent and pack our gear. We remained silent and did our best to stay composed. Occasionally one of us would lose it and start running and swatting and shrieking and cursing. Luckily this never happened to both of us at the same time. At the last moment, we tore off our jackets, stuffed them in our packs, and ran! We jogged about four miles per hour for a couple hours then dropped the packs, pitched the tent in record time, dove in, and caught our breath.

Craig wrote in his journal, "Did fifteen miles or so to get here and the skeeters are unforgiving. We set up the tent around one and stayed in for two hours eating moldy bagels, but away from the bugs!" Each break, I assessed the recent damages and scratched furiously at countless red bumps. My stick of Cortaid became my most treasured possession. Craig and I lay in the tent, watching the mosquitoes, their needlelike proboscises probing for flesh, drilling for blood. Day and night, we were haunted by their constant buzzing and intrigued by their lack of sleep. Do they sleep in midflight? Do they take shifts patrolling the tent? How are they always around us?

A few always managed to follow us into the tent before we could zip the door shut, so the first few minutes in the tent were spent locating and killing the intruders. The white walls of the tent interior became smeared with mosquito parts and streaked with blood. We then stripped down to our underwear, lay back, and treasured the calm as our thighs and backs stuck to the sleeping pads. "Honey," I said, "stop swatting. We've killed them all."

"I know," said Craig, "but it feels like they're all over me, in my ears. It's the buzzing. It drives me crazy."

For days we were unable to cook. We ate pop-tarts and trail mix and granola bars for every meal, or we went without. "I did not come out here for *this*," Craig said. But there was no way out. We had to keep going and hope that the trail would eventually rise out of the swamps and into the Green Mountains.

It was near the eighty-fifth mile of Massachusetts rain and swamps and mosquitoes as thick as falling snow that something clicked inside me and I swore that these measly little bloodsuckers would not stop me from going to Maine. They would not drive me off the trail. We rode a roller coaster of joyous moments and painful times, mental deterioration and spurts of positive thinking and relentless humor. But this time it was personal. I was driven by a deep hatred for mosquitoes, and I acknowledged that, no, this may not be fun, but, by God, I'm going to finish this trail.

Craig, on the other hand, was showing some doubt. He was covered with red bites, and he had reached his threshold of tolerance for heat and humidity.

"Come on," I reassured him, "We're just about to get to the good stuff. Vermont is right around the corner."

His ankle was bothering him as we descended Mount Greylock. He looked haggard. We were exhausted from our frantic sprints and snack-food diet, and Craig started to lose his cool every time a mosquito got near his head, which was often. Our sleeping bags were damp and the tent was waterlogged and never had a chance to dry out. Wet gear added considerable weight to his load. "All I can think about is getting out of here," he said. "I'm serious. I'm about ready to quit this trail. I don't care; it's not worth it."

When we got to Williamstown, Massachusetts, Craig still felt the same way and I was nervous about what he'd say next. It wasn't that long ago that I was feeling the same way. He was so strong in Pennsylvania; I didn't understand how he could fall apart now. And I didn't know what quitting would mean for us. It seemed to me that if we didn't finish the trail together it would say something about our relationship, like we might walk out on that too. I never told Craig this, but as we walked in silence toward Williamstown, I felt there was more at stake than a hike.

We found the little bus station and took a seat on our packs. "What do you think?" I asked him.

"I don't know," he said, "it seems like we're so uncomfortable out here. We're a mess, Honey. Just look at us." I agreed we looked pretty bad. "And we have so much farther to go," he said.

"I know," I said. "I'm not sure what we should do to make it better, but we need to think of something. I don't think quitting's the answer."

"Wouldn't you like to start a new life together?" he asked. "We could leave now and move to Utah and be with Kodiak again and get a house with a real bed."

I was starting graduate school in Utah in the fall and was delighted to hear that he wanted to move there with me. It was one of those things we never talked about—commitment after the trail. I knew I was heading west and I figured it would be up to him if he decided to follow me there. As badly as I wanted that to happen, I knew right then was the wrong time to go.

"It's tempting," I said, "but you know something? If you quit now, it's going to eat you up. You're going to think about all the 'what ifs' every damn day. I know you and I know you'll become obsessed with this trail. It will drive you crazy until you come back and finish it."

We sat in silence, staring at the concrete, and I wondered what I would do if he left. Would I go with him? Should I continue on, by myself? Could I really survive this trail alone? It felt so sudden; I needed some time to think about my options. I wasn't sure I could make a decision right there at the bus stop.

"Okay," he took a deep breath, "let's keep going. But I think it would help if we skipped ahead a little. Actually, there is no goddamn way I'm going back to the trail until we're deep in the Green Mountains and out of the swamps and bugs."

It was decided. We yellow-blazed luxury style in the front seat of the Bonanza bus and headed to Manchester, Vermont, about fifty miles up the trail. We actually saw the best views of the mountains we had in all of Vermont. From a distance they're beautiful, soft, thick, and green. Once we were inside the forest, it felt a bit claustrophobic. It was hard to tell where we were and which direction we were heading.

Before we entered the Green Mountains, we stocked up on survival gear: a can of OFF!, two bug nets, and a tiny radio Walkman. The OFF! worked occasionally. The bug nets were essential for breaks, but walking all day with blurred bug net vision was enough to make us crazy in itself. The Walkman was necessary for sanity maintenance in the tent; it was either music or the buzzing of mosquitoes, and I think at that point Craig and I would have preferred even opera to mosquitoes, which is saying a lot.

That night in our tent, Craig finished writing in his journal and slid it toward me. I read his summary of the last few days and of our struggle to stay on the trail. At the end of his entry was a note: "Adrienne, every time I think I can't love you any more than I already do, I prove myself wrong." We made a pact, once again, not to break up the team. This is the last time we need to reassure ourselves, I thought. No matter what, we're going all the way.

Some warm summer evening, when my belly is full and my body clean and dry, I'll take a seat beside the window. As daylight becomes fuzzy and faint, the pane blackens and my reflection is framed. I smile at myself. Life is pretty good. I squint past the glass and scan the backyard. I look out and notice a few mosquitoes flitting about. Maybe then I'll think to myself, They're not so bad. Maybe then.

$$\oint$$

We walked anywhere from twelve to nineteen miles a day in Vermont and tried to resupply every three or four days to keep our pack weights down. I was happy carrying twenty-five-to-thirty pounds and Craig's goal was to keep his pack below thirty-five. We managed to resupply often, but not without a few scary hitchhiking encounters. When we got to the junction of the Appalachian Trail and the Long Trail, Craig and I decided to scoot to town and grab some groceries. A woman in a minivan picked us up and immediately began talking about her tennis game and her ex-husband (I'm still not sure how the two are related), which right there sort of made me wonder. She was too busy with her monologue to bother looking across the two lanes of traffic she needed to cross, so when she peeled out into the middle of the highway she was a couple inches shy of taking out a small pickup. The truck swerved off the road to avoid crashing into a small blue car.

Three cars behind the blue car came to a screeching halt, and when I looked back, the drivers were shaking their heads and fists. "Ooops," is what the lady said. Then she said, "Sorry," and continued on about her ex-husband.

This particular incident was not as bad as a couple other rides we survived down south. One time in Virginia we got picked up by a man in his late twenties driving a tan Oldsmobile with rust spots and a small dent where the front left headlight used to be. As soon as I pulled the seat forward to climb in the back and saw a case of empty Budweiser cans on the floor, I knew we had made a mistake, but it was too late to decline the ride without causing a scene. The man wore a black T-shirt with the sleeves cut off. His belly was bulging just over the edge of his pants, and his hair was long and brown and greasy. We shut the door and he popped open a can of Bud. It was Sunday morning about 9:00 A.M. He sped along the curvy back roads faster than I would travel on a highway. I clenched the door handle and almost started to cry. At the trailhead he asked if we had anything to smoke. He was talking about marijuana and he didn't believe us when we said no.

In another instance, Craig and I hitched a ride from a sweet old man in Tennessee, but as he gripped the steering wheel, we noticed that his forehead barely rose above it. I took the back seat and Craig sat shotgun. The old man pulled onto the road and after a minute we had accelerated to a speedy fifteen miles per hour. The road was plenty wide and gently wove through the country. Even at a crawl, the man had trouble staying between the lines. He'd veer over to the right, just barely graze the guardrail, swerve left until he was clearly over the yellow line, and then bring it back too far to the right so we'd almost, but not quite, go off the road. The swerving was calm and graceful, and the man didn't miss a beat of the conversation. Craig sat with his hand poised inches from the steering wheel. He looked back at me and I nodded at his hand. He nodded, assuring me that he would grab it if he had to.

Thankful to have survived all of five treacherous minutes in the minivan, Craig and I headed back to the woods and continued on.

We met a number of thru-hikers in Vermont: Bob the River Bum, Glider, Bedowin, the Cornell Crew, and a couple speedy hikers who had started much later than we did and who would complete the trail much sooner. The hikers we met had 1,600 miles of thru-hiking stories and 600 miles of hopes and dreams; never was there a dull moment. Bob the River Bum was an older man, a truck driver who carried a big umbrella, crept along at what he called a snail's pace, and said if nothing else, hiking would get rid of his truck butt. Bob had something positive to say even on the lowest days, and of all the people I met, I think it was he who had the best attitude. Others came close. Glider carried a small pack that never weighed more than twenty-five pounds. He was quiet and smiled a lot and seemed to be happy about life in general. A young college boy, Glider was traveling alone, seeing the country, finding himself. Bedowin was on a similar journey and carried a small mandolin. We also shared many nights with the Cornell Crew, two recent graduates out for a postcollegiate adventure and certainly finding it. Everyone loved and hated the trail as we did, but when we were all together, we mostly loved it.

After more than four months on the trail, hikers were getting a step closer to discovering something important about themselves and were cluing in to what makes them tick. For the young boys it may have been about recognizing what makes them happy and possibly defining certain life goals and a sense of direction. Before bed, the Cornell Crew would toss around ideas about jobs and school after the trail. Every now and then they would say something like, "I just want to make sure I never forget what it feels like to live this way," and, "If only we could live like this forever; I bet we could find a way to make it happen." For Bob, the trail may have been a time to reflect and put life in perspective. His AT thru-hike may have come with an understanding that far fewer adventures lay before him now than thirty years ago. For Craig it had a lot to do with grappling with the whys of his brother's death. He was beginning to let go of the search for an explanation and accept that there may be no simple answers. I too was figuring some things out. It began with defining my role as a woman thru-hiker on the Appalachian Trail.

§

My first attempt at figuring out how my little life fit into the big picture happened the first time I saw a globe. When I was five, I pinned Pennsylvania under my index finger and spun the world. I sat there feeling a bit concerned, trying to pronounce names like Indonesia and Thailand, and I felt very, very small. It suddenly occurred to me that my house and my family were not on the map. That moment initiated a process of self-discovery that, as I realize now, may continue until my final breath. I believe that every person goes through this process and, to some degree, becomes aware of his or her place. On the trail I had hoped to reveal not only who I am or what I want to be, but my place in the universe.

Think about something as simple as a raindrop. A single drop, round and robust, plummets from the heavens, smacks the surface of a pond, and melts into the pool. Ripples radiate toward the shores, and, assuming elements have consciousness, the raindrop realizes that it is only one drop in a little pond. There is an area surrounding the pond where space is no longer filled by water but by land, and the raindrop learns boundaries. The pond sits in a dip on the landscape and appears as a dot on the continent. The continent floats on the planet and the planet spins somewhere in the universe, and then things become sketchy. It requires some energy and the willingness to feel small and inadequate, but you can eventually find your position. The key to it is this: Once you see the continent and the planet and the universe and you can't seem to expand the scope any further, you should once again see the raindrop. It is then that you realize you *are* significant, for the drop is the universe. You are the substance of it all.

When I was younger, like other children I had no concept of place. The universe was a seashell, an anthill, or the bank of a river. The continent had not been discovered. I was a tomboy. I raced remote-control cars with my brother, played sports with the boys and usually beat them. I plowed dump trucks through dirt piles and cut the head off a Barbie Doll that some unknowing friend had given me on my tenth birthday. My brother, Scott, was three years younger and I beat him up regularly.

I'll never forget the day that Scott refused to do what I ordered. He grew almost overnight. He grew taller and stronger and faster, and I stayed the same. Neither of us understood it. He was appalled that I couldn't bench-press eighty pounds; I told him the *bar* was heavy. During our teenage years my 6'3" brother took every opportunity to get revenge on his tiny sister until one day, I guess, he felt he had evened things up.

It took me a long time to accept my physical inferiority to athletic men, and to this day I occasionally forget. I still challenge men to contests of strength, although I have been advised to stick to ping-pong and horseshoes. I was born under Libran skies and so am plagued (or blessed, depending on the situation) with a remarkable stubborn streak. It took years of high school and college sports and a few feminist friends for me to begin to see myself as a strong *woman*, not an average person. So I graduated from college proud of my role as a woman, confident of who I was, and ready to take on the world.

When I started hiking the Appalachian Trail, I had no doubts about my physical ability and no doubts about finishing. Even if I found myself challenged, I knew I would be too stubborn to quit. On the front page of my journal I made a list of goals for the trail. These included feeling my place in Nature through meditation and observation, strengthening my relationship with Craig, getting in great shape, and writing every day. Completing the trail was not on my list; it was a given. I did not set out to prove anything. My niche was well defined. I was a strong woman, mentally and physically. I never thought I wouldn't be able to keep up.

Veteran hikers had warned against being in a terrible hurry. I had lived most of my life around people who were perpetually in this hurried state, and I knew the consequences. I would not be like them. I would take my time and absorb the journey. Maybe it was because we weren't physically capable of long days, but we did take our time in the beginning. Then we pushed for longer and longer days. I slipped into a phase of competing with myself and with Craig. By the time we reached Virginia, I found myself in that terrible hurry.

Looking back through my journals it's easy to see what I did. I reverted to my old tendencies of competing with men and expecting to win. And at first I did. I began the hike in good shape. I had always been active and worked out with extra vigor prior to February. It took Craig a few weeks to strengthen his hiking muscles, but after a few hundred miles he had shed more than twenty pounds and was solid as stone. In Pennsylvania I found myself wishing he would slow down. My lungs burned, my legs ached, but it was my pride that hurt the most. I spent many angry miles cursing myself for not being able to keep the pace. I resented Craig, and all the men I met on the trail, for being stronger and faster and able to glide over all the rocks that I cautiously plodded over.

I began to notice other differences between my male counterparts and me. My bony hips had been bruised and chafed from carrying a heavy pack. I walked for weeks with two bloody welts, cringing every time I cinched the straps and secured the load. I knew the guys could not possibly be in this much pain. Every time I had to relieve myself, I had to strip my pack from my back while my wet shirt instantly froze to damp skin. Remounting my load meant pressing the icy cloth against my spine. The men never knew this discomfort. And then that special time of the month would come. I carried the extra bulk of tampons and pads and lived with a sticky, smelly, bloody mess for a week, each day hoping for a chance to take a shower.

After a month on the trail it occurred to me that I hadn't seen another woman. I started becoming more aware of my role as *the* woman, although I never managed to be proud of that role. Somewhere between the Georgian steeps and the Pennsylvania boulder fields that memory of women's strength dissolved.

After four months I met another female thru-hiker. Our acquaintance was brief since we were about to take a day off in Connecticut and she was to continue on. So, for most of my thru-hiking experience, I carried the burden of being the female representative. I was Raindrop, ambassador to the World of Men. I never bid for this job but it somehow stuck with me like the scent of dirty socks. If I lagged behind or complained about the weather, I was afraid people would think I couldn't take it because I was female. So I was going to smile and take it. I stopped looking around. I had miles to travel and I wasn't about to let my gender down.

I have to admit there were times on the trail when I did like being a little different; I always have. I prided myself on being able to rough it and to feel at least sometimes like one of the guys. I often felt the bond between thru-hikers was stronger than the bond between genders. We were a select group of people on a unique mission. We were bound by the desire to walk the length of our country, and that was a desire few others possessed. I enjoyed being part of that group, and I knew the others respected me for being the only female.

Still, it was tough spending nearly every night in the shelter as the token female. The men changed their sweaty shirts in the warmth of their sleeping bags while I shuffled out in the rain or snow to change clothes behind the shelter. I resented the fact that I was the only one who had to leave, and I wanted more than anything to share my experiences with another woman. The majority of our nights were spent alone or with a couple others, but we would occasionally share the shelter with eight to twelve strangers. Those were the times I felt I never quite fit in. I longed for a female companion with whom to share my experiences. "Craig," I said, "how would you feel if you were always with women and hadn't seen another man in three months?" As a smile strung across his face I knew my example had backfired. Maybe it's different for women. Maybe we need each other more than men need the company of other men.

Along the trail, I found myself accomplishing all my goals except the spiritual one—feeling my place in Nature. I got caught up in the male-dominated culture of the trail and lost sight of why I was out there and what I had hoped to gain. Back on the playground, I was a child again and the dirt path was my world. I had lost my peripheral vision and lost my sense of place.

I had to stop and force myself to answer some vital questions: What is my role on the trail? Why is my experience different and what does that mean? How do I define my goals? How does my life fit into the big picture? Many people take to the woods to find their place in the world. Nature and solitude are a good combination for a healthy dose of self-reflection. I learned that the hard way. I had to lose who I was before I was able to see myself clearly, and even then that clarity would dim and fade with bouts of mosquitoes, hunger, and self-doubt.

It has been a long process of stargazing and soul-searching, and I often grapple with questions to which I have no answers. But there's one thing I know for sure: My life always shines with renewed clarity when the landscape unfolds into a canyon at my feet and exposes those rocks of times long forgotten by everything except our primal souls. Somehow the process of self-discovery is facilitated by wild places and experiences that reduce your needs to the most basic ones.

For brief moments on the trail, I felt deeply connected to my surroundings and I felt that I was close to finding my place. At times, a feeling of peace would rush over me and I would be content with myself. I saw my role as a woman as something worthy and unique. Still, it is difficult to accept some of the differences; compared to most men, I will never be as agile on the rocks or as strong in the swift currents or as fast on the uphill climbs. But I am connected to the earth in a way that no man will ever be. It is only the female form that has the ability to give life. I am an infinitesimally small unit on the earth, but I am also part of the energy of the universe and of the creation of life. That is the role I glimpsed on the trail.

§

One afternoon I woke from a nap at an overlook somewhere in the Green Mountains of Vermont. As I slowly drifted back to consciousness and blinked through sleep-shrouded eyes, something in the thick green hills caught my attention. There was a form, a female form, birthed from the mountains in front of me. Two voluptuous mounds rose side by side, a lower ridge extended outward, lesser rolling hills seemed to form legs and arms, and the land rose again into a shapely mound near the pubic area. I sat up to study the land and, sure enough, the resemblance was uncanny. Poised on that overlook, I wondered how many clusters of mountains resembled women; how many goddesses on the Appalachian Trail had I hurried past? In this gentle, swollen, rounded range it is easy to see the female form, this Earth Goddess, everywhere. And if that was the only female companionship I would find on the trail, then so be it.

That was not the first time I had felt a strong connection to nature, and I always assumed there was something uniquely feminine about the Appalachians. By now I knew that seeing a female form in these mountains was not just a desperate attempt to feel part of something larger than myself, but that it signified a bond between the earth and women that went much deeper. There is, there has to be, some connection between women and the earth that is not fully acknowledged in our society.

I never paid much attention to history—maybe because the history I learned in school seemed to have more to do with war and power and men in suits than it had to do with me. History lessons began and ended with Christian cultures and patriarchal societies. Once I embarked on my own journey for knowledge, which started with tossing the biased school textbooks in the dumpster behind my apartment, I discovered that I could relate to much of what has occurred in the past. I discovered that, as a woman who loves Nature, I have a history, I have a legacy, and I'm not the first to feel connected to the natural world in a spiritual way. With the help of other women on a similar quest, I've unraveled years of lessons and reconstructed a history that includes us. It is comforting to know that I am not alone in my dissatisfaction, nor am I alone in my search for a more accurate history.

From artistic creations and material remains found in various parts of southeastern Europe, the Near East, and India, we can infer quite a lot about how peaceful tribal societies viewed the natural world. These cultures flourished from the late Paleolithic age, around 35,000 B.C.E. (before the common era), through the Neolithic Age, which ended between 3500 and 1500 B.C.E. Evidence of their rituals, spiritual beliefs, and gender roles suggest that these early tribes were largely matriarchal (that is, women assumed leadership and important spiritual roles). They worshipped either one main goddess or a combination of goddesses, and they took symbols of nature (birds, snakes, trees, flowers, moon, stars, fire, bears, bees, toads, fish) to represent divine qualities. The Earth Mother, in one form or another, was the central figure of worship.

Although it is difficult to generalize about several thousand years of global history, there is agreement among historians of culture and religion that these societies respected the natural world, saw themselves as connected to their surroundings and to natural cycles, and assigned natural symbols to represent the things that were most sacred to them.

Dr. Miranda Shaw, author and professor of religion at the University of Richmond, explained that this all began to change in the fourth millennium B.C.E. when warlike nomadic people from the Asiatic and European north overran the centers of goddess culture. "They introduced their sky gods and saw to it that the goddess worshippers and their values were suppressed," she said.

When I started studying goddess cultures in college, I knew instantly that I would have liked to live in the Neolithic Age. I started to wonder if it would be possible to create my own little goddess-worshipping commune, and my friends and I, half-heartedly, began to conspire. Although Dr. Shaw tells me that today there are pockets of goddess-centered cultures scattered throughout the world, and that the goddess and her symbolism can be found in nearly every religion from Buddhism to Hinduism to Christianity, most of the large societies were annihilated a long time ago.

During the Roman invasions, which lasted from about 300 C.E. (common era) to 500 C.E., patriarchal societies rewrote the old myths into a new religion that took the sacred symbols of goddess religion, like trees and snakes and women, and assigned them evil properties. They shifted the paradigm of the culture from a holistic world view to a more dualistic one, characterized by a conflict of opposing forces: man versus woman, good versus evil, life versus death, light versus dark, and humans versus nature. I was floored when I discovered that dualism and patriarchy were once revolutionary concepts and that they made a relatively late appearance on the historical scene. "For more than 30,000 years," Dr. Shaw explained, "humans were seen as part of nature, all things were cyclical, life and death were simultaneously part of the natural cycle, and there was no distinction between good and evil." The traditional goddess-worshipping societies were holistic, not dualistic. There was no distinction between humans and the divine. Similar to Native American beliefs, everything was connected, so everything was sacred; a divine presence existed in everything. And crucial to our understanding the connection between women and nature, goddess religion was earth-centered while the new religion, which became Christianity, rejected the sacred earth and shifted its vision to a heavenly afterlife and to a god who ruled from on high, while men were given dominion over the earth—and women.

Throughout the Middle Ages, the Inquisition further extinguished the women- and earth-centered religions by killing everyone who was thought to stray from the new patriarchy guided by one male god. Millions of people—most of them women—who posed a threat to the patriarchy were brutally tortured and executed. These groups included witches, prostitutes, gypsies, gays, herbalists, midwives, village healers, and anyone advocating female power. Any woman who practiced the old earth-worshipping rituals and celebrated the power and energy of the female form was a threat to the patriarchy and was branded as a witch. The Inquisitors also targeted gays and lesbians who, in the old cultures, were often assigned special roles since they were believed to be able to connect with two different worlds; they had special powers to "cross over" and understand both men and women, and lesbians were able to commune with the goddesses. Historians estimate that at least 6 million and possibly as many as 9 million women/witches were killed.

During the Inquisition, the symbols and myths that had been an integral part of peaceful societies underwent patriarchal inversions. Their earth- and female-based symbols were assigned new meanings that would better suit the new male rulers. It was necessary to make the old sacred symbols as hideous and threatening as they could so people would not be tempted to return to the old religion. That was bad news for wilderness, since many of the old symbols of nature were now assigned evil properties. These new beliefs and ideologies were readily incorporated into Christianity. The snake, for example, which goddess cultures revered as a sacred animal, was transformed into a symbol of corruption and evil in Christianity.

I began to notice goddess symbols everywhere—in modern art, in coffee shops, in advertisements—and I developed a new appreciation for snakes. Before long, my best friend and I were giddy with delight, knowing there was something about the feminine, something about us, that was powerful enough to cause people to fight for thousands of years to suppress it. Goddess traditions, we thought, were something that we wanted to reclaim. It was only too peculiar when the two of us went to a psychic in Virginia Beach and were told that in a past life we were part of a powerful circle of women. We were delighted that our suspicions were confirmed, that our roots are grounded in goddess traditions. It is true that we were silly college kids, and our plans to form a goddess commune never amounted to anything, but what we took away from our research was a feeling of empowerment and connectedness to something that went deeper than the shallow roots we had grown in our present patriarchal society.

Worldwide, people are realizing that throughout much of history, the earth and women have been viewed in the same light and have been subjected to a similar pattern of mistreatment. The paradigm that links women and nature forms the foundation for the modern movement called ecofeminism. Traditional goddess cultures recognized the inherent connection between the earth and women, and they celebrated the life-giving and nurturing powers of them both. Today, many women are rediscovering that connection and are celebrating the power of the female form.

I often wonder if my frustration with the trail had something to do with glimpsing that connection but never allowing myself to fully realize it. Maybe I needed other women to help me understand my place. I lost my perspective and couldn't help but feel that I wanted something from the trail that was different from what the men wanted, but the men's goals often became my goals even when they didn't feel right. Many of the men, including Craig, liked to hurry through the day's mileage and relax at camp in the afternoon. I found myself racing to make miles instead of stopping along the way to take in my surroundings. Parts of my AT experience didn't feel like my own, and I wrestled with ways to claim my own experience. I tried to take my time, feel the connection, and be proud of my place and my identity. I tried to walk my own walk and nobody else's. Every mile I had to make a conscious effort to slow down and demand my own experience.

Recognizing that my experience may be different from the experiences of my male friends was the first step. Understanding that my feelings are grounded in a history of women communing with nature was the second step. To define my own journey and feel confident in pursuing it was the hard part. It was something that would take more than one hike to work through. It may take a lifetime to truly see my place and define myself, but on the Appalachian Trail I got one step closer.

## CHAPTER EIGHT

# FRAGILE PEAKS
# AND TRAIL ANGELS

I woke up hurting all over. I sat up, swallowed three Advil, and attempted to stand. My knees shook, remembering yesterday's steep descent. The mountains beat me up. I have the wounds to prove it.

Craig was still bundled in his bag so I lay back down, closed my eyes, and drifted in and out of consciousness. I was thinking about wearing a dress. I pictured my swollen, bruised feet squeezing into pretty shoes. I could see my hair, which had not been washed in fifteen days, shiny and straight, falling around my shoulders. I'd put in a pair of earrings too, if the holes haven't closed. I guess after hiking close to 2,000 miles, this is a relatively normal fantasy.

In my sleeping bag I was warm and dry. The dress could wait. Rest was all I needed. After a strenuous few days I could feel the lactic acid building up in my muscles, damming the river, jamming the crank. I needed a lube job, a good oiling, a long nap.

"Honey, can you pass the Advil?" Craig groaned.

"Yeah," I said, sliding him the Ziploc bag. "We have to ration it. We're almost out. I don't think I can walk without it."

"Damn East Coast," said Craig, "They don't believe in switchbacks out here. Can you remember the last time the trail *traversed* up a mountain?"

No, I couldn't. It had been straight up and straight down since the Green Mountains in Vermont. Steep and rugged, the Northern Appalachians reminded us of the terrain in North Carolina. Ascents and descents were many miles long, making the climb over one mountain a full day's work. We climbed up and over a number of Vermont's finest ski mountains, including Stratton, Bromley, and Killington. Unrelenting rain created mud chutes and rock slicks along the trail. Our daily mileage dropped from twenty in Connecticut to fifteen in Vermont to ten in the White Mountains of New Hampshire.

We were a little discouraged when we felt our mileage slipping, and for a few days we tried to sustain high-mileage days even though the terrain demanded we slow down. It was toward the end of our overly ambitious mileage attempt when Craig and I crossed a road and noticed a truck pulled over on the shoulder. A group of hikers circled the tailgate.

As we got closer, a woman turned to us and smiled. "You thirsty?" she asked.

"Yeah," we said, limping along.

"Well, help yourself." She removed the lid on the cooler to reveal dozens of sodas and beers. The other hikers stepped aside and we reached into the cooler for our icy drinks. The group, it turned out, was a Boy Scout troop from Vermont. They were out for a week and clearly ecstatic about their good fortune. The two troop leaders sucked down beers and the five boys grinned through sticky soda lips. The woman, a New Hampshire local, introduced herself as Dizzy B. She doesn't hike, she told us, but she experiences the trail vicariously through those who do. "I know it's a tough trail," she said. "I just want to do what I can to help." In addition to roadside tailgates, Dizzy B. leaves jugs of drinking water along the trail in spots that often experience droughts, and she has been known to take hikers into her house and feed them a hot meal. Dizzy B. is what we call a trail angel.

Trail angels are people who offer us rides to town, who give us advice or tell us a weather forecast, who spend their weekends maintaining the trail, who build shelters, who clean up the shelters when day-hikers don't pack out their trash. Along our journey we met angels who gave us cookies, pop-tarts, wine, and Coleman fuel. They are the people who keep the spirit of giving flowing through the woods on a narrow corridor called the Appalachian Trail.

Craig and I were blessed by trail angels the entire trip. I remember one time in North Carolina when we emerged from the woods to cross a road, and in our good fortune the only car on the road suddenly stopped. A man shouted out the window, "Hey, do you want some fresh fruit?" The man and his wife told us they could tell we were thru-hikers and thought we'd enjoy a couple oranges. "We hiked the trail in '88," he said. "We know what hikers crave." They also understood the importance of a well-maintained trail and were volunteering their Sunday afternoon to clear a section of trail near their home. We headed north with pockets full of chewing gum and oranges.

Another encounter with trail angels occurred in Tennessee. After resupplying in a small town five miles off the trail, we were walking back to the trail when a young man in a truck pulled over next to us and asked if we wanted a ride.

"Yeah, sure do," I replied.

"I work for a furniture company," he said. "We do a lot of hiking ourselves, and it's our policy to help hikers whenever we can." Craig and I looked at each other. I searched for the connection. Furniture company? Your policy? We never asked for an explanation. We simply said thanks.

Trail angels always seemed to appear when we needed them the most. I remember an afternoon in Virginia when Craig and I were frantically trying to pitch our latest investment, the two-pound teepee. It was a warm, humid evening near McAfee Knob and the biting flies arrived in swarms. I ran in circles trying to lose them, but they swarmed as soon as I stopped. Craig was attempting to stake the teepee as close to the ground as possible, and I was shouting about what a stupid idea this teepee was and how the hell were we going to get away from the flies when the sides of the teepee were four inches off the ground. Just then, a thru-hiker named Ishmael appeared with a stocky older man with long dark hair. They invited us to spend the night in the older man's cabin. We quickly accepted. It turned out that the man goes by the trail name Habitual Hiker, and he is one of the most experienced backpackers in the world. He has thru-hiked the AT four times and has completed the Pacific Crest Trail, most of the Continental Divide Trail, the Colorado Trail, long-distance trails in Iceland and France, and many others. He was caretaking a cabin on the ridge, overlooking miles of mountains and the Roanoke Valley. We spent a bug-free night on a carpeted floor and took showers, and in the morning the Habitual Hiker and his partner, the Umbrella Lady, fed us piles of pancakes. Saved once again by trail magic.

Trail angels are perpetuating the cycle of kindness, knowing that those who receive it will return the favor to someone else down the road.

"Sometimes I wish I was still living in Connecticut," Craig said.

"I'd hang out by the trail all summer and give hikers rides to town and bring them cold beer and cokes. I bet we could do it later this summer and meet a bunch of the southbounders."

The idea of helping other people complete the trail was, at that moment, appealing because it would mean sitting on a tailgate with a cooler instead of knocking knees on some of the most rugged country in the East. I figured our time would come when we'd be in a position to reciprocate the kindness. As it was now, we were the recipients of good fortune and we needed all the help we could get.

§

Our preview of the Whites began with Mount Moosilauke, the trail's first ascent above treeline. From the hamlet of Glencliff, we climbed four and a half miles up. I felt like I was climbing a rock staircase that was missing three out of four steps. We approached treeline and the thick, stunted spruces looked like waves in a green ocean. Washed in the tide of wind that rips across the summit, they were only three or four feet tall and were all leaning in the same direction.

With each thousand feet of elevation gained, the warm sunny day became cooler and darker. Less than a mile from the summit of Moosilauke, we changed from shorts and T-shirts into rain pants, thermals, and Gore-Tex jackets. The cold gusts raced across the treeless peak, whipping my hood against my face and chilling the sweat on my back. We kept walking, trying to absorb the panorama that was unfolding around us. Crouched behind a rock on the summit, we were shielded from the wind.

"What a view," said Craig, gazing at ripples of ridges cloaked in varying intensities of blue and green.

"Where does the trail go?" I shouted over the wind. Craig pointed to the enormous mountains to our left. We could see a faint ring around the mountains where the trees could grow no higher and where the rocky, alpine tundra crowned the summits. The Franconia and Presidential Ranges of the White Mountains awaited our footsteps.

The descent off Mount Moosilauke paralleled a 3,000-foot cascade. Trail-builders had bolted wooden platforms into the slippery rock to give hikers' boots some purchase on an otherwise sheer rock face. The descent was a bit unnerving, but the creek beside us danced around mossy boulders and slid over cliffs. The spray freckled my face when I paused to admire the falls. There were times during the descent that I took off my pack and crawled on all fours, clutching roots, trees, and jutting rocks. I found myself employing this technique rather often during the remainder of the trip.

Later that day we climbed Kinsman Mountain and crossed the rolling stretch of hills leading up to the impressive and ominous Franconia Range. For days we had been staring at this ridge. Every day it was a little closer. Now, the base was at our feet.

After a long, grueling ascent, deciduous trees gave way to balsam firs. At about 4,000 feet, the firs became flagged and stunted. Biologists call this wind-swept community of high-elevation trees krummholz, a German term meaning "crooked wood." In addition to battling the wind, the trees are stunted by supercooled clouds that coat the trees in a type of ice called rime. The conditions eventually become too much for trees, and at a certain elevation they disappear altogether. We emerged onto the alpine tundra and walked the ridge for two and a half miles while howling wind slammed sheets of rain at our backs. My hands began to numb.

Without the protection of trees, it is a harsh world. The lichens, mosses, grasses, shrubs, and wildflowers that inhabit the alpine tundra remain close to the ground and often take years to mature. Growing out instead of up is just one of many strategies alpine flora have developed to survive. As Craig and I scrambled through the wind and hopped across gigantic lichen-covered rocks that formed the backbone of the ridge, I began to understand the practicality of this strategy. When I felt like I was about to get blown off the ridge, I understood why the plants don't grow too tall.

In addition to combating wind, alpine plants have to deal with extreme cold and dry conditions. Although it may seem damp up there, especially when rain is blowing sideways into your face, the alpine system is similar to a desert in terms of water availability. The soil consists of a thin layer of glacial till that doesn't retain water very well. These conditions have forced plants to develop innovative ways to trap moisture. Some plants, like alpine azalea, have waxy leaves that help keep the plant from drying out. Others, like Labrador tea, grow hairs on the underside of the leaves; the hairs help trap water and keep the plant warm. Some plants like *Diapensia* form cushion communities; that is, they grow in clusters or cushions, thereby insulating one another. The temperature inside a cushion community can be ten degrees warmer than the air temperature. The cushions are also aerodynamic, which enables the plants to withstand hurricane-force winds.

The growing season in alpine communities in New Hampshire is only about seventy days. With the additional strain of wind, lack of moisture, and cold temperatures, when plants do grow it is slow; a cushion community may take 25 years to grow to the size of a quarter. *Diapensia*, for example, grows only three new leaves each year. It may take 100 years for it to grow six inches off the ground and cover an area the size of a Frisbee. To combat the short growing season, some plants called snowbank communities have developed a way to get a jump on the growing season. Alpine azalea and crowberry are two of a number of plants that start photosynthesizing under the snow. Many alpine plants also are able to photosynthesize at much lower temperatures than low-elevation plants.

The alpine ecosystem is as delicate as it is unique; the forces of nature that led to the unusual plant adaptations also make the ecosystem highly susceptible to disturbance. That is why the Appalachian Mountain Club (AMC) and the Forest Service are actively trying to protect this ecosystem and maintain the delicate balance. Since a single boot print can destroy decades of growth, the biggest challenge is to keep visitors on the trails. When hikers leave the trail, they dislodge root systems that took years to find purchase on a sprinkle of soil. The AMC and the Forest Service have launched a major visitor-education program that includes information at Pinkham Notch below Mount Washington and nightly lectures at the alpine huts. It is the backcountry equivalent of neon flashing signs. If you learn nothing else during your visit to the Whites, you will somehow grasp that what you're walking through is fragile and that you are supposed to stay on the trail. It was a message that seemed virtually impossible to miss. To our disbelief, Craig and I saw people leave the trail anyway. We asked them to stay on the trail and they said they were sorry. I guess for some people, education goes only so far.

⚜

"Where's the trail down?" shouted a man wrapped in a plastic garbage bag. It was more than pouring; it was slinging rain and hail and drenching the dozens of day-hikers who were now stranded on top of Franconia Ridge in shorts and T-shirts. Everyone was scurrying along the mountains—Liberty, Little Haystack, Lincoln, and Lafayette— trying to find a way down. It was one of those uncomfortable moments when I wanted to sit down and cry, but instead I looked down and kept walking.

The next couple days were spent maneuvering up and down slick, rocky chutes, bobbing above treeline, and descending into the valleys. I had a tough time doing ten miles a day. Then we faced the Presidentials. Each of the seven Presidential peaks towers above tree-line. The steep connecting trails rattled our knees and burnt our quads. At 6,288 feet, Mount Washington is the highest peak in the Northeast and claims the worst weather in the world. It is easy to believe when you consider the statistics: a record wind speed of 231 mph was once measured on the summit, and Mount Washington witnesses an average of 300 cloudy days a year. You can imagine our surprise when we walked the ridge on a sunny, still day—a rare event for sure. It was a terrific climb and took us about four hours to reach the summit.

We climbed across the lichen-covered rocks toward the parking lot and visitor center and followed a stream of people through the main entrance. Craig and I had sent ourselves a mail drop at the visitor center just to see if it was really possible to get a package on top of Mount Washington. We opened our mail drop while obese tourists in dresses and high heels stared at our delight at receiving a box of animal crackers and turkey jerky. It was hard to share a mountain that we'd spent all morning climbing with people who drove up in their minivans or who rode up on the cog railway, the old train that belches black smoke across the fragile alpine environment. Of course, hikers and guidebooks had forewarned us about the gift shops and cafeteria and hundreds of vehicles, so when the man with the video camera and poodle told us he was alarmed that we would go hiking without a cell phone, we weren't surprised. At least people were getting out and appreciating the land in their own capacity.

$$\text{\it \&}$$

In addition to being a tourist attraction and having the capacity to measure high wind speeds, Mount Washington also is equipped with air-quality monitoring devices. The air-quality problem in New England is a result of the same pollutants that sweep across the Southern Appalachians, but it has a slightly different twist up north. In the South, the spruce-fir forests are weakened by acid rain and are dying because of an exotic insect. In New England it is believed that acid rain has inhibited red spruce's ability to withstand New England winters.

Andy Friedland, professor of environmental science at Dartmouth College, explained that throughout the '70s and '80s there was almost a 50 percent mortality rate of red spruces in the Green Mountains and a 30 percent mortality in the White Mountains. In 1983, a cloud and rain collector was installed at Lakes of the Clouds Hut. Since then, it has showed that rain and cloud water can be 100 to 1,000 times more acidified than natural rainwater. Scientists at the Hubbard Brook Experimental Forest demonstrated that acid rain has leached calcium and magnesium from the soils, elements the trees need for growth. Bruce Hill, air-quality specialist at the AMC, told me that acid rain has created a condition he once heard cleverly termed "invisible clearcut." "The trees are growing," he said, "but the forest is not maturing the way it would if it were healthy and unaffected by the depletion of these nutrients."

Andy Friedland cowrote a 1996 study that determined that high-elevation forests showing high mortality rates were comprised of trees that had exceptionally high levels of compounds called phytochelatins. Trees produce phytochelatins to combat heavy metals like cadmium. The study proved that the trees were fighting an onslaught of heavy metals, toxins which probably blew in from the industrial Midwest and bathed the forests in a deadly, acidic stew. Friedland told me some scientists believe that in addition to heavy metal damage, acid rain decreases calcium levels in the soils, which in turn inhibits the tree's ability to withstand freezing temperatures.

Friedland believes, however, that the spruce decline is over. He suggests that red spruces may have been only marginally tolerant to cold to begin with and the high acid deposition in the '70s and '80s made them more susceptible. It is also possible that spruces varied in their ability to survive the harsh New England winters. Trees that were less tolerant to cold died. What we have now are trees that can withstand cold, despite being weakened by air pollution or other environmental factors.

When Craig and I stood on top of Mount Washington, the views, although a little hazy, were truly spectacular. We were told it was a rare event. As a result of sulfur particles in the air, the average visibility on Mount Washington is about 35 miles, when it should be 130 miles. During the last decade, sulfur emissions have decreased nationally, but it hasn't been enough to improve visibility.

In 1987, scientists from the AMC and the White Mountain National Forest began measuring ozone levels on Mount Washington, and they found that we have exceeded the EPA's ozone standards on the summit. One of New Hampshire's problems is that ozone pollution blows in from urban areas like Boston and New York City. I found that this is a common problem throughout New England. Maine has been saying for years that it can't meet standards until the air coming in from the west and the south is cleaned up. Massachusetts reduced its ozone-producing chemicals by 65 percent in the last decade, but its air quality hasn't improved much.

In August 1997 eight northeastern states formally petitioned the EPA to set tougher standards for midwestern utility plants, the main culprits in New England's pollution problem. In October of 1997, based on comprehensive studies from the Ozone Transport Assessment Group, the EPA tightened standards in twenty-two states. But in 1999, the American Trucking Association; the oil and gas industry; and the states of West Virginia, Ohio, and Michigan took the case to court to try to get the eight-hour air-quality standard for ozone lifted. In May 1999, the three-judge panel of the U.S. Court of Appeals overturned the EPA's ozone smog standard, ruling that EPA did not establish clear criteria for setting standards. The court said, "Although factors EPA uses in determining the degree of public health concern associated with different levels of ozone and particulate matter are reasonable, EPA articulated no intelligible principle to channel its application of these factors." The nondelegation doctrine, the court said, requires such a principle. The court's decision was based on an arcane doctrine of separation of powers from the 1930s. According to the court, by delegating the setting of standards to the EPA, Congress is giving too much power to the executive branch.

I was shocked when I learned about the judges' decision to jeopardize human health, especially the health of children and the elderly, who are more susceptible to problems caused by poor air quality, to appease the industry. Environmental groups were equally appalled. "The trucking industry was really searching for a long shot when they resurrected that old doctrine," said Mary Peterson, an activist from Maine. Of course, dozens of standards have been created and implemented by the EPA just as the ozone standard was, and none of them has been challenged by the old doctrine. "It's all political," she said, "and two of the three judges who heard the case are very conservative."

The EPA petitioned for a rehearing. In October 1999 their request was denied. However, a minority of the 11 judges of the D.C. Circuit Court strongly opposed the decision to deny the EPA a rehearing. Three judges concluded that, "Not only did the panel depart from a half century of Supreme Court separation-of-powers jurisprudence, but in doing so, it stripped the EPA of much of its ability to implement the

Clean Air Act, this nation's primary means of protecting the safety of the air breathed by hundreds of millions of people." Many environmental and outdoors organizations, like the AMC, continue to petition the courts to uphold the EPA's standards. Progress often seems slow, but, like walking the Appalachian Trail, every step, no matter how small, brings you a little closer.

§

We left the tourist mecca of roads, parking lots, and cog railway that cloud and clutter Mount Washington's summit, and scrambled through the boulders to the Madison Hut. The Appalachian Mountain Club maintains a system of eight huts, enclosed units with kitchen facilities and large bunk rooms, all about a day's walk apart. The largest hut can accommodate up to ninety visitors, and during the summer all the huts are almost always full.

For $30–$62 visitors get dinner, breakfast, and a bunk. Thru-hikers, however, are allowed to work at the huts in exchange for meals and a place to sleep. Craig and I arrived early to secure a spot and played board games with some of the other guests. That evening we helped the staff wash dishes and bus tables, and although we felt a little out of place sitting next to the paying guests who needn't carry more than their wallets and a change of clothes on their wilderness experience, it was a unique experience and an easy way to get a good meal and a warm bed. That night, all forty-eight bunks in the Madison Hut were filled.

In 1996, the AMC's permit to operate the huts had expired; when Craig and I were in the White Mountains, the AMC was operating the hut system under a temporary permit until the Forest Service could determine if it was appropriate to extend their permit for another thirty years. In the following years, the repermitting debate became quite heated. The Appalachian Mountain Club, America's oldest hiking and conservation club, boasts a membership of more than 83,000. It has operated huts since 1888, before the White Mountains were incorporated into the national forest system. Now, six of the eight huts are located on federal land, one is on state land, and one is on private property.

Critics of the hut system feel that the AMC has a monopoly on the forest, that $62 per night is too expensive, that the huts and their users degrade the wilderness, that it is unethical for the AMC to operate the huts rent-free on public land, and that the AMC is using public land to influence people about environmental issues that are sometimes contrary to the interests of the timber industry in the region. During the repermitting process, millworkers from surrounding communities joined forces with other residents and environmental groups to pressure the Forest Service into denying the permit or reissuing it with certain restrictive provisions. For the paper industry, it was payback time for the pressure the AMC put on them in the past to clean up their act. Environmental groups were also skeptical, saying that if it were anyone else trying to operate a hut system, a hotel chain for example, the AMC and the environmental community would be up in arms. Some people cited the numbers: 54,000 people stay in the huts each summer and fall and 7 million people visit White Mountain National Forest each year—that's more than Yellowstone and Yosemite combined. That many people certainly have the potential to strain one of our most fragile ecosystems.

In 1996, after thousands of letters were written and after 400 people attended three public hearings, the Forest Service ordered an Environmental Impact Statement (EIS) to assess the effects of various alternatives ranging from continuing the hut system to demolishing the huts. After more than two years and $200,000, a 350-page draft EIS was completed. Back in 1965, when the AMC last applied for the same thirty-year permit, the five-page document it submitted to the Forest Service was approved in three hours.

But now the debate was more complicated. The AMC pledged to be good stewards to the land and cited its 100+ years of service to the land and its people. Volunteers from the AMC contribute more than 30,000 hours a year to trail maintenance, the AMC contributes $40,000 a year to search-and-rescue operations, and visitors to the AMC's facilities spend almost $5 million every year when they visit the White Mountain region. In 1999, White Mountain National Forest agreed that the AMC had been a front-runner in research and conservation in the region. Forest managers recognized the hut system as filling a critical niche, and they issued the AMC another thirty-year special-use permit.

Along with the permit came a few provisions to ensure minimal impact to the environment. The AMC is required to monitor water quality and impacts to vegetation around the huts, eliminate mid-summer helicopter supply flights to protect nesting birds, and develop a soil-erosion-prevention plan. Although the Forest Service doesn't have the authority to dictate what material is presented in the AMC's outreach programs, the AMC agreed to work with agency people to develop the programs. The Forest Service decided that the huts allow people who otherwise wouldn't be there to enjoy the land and that the AMC is working to foster an appreciation of the land and instill in the public an environmental ethic. I suppose the Forest Service feels that sometimes people need to experience the land in their own way in order to appreciate it, and the hut system allows them to do just that.

§

"Weather doesn't look so good," Craig said the next morning. Thick clouds hung above and below us when we left the Madison Hut and worked our way through jagged, lichen-covered rocks. My foot got wedged between rocks a few times and I had to stop and work it out. For about seven miles the trail wound its way through this mountain environment. At first there were no trees to shield the wind and rain. Clouds rose, washing white wind around our feet, bleeding into every crevice. They swirled around our bodies and then we were in the middle of the clouds, in the middle of a storm. It took five hours to walk the seven miles to Pinkham Notch. I wanted so badly to take in the beauty, to sit and listen, to notice the details. But it seemed we were always running from rain and wind and cold.

Every day there were moments when I felt it was a wonderful way to live: that first sip of hot tea in the morning, the first stretch of the legs, the way Craig and I would sometimes walk funny or talk funny to break a smile in each other, an overlook on a clear day, stopping for lunch on a warm rock, watching Craig's calves propel his body up a mountain, and watching muscles bulge in my own legs. But then there were moments when I was barely hanging on. Things got more painful than I ever expected. We tried to make each other laugh as much as possible, but we often walked for hours in silence, me far behind with tears in my eyes. When I saw Craig waiting for me, I'd wipe away the tears and hope that my eyes didn't look too bloodshot.

When we got to Gorham, New Hampshire, it was time for a break. Bruno and Mary Ann Janicki run the Hiker's Paradise hostel and motel. Craig and I booked ourselves a room in the hostel and shared a kitchen and bathroom with a number of other thru-hikers. Everyone seemed happy to be there. Craig went outside to get a feel for the place and came back nearly skipping with delight. "They have breakfast here!" he said. Breakfast was one thing that was guaranteed to raise his spirits. Bruno had a full breakfast menu, and the next morning we stayed until we couldn't eat another pancake. "You want real or plastic syrup?" Bruno asked in his enchanting accent. I got a scornful look when I requested the plastic syrup and I knew I had violated some sacred New Hampshire rule. (I grew up with Aunt Jemima and, hard as I try, I just don't have the taste for real maple syrup. I've learned to apologize profusely in the presence of New Englanders.) Craig requested the real stuff and Bruno beamed. He whirled around the room, bringing more coffee, more bacon and sausage, more potatoes and toast, making sure every person was satisfied and smiling. He treated every one of his ragged guests like a king or a queen.

A number of Southbounders were at Bruno's hostel and they were fresh and giddy. With 300 miles under their belts, they were certain they would go the whole way. Many of them treated us like celebrities; after all, we had been living the dream they had just begun to experience. They reminded us of ourselves just five months ago. "They still think they won't get sick of oatmeal and they think they'll walk every blaze," said Craig.

Their packs seemed awfully heavy, and they quizzed us about our gear and made notes about what they could send home. Craig and I noticed right away that they were still trying to be polite to their partners. There is a certain initial formality between partners that gets lost somewhere along the way. There comes a time when divvying up your loads, assigning camp chores, and studying the guidebook together gets left behind. At first you feel obligated to make conversation. You spend a few weeks covering the deep and personal topics of dreams and life ambitions, relationships and personal traumas. Eventually you can read your partner's mind and you understand that most of the time there is no need to speak.

By this time Craig and I were inseparable. We were comfortable with our routine and no matter where we landed at night, we were at home with each other.

"Talking with them made me feel like we've come a long way," he said.

"Yeah," I said, "we have. You know, I finally feel like we've made some progress. I finally feel like we may see the end."

Our spirits rose when we crossed the border into the fourteenth state of the trail. For five months we had been telling people that we were walking to Maine. Now we were finally there. Craig and I did the dance of joy at the sign that welcomed us to the last state. We took off our packs and jumped around in circles, thrilled at just being in the woods and knowing that Georgia was a long, long way away. Then we took a deep breath, smiled at each other, strapped our packs on our backs and put one foot in front of the other. That was the only way to make it to Katahdin, and we knew that the end of the trail was still a long way from Maine's southern border.

## CHAPTER NINE

# THE JEWEL OF MAINE

It had been a long time since Craig had asked me on the six-month date. The invitation, as I remember it, didn't come with a promise of perfect weather, but I had a good feeling about it. Even though I didn't know what to expect, I remember trusting him and trusting that a journey into the unknown would be a good experience. I knew that hiking the AT may not be the most logical thing to do, but I said yes with all my heart.

Many times during the date I wondered why we were still following each other up and down all those mountains. Couldn't we go out to dinner? Go to the movies? Sign up for country line-dance lessons? Isn't that what normal couples do? Instead, we led each other into blizzards, over swamps, through fields of rocks, through swarms of mosquitoes, up sheer rock walls. We had been walking for five months, and the longest time we had been apart was three and a half hours. Craig made a trip to town one day while I continued to the shelter. "It was so strange to be walking without you," he had said. "You're part of me now." It was true. Somehow our lives had literally wrapped around each other, growing deeper into the other's matrix of personality and thought.

"You know," I said jokingly, "I've been on dates that were a lot more fun."

Our initial adventure in Maine was the infamous Mahoosuc Notch, a one-mile section of house-sized boulders and crevices lined with glacial ice. Craig was agile, leaping over gaps and squirming through cracks, but it was a slow half-mile-per-hour crawl for me. The trail continued to climb straight up rock faces. We wriggled, slid, squeezed, and pulled. We heaved ourselves up and held on for dear life. It was frustrating when a couple miles took hours and we were rewarded only with throbbing knees and strained ankles.

Each step was excruciating. Craig suffered silently; his right ankle, which hadn't properly healed after a childhood break, was gradually giving out. My kneecaps felt like they were connected to my legs by a single skinny sinew. I took Advil by the handful. One morning I told Craig, "Except for the fact that I can barely stand, I'm in the best shape of my life." But we had come so far.

Sure, we had our share of challenging conditions, and the painful times often stand out most vividly in moments of recollection. But there was a sense of excitement and adventure in the challenge, and we knew we were of the breed that lived for that sort of experience. At the end of each day, we knew we had spent the last twenty-four hours the best way we knew how, and we knew we had reason to be proud of ourselves. There were many times when I would not have wanted to be anywhere else. The first week in Maine was a good example.

Tiny one-street towns were separated by many miles of wilderness. Patches of clearcuts scarred some slopes, but there were no houses, roads, or power lines as far as we could see. We enjoyed long stretches above treeline and views of more green than I had ever seen. The smooth fingers of Mooselookmeguntic Lake swelled into the valleys. The shimmering blue was a stunning contrast to the sea of deep-green forest rolling in waves from the horizon. Near Rangeley we saw our first moose. It stood knee-deep in ferns and munched the plants at its hooves. Its long, bulbous snout and dark, liquid eyes followed us as we slowly walked by.

Although there were few signs of civilization, the Maine woods were certainly popular with summer recreationists. At the Bemis Mountain shelter, Craig wrote, "Holy crowded campsite Batman! Six Southbounders, fifteen young French-Canadian ladies, and ten Boy Scouts. No more nude backpacking!" To be quite honest, we weren't bothered by the numbers. The landscape, it seemed, could accommodate us all. Craig and I went about our business as if we were living in our own little thru-hiking bubble. We laughed at our inside jokes, laughed at the unique private language we had developed on the trail, and continued our bizarre rituals like talking for our sleeping mattresses and spoons, to which we had also assigned trail names. One of our more serious rituals, though, was swapping journals before bed. Somewhere in Virginia we got in the habit of writing little notes to each other at the end of our entries. We'd write things like, "I love you," or, "Good night," or, "Craig has the nicest smile I've ever seen; sometimes it's all that keeps me going." It is the sort of cheesiness that most couples don't admit to in public, the sort of thing they reserve for the privacy of their own homes. The notes were usually sweet and light, until one night I read, "I want to spend the rest of my life with Raindrop." I blushed when I read it and debated the seriousness of what he'd written. Neither of us said anything, but it started me thinking. I anguished over the status of our relationship. At twenty-two I hadn't considered marriage to be something in my near future. All of a sudden it felt like a major life decision was looming on the next mountaintop. I was certain that if Craig asked me to marry him it would be on Katahdin, so I figured I had some time to think about it.

A couple weeks remained in our date, but two days after that journal entry, Craig and I were no longer dating.

That morning we climbed across the alpine sweep of the northern end of Saddleback Mountain. For the first time, Katahdin, the northern terminus of the Appalachian Trail, was in sight. It loomed in the distance, 200 miles away, as a blurred, blue volcano. We sat on a rock and stared at our final destination and at unbroken wilderness in every direction. A gentle breeze blew across the summit and shook the pink and white flowers at my feet. When Craig turned to me and knelt, my heart froze. It must have been less than a second before he looked into my eyes, but I knew what was coming. At that moment my mind shut off and all the confusion I had been feeling was gone.

The invitation didn't come with a promise of perfect weather, but I was beginning to trust the tug at my heart that wanted to commit to journeys into the unknown. Like the invitation to hike the AT, I had a good feeling about it and I said yes with all my heart.

§

What a strange day: To commit the rest of your life to someone and to have your life remain exactly the same. We kissed up there and did a couple hoorahs but then we kept walking, with enormous smiles, of course, but it was the same as every day for the last 150 days. We looked at each other every now and then to make sure we understood what had just happened. After a while, Craig turned to me. "You haven't changed your mind yet, have you?" I assured him I hadn't. As we moved away from Saddleback Mountain, we kept looking back at the sweeping alpine saddle, trying to memorize the wildflowers and the tiny ponds and trying to brand the vista in our minds. We both knew it was a place we wouldn't return to for a long time, and with a pending ski area expansion there's no guarantee that our beautiful mountain will escape development forever.

§

In 1938 the Appalachian Trail Conference, National Park Service, U.S. Forest Service, and state agencies created a pact known as the Appalachian Trailway Agreement. Under the agreement, a two-mile wide corridor on either side of the trail was to be protected from development. The corridor was reduced to a half-mile where it crossed state-owned lands. Supporters of the trail were thrilled by the agreement, but after a number of years they realized that development on private lands was pressing in with nothing to stop it. The region around the original southern terminus, Mount Oglethorpe, became too developed to support the trail, so the terminus was relocated to Springer Mountain. Congress was planning highways in Georgia, Virginia, and New Jersey that would displace the trail. Ski resorts, housing developments, and logging and mining activity threatened to relegate the Appalachian Trail to roads. Myron Avery, trail pioneer and former chairman of the ATC, wrote about the need for federal protection: "The problem lies in the connecting units of privately owned land, much of which will soon become subject to intense development. Protest against federal or state domination is, of course, a popular theme these days. However, the unexpected penetration and development of areas in private ownership will serve to fortify our conclusion that some form of public protection must be extended to the Trail system if it is to survive . . ."

Finally in 1968, after a number of failed attempts, Congress passed the National Trails System Act. The act established the Appalachian Trail and the Pacific Crest Trail (PCT) as National Scenic Trails, giving them federal protection and funding, and it set the stage for a number of other National Scenic Trails and National Historic Trails. The law declared that National Trails "will be extended trails so located as to provide for maximum outdoor recreation potential and for the conservation and enjoyment of the nationally significant scenic, historic, natural, or cultural qualities of the areas through which such trails may pass."

The Park Service was charged with managing the AT and the Forest Service was responsible for the PCT. The law gave states and local authorities two years to acquire land for the trail. After that, the Park Service was allotted $5 million to acquire land through cooperative agreements, acquisition of fee title, easements, exchanges, and as a last resort by condemnation under the principle of eminent domain.

I believe the most critical part of the trails act was that it allowed the Park Service to enter into agreements with private groups like the ATC to operate, develop, and maintain the trail. Since there was an enormous amount of public interest in creating, protecting, and hiking the AT, it made sense to let the public take on many of the management responsibilities. Some managers suggest that the Park Service welcomed the help because they didn't know what to do with the new linear park. To most managers, the AT must have been a jurisdictional nightmare: it passes through fourteen states, six other units of the national-park system, and eight units of Forest Service land, and it involves sixty state parks and forests, altogether crossing about 250 local, state, and federal jurisdictions. The best part about the public/private partnership was that it allowed local people to work within their own communities. All along the Appalachian Range, trail clubs and conservation groups emphasized the importance of the trail and got local residents to sell or donate their land for the protection of the trail corridor. People, it seemed, were more willing to work with their neighbors than with an unknown government official from Washington, D.C.

Private and local groups protected a considerable amount of the trail corridor, but they couldn't win the tough cases without the strong arm of the Park Service. When commercial development pressed in, the trail was forced back onto roads, and local trail clubs didn't have the authority to stop it. Frustrated by the lack of effort shown by the Park Service, local groups spread the word that the Park Service hadn't made any real progress in acquiring land for the trail. Less than 60 percent of the trail was on public property, and the public became increasingly dissatisfied. In the mid-1970s, the ATC testified before Congress that the agencies were not protecting and managing the AT in accordance with the law. The result of public insistence was the 1978 amendment to the National Trails System Act, which authorized $90 million to purchase land or easements. Although appropriation of funds didn't match the anticipated timeline of Congress, it was a step in the right direction and funding was provided over a number of years. Congress directed federal agencies to step up their trail-protection programs, and Congress expanded the agencies' authority to condemn land to obtain a trail corridor averaging 1,000 feet instead of 200 feet. The Park Service began title searches for 1,750 privately owned tracts of land, and throughout the following years land was bought and easements, lease-backs, and reserved interests were used to secure the corridor. The ATC established the Trust for Appalachian Trail Lands, and when the Park Service wasn't able to work on a critical segment, the ATC would buy the land itself.

Then the state of our nation's trails took a turn for the worse. Reagan's secretary of the interior, James Watt, disbanded the Heritage Conservation and Recreation Service, thereby removing the trail's only sponsor in the government. As has been the case for so many environmental crises, when the government slips, the public picks up the slack. The 1974, 1984, and 1994 Management Delegation Agreements encouraged the public to do so by institutionalizing the long-standing tradition of volunteer stewardship of the AT. The agreements imple-ment the original act's authorization for public/private partnerships, and they are renewed every ten years. The agreements give the ATC respon-sibility for managing the trail and the trail corridor on public land. This is an unusual arrangement, for the Park Service is rarely willing to share its authority with the private sector. The ATC develops and publicizes standards and policies for trail design, protection, maintenance, and use, and it delegates responsibilities to the trail clubs. The clubs, large and small, have taken the reins. Clubs like the AMC and the PATC have lobbied Congress extensively, educated millions of people about the trail and the challenges it faces, and contributed hundreds of thousands of hours to trail maintenance and management. The delegation agree-ments essentially put people in charge of the trail who know most about it and who, by living near it, have a vested interest in it.

Despite the lack of support from the Reagan administration, the Park Service stepped up their efforts to acquire land in instances where local efforts were met with opposition. Shared responsibility for the AT allowed the Park Service to focus their energies where they would be most useful and allowed local groups to do a tremendous amount of work. For example, in Maine, 167 miles of trail crossed property that was owned by the major pulp and paper companies. In the 1970s the Maine Appalachian Trail Club (MATC) told the Park Service it had things under control and suggested the Park Service focus its acquisi-tion efforts elsewhere. Throughout the '70s and '80s, the MATC led a campaign to acquire a corridor for most of those 167 miles. Many of the trail miles were located on logging roads in the valleys, so the MATC worked with the paper industry to relocate the trail to the ridges. The arrangement pleased everyone: hikers got better views and more-natural trail conditions and the industry didn't have to worry about gauging their activities in the valleys to accommodate a trail. Today, the MATC, like all the other clubs, continues to assist the Park Service with many of its management responsibilities. The MATC builds and maintains trail, publishes the *Guide to the Appalachian Trail in Maine*, works to ensure that the AT corridor remains wild and pro-tected, and cares for shelters, privies, signs, and campsites.

By 1988, the Park Service and AT supporters had acquired most of the AT corridor; out of more than 2,100 miles, only 149 miles of trail remained on private property. As of June 1999, only 26.4 miles of trail still remained under private control. The longest stretch of trail that passes through private property is the 3.5-mile stretch across Saddleback Mountain in Maine. This time, local efforts aren't enough. The protection of the trail depends on the outcome of a battle against the powerful Saddleback Ski Area, a battle local groups aren't equipped to fight on their own.

§

The controversy surrounding the AT across Saddleback Mountain has been ongoing since 1977, when the MATC met with Georgia-Pacific to negotiate the protection of a trail corridor. No agreement was reached. In 1984, Donald Breen, the current owner of Saddleback Ski Area, purchased 11,000 acres, which includes Saddleback Mountain. Shortly thereafter, the Park Service resumed negotiations with Saddleback Ski Area to protect the trail. In 1987, the Park Service drafted three alternatives for the protection of the Appalachian Trail corridor. More than 1,100 people responded to the Environmental Assessment and most were in favor of the alternative that the Park Service preferred, an alternative that would protect close to 3,000 acres of the mountain. The same year, Breen submitted a proposal to the Maine Land Use Regulation Commission (MLURC) to significantly expand the ski area.

The MLURC approved the proposed development with a number of stipulations, one of which charged the ski area with finding alternative locations for the upper terminals of two proposed high-elevation ski lifts in order to minimize impacts on Saddleback's fragile alpine and subalpine vegetation and to reduce visual impacts to the Appalachian Trail.

Negotiations continued between the ski area and the Park Service. In 1991 the ski area agreed to sell most of the 2,860 acres outlined in the preferred alternative from the Environmental Assessment. An independent appraisal of the land was made and the Park Service sent an offer to Donald Breen. Breen insisted the land was worth more and rejected the offer.

In 1997 the Park Service offered to buy an 893-acre parcel to protect the delicate alpine and subalpine zones, Eddy Pond (a pristine nine-acre pond at the base of the southwestern ridge), and the high-elevation undeveloped saddle area (the sway in the spine of the mountain between the summit of Saddleback and the Horn, which represents the visual foreground of the AT). Included in this offer was an assurance from the Appalachian Trail community that they would not oppose the ski area expansion. Again, Breen rejected the offer.

In 1999 Donald Breen offered, in what can only be construed as a rather hollow gesture, to donate 660 acres to the Park Service. Under the agreement, however, was the stipulation that the ski area maintain the rights to develop the area it "donated." These included "the rights to construct, repair, maintain, and use new ski lifts, structures, buildings, skiing trails, wind barriers, snow fencing, signs, snowmaking pipes, electrical, water, telephone, and other utility lines, and other recreational facilities; the rights to excavate, grade, work, and build terrain for ski trails, pipes, lifts, buildings, and other ski-related facilities; the rights to cut and control trees and other vegetation; the rights to cross the Appalachian Trail with two ski trails; and the water rights to Eddy Pond for storage and snowmaking purposes, including the rights to dam and control water depth and withdraw water from Eddy Pond and construct and utilize facilities for doing so." Breen couldn't understand why the Park Service rejected his offer.

In 1998 the Park Service issued a scoping notice for an Environmental Assessment to protect the Appalachian National Scenic Trail across Saddleback Mountain. Hundreds of people wrote letters expressing their concerns about how development would affect plant and animal communities on the mountain. The glacially polished bedrock that sweeps across its 4,116-foot-high summit makes Saddleback one of the most spectacular spots on the entire AT. I would argue that, next to Katahdin, it is the most beautiful mountain in the range. Nineteen arctic-alpine species grow on Saddleback, making it the third most diverse arctic-alpine community in Maine. Because of its rare alpine vegetation and krummholz community, it is registered as a Maine Critical Area. Saddleback Mountain also supports a gray-brown migratory songbird called Bicknell's thrush. This bird spends winters on islands in the Caribbean and returns north to breed in high-elevation spruce-fir forests. Bicknell's thrush was ranked as a Category 2 candidate under the Endangered Species Act and is now listed as the top priority among neotropical migratory birds in the northeastern United States.

Some people felt a ski area expansion just wasn't necessary. "There are hundreds of ski areas," wrote one person, "but there's only one Appalachian Trail." Some people wondered if an expansion was even a logical business move in a time when ski areas all over the country are in financial jeopardy. The number of ski areas across the country has decreased from 800 in 1979 to 520 in 1996. Although a number of resorts in Maine have been quite successful, there was some doubt that skiers would travel to a remote resort like Saddleback when other resorts were more easily accessible. The town of Rangeley is quite small, and many people feared that the town could not support a large number of visitors should the ski area expand and draw the number of visitors it hoped to.

Some people, however, favored the expansion. They believed it would boost the economies of surrounding rural towns. Others felt that in order to be competitive with other ski areas, Saddleback Ski Area had to expand and upgrade its facilities. Some people simply wanted to pick a fight with federal agencies.

After considering public input, the Park Service came up with four alternatives. The first alternative would protect 2,860 acres of critical habitat, protect most of the viewshed of the AT, and allow the ski area to add three lifts and nine ski trails. The second alternative would protect 893 acres and the visual foreground of the trail, but would allow the ski area to add nine lifts and thirty-two trails, many of which would be visible from the AT. Under alternative #3 the ski area could expand to eleven times its current size, expand on both sides of the mountain, operate nineteen lifts and ninety-four trails, and provide facilities for 14,500 skiers at a time, as opposed to the 1,300 skiers it could accommodate in 1999. Currently about 33,250 skiers visit Saddleback each year. This alternative would make it possible for 230,000 people to visit the ski area. I can't help but wonder where the ski area gets the impression that 200,000 more people are suddenly going to want to come to Saddleback. Alternative #3 is proposed by the ski area in its bogus 660-acre "donation" offer. Developed by Sno Engineering, Incorporated. Alternative #4 is an optimal ski area development plan, allowing six times the current visitation, and although it would protect 784 acres, it would have a serious impact on the AT and the fragile subalpine environment. According to the Environmental Assessment, under the fourth alternative "the Appalachian Trail experience north of the summit would no longer be perceived as remote or natural."

Pamela Underhill is the National Park Service manager for the Appalachian Trail. After graduating from the University of California at Berkeley, Pam returned to the East and went to work for the Park Service. She got her foot in the door in 1977 by working as a secretary. After the 1978 amendment to the National Trails System Act increased funding for the trail, new positions opened and Pam began climbing the ranks. During the past twenty years, she has moved through various positions at the Park Service's Appalachian Trail headquarters in Harpers Ferry, West Virginia—realty specialist, trail project assistant, environmental protection specialist—to her current position as manager. When I spoke with Pam she was absolutely delightful, energetic and wholly dedicated to the trail. If you ask Pam about Saddleback, she'll tell you that she eats, sleeps, and breathes it.

As manager, Pam set out to solicit public input on the four alternatives. In August 1999, public hearings in Rangeley, Bangor, and Portland drew more than 400 people. The Park Service was eager to share information and facilitate communication between the interested parties, but the hearing in Rangeley turned into, as she put it, "one of the more humiliating and frustrating experiences I've ever had to endure."

Chuck Cushman is the director of the American Land Rights Association (ALRA), a private property rights/multiple-use advocacy group. His website proudly states that he has been nicknamed

Mr. Rent-A-Riot "as a result of his aggressive and successful efforts to protect landowners and permittees from overreaching Federal, State, and other land-use controllers." Traveling from their headquarters in Battle Ground, Washington, Cushman and his cohorts descended upon Rangeley and took over the hearing. The Park Service designed the hearing as an open house, but Cushman wanted a platform. According to Pam, when a critical mass had assembled, Cushman stood on a chair, told everyone to gather 'round, and launched into a tirade against the Park Service. Not only does the Park Service lie and cheat, he says, but it is trying to divide and conquer the people. Having said his piece, Cushman turned the chair over to another gentleman who wanted to speak. After a few moments, the speaker became convinced that Pam wasn't listening to him. He moved towards her and shoved his notes in her face. "Then he started body-shoving me," she said. "That's about as close as I came to losing it. I can pretty much deal with verbal assault but I like to think there's a little invisible circle around me that you have to be invited into." A hint of bewilderment lingers in her laugh as she relays the story to me. I tell her I'm impressed by her ability to maintain a sense of humor. "If I didn't, I'd be a bundle of tears in the corner," she replied. Then she added, "That won't do."

By now, Pam is used to the attacks. She has stood her ground under pressure from her share of politically prominent people. Senator Olympia Snowe has tried continually to dissuade the Park Service from using eminent domain to acquire land on Saddleback. Earlier, state senator John Benoit told the press that Pam personally had lobbied the legislature in Augusta against Saddleback Ski Area. "I was dumbfounded when I read that," she said, "Not only would that have been illegal, but I just never would even *think* of doing such a thing."

Kitty Breen, daughter of Donald Breen, has taken over as the principle spokesperson for Saddleback Ski Area. She is convinced that Alternatives #1 and #2 are illegal and, as Pam says, "you can't tell her otherwise." Kitty has been dedicated to getting a fresh slate of players from the Park Service; she has no qualms about telling everyone that Pam has lied and misrepresented information. These tactics have not been successful. Pam is still there, and she still responds to the attacks in a professional, nonconfrontational way. The Park Service would like to resume negotiations with the Breens, but the Breens are demanding $16.1 million for the land, a price that independent appraisers feel is at least $10 million too high.

The hearings in Bangor and Portland went more smoothly. Chuck Cushman didn't make such a fuss, although he did have a number of people dress up in black-and-white-striped prison outfits, dragging a plastic ball and chain. The message behind the costume was to free the prisoners from the Park Service.

In addition to the comments recorded at the hearings, the Park Service received more than 4,000 written comments, and Pam is dedicated to reading every one. Despite the vociferous opposition by Saddleback Ski Area and the ALRA to federal protection, it appears that the majority of respondents support Alternative #1, the plan that would give the trail and the mountain the most protection. "There are a huge number of people out there who care about the AT and who want to see it protected," says Pam. "A clear picture is forming of what is fair and what is the right thing to do. It becomes a matter now of figuring out how to make it happen."

After an alternative is selected, the Park Service will resume efforts to acquire the acreage outlined in the selected alternative. Although the Breens appear to be in denial that acquiring land by eminent domain is a legal alternative, if no settlement can be reached, it may come down to that. All parties involved—Saddleback Ski Area, the Park Service, rural communities in Maine, and everyone interested in the Appalachian Trail—would like to see more than two decades of controversy laid to rest, but as of this writing no one can predict how or when the issue will be settled.

§

We left Saddleback, walked all day, and didn't see a soul. I wanted to tell everyone—my parents, my brother, my friends—but we were miles from the nearest phone.

The next night we climbed Maine's second highest peak, Sugarloaf Mountain, while Hurricane Bertha whipped around Maine's coast, creating rainstorms and high winds inland. We made it to the top and took refuge on the worn, wooden floor of the old, abandoned summit house. The house was damp and drafty, and although we felt a little silly pitching the tent inside, we were glad we did. The roof leaked all night. By midnight the floor was under an inch of water and we struggled to find a dry spot to relocate the tent. One southbounder shared the summit house with us. Together we built a fire in the wood-burning stove and shared stories and chocolate. We knew him for only a couple hours, but he was the first person we told of our engagement.

That night I asked Craig why he decided to ask me on Saddleback. "Actually," he said, "I've wanted to ask you for a while. I knew a month ago that I wanted to be with you forever. But it was never the right moment. There were always other people around or it wasn't the perfect mountain." Craig's journal entry indicated that it was a combination of his brother, Marc, and the magic of the mountain that inspired him: "Raindrop and I got to the first hump of the saddle which was above treeline, not too rocky and there was even an alpine pond! We decided to wear headphones and when I put mine on, 'Fire and Rain' by James Taylor was playing. That's the song that reminds me of Marc. After thinking about Marc and knowing his approval, and seeing the beauty of Saddleback Mountain, I decided it was right. I sat at the northern end of the saddle and waited for my AT hiking partner. We sat for a few minutes until the mountains gave me courage, then I slid down on one knee and asked her to marry me."

Craig proved there is value in natural places that cannot be measured in economic terms. For Craig, the beauty of an undeveloped mountain provided inspiration that couldn't be found in town or on a mountain scarred with roads, power lines, or ski lifts. To degrade the natural beauty of Saddleback would devalue nature in a way that would destroy the potential for moments that are set into motion by natural inspiration, moments that change people's lives.

After two full days we were anxious to share the good news with our families and friends, so we bushwacked down the ski slopes to the town of Stratton. From a pay phone on the side of the road we made the calls. My family was a little stunned by the news, because since I was sixteen I had sworn I would never get married. Craig's family was less surprised and everyone was happy. Telling our families seemed to make it official. That night we found the nicest restaurant in town and celebrated with steaks and wine. In many ways we wished the trail would have ended there, and in many ways it did. Mentally we were over it; we just needed physically to get our bodies to Katahdin, which, without the mental capacity to guide our bodies, would demand from us everything we had left.

§

It was a dark, rainy morning in mid-July. If I had been at home, I would have curled up on the sofa with a book and a cup of tea and turned the phone ringer off. It had been that book-and-tea type of morning for weeks. The rain was incessant.

It had rained six out of seven days for nearly two months. Locals said it was the most rain they had seen since the turn of the century. I learned later that Maine and New Hampshire saw the wettest summer since people began keeping records. The ground was saturated. The lightest drizzle could create a flood. The rivers more than jumped their banks—they devoured them. With wet lips, white-capped teeth, and a frothy smirk, the rivers seized the shores and slurped them down. The currents raked the land, taking with them anything that was loose, broken, or buoyant.

There are no bridges on the AT in Maine, and the trail crosses these surging waterways frequently. When we talked with southbounders about the upcoming fords, the responses were less than encouraging.

"I saw one guy use 100 feet of rope to haul gear and his partner across this gushing stream," said one hiker.

"I carried my pack on my head," said another man. "I bobbed up and down in neck-deep water and slowly made my way to the opposite bank."

"Isn't that dangerous?" I asked.

"Yeah," he said, "if I was a couple inches shorter, I probably would-n't have made it."

Our first major ford was the infamous crossing of the Kennebec River. Unannounced releases from the power-company dam upstream cause water levels to rise faster than you can cross. We found the river 100 yards wide, sixteen feet deep, and streaked with powerful currents. A man had drowned in the river two days earlier. Fortunately, the Maine Appalachian Trail Club provides a canoe to ease this treacherous ford. We hugged the shore and paddled like hell through the eddies until we were about 100 yards upstream. Then we turned into the river and paddled across the currents to the opposite shore.

The next few crossings involved jumping across rocks, a tightrope walk across a cable above Baker Brook, and a couple fords through waist-deep water.

At one point, the trail dead-ended into a beaver pond, and the only way across was to balance on slick floating logs.

"Ummm," I said, surveying the route, "no way in hell."

Fortunately Craig agreed that a swim with the beaver family was not the best option. "We'd have to wade out about ten feet just to get to the logs," he said. "We'll have to bushwhack around it."

"The vegetation is so dense I don't know how we're going to get anywhere," I said.

Craig turned into the forest, swatting furiously at mosquitoes that had formed a cloud around his head, and began a long, painful bushwhack. We pried the spruce trees apart and squeezed through, getting scraped by their sharp needles and branches. The ground was covered with rotting logs and sinkholes.

"Which way is the trail?" I shouted. "I can't see anything."

"I have no idea," he said, "I'm just trying to get through this." It took about forty-five minutes to bushwhack around the beaver pond, but we finally reconnected with the trail.

Before the bushwhack I had doused myself in DEET. After experimenting with nearly every mosquito repellent on the market and even mixing repellent in odd combinations, we had worked our way up in potency from citronella to 100 percent DEET. By the time we stopped for lunch that afternoon I was flushed and dizzy. After resting for an hour or so I began to feel a little better. Before we resumed walking, I again sprayed myself with DEET and almost instantly became hot and sick. After that, we left the DEET in my pack and decided OFF! would have to suffice.

Some river crossings were too treacherous to attempt with all the flooding. Rangers waited near Monson to direct hikers around dangerous fords, and I eagerly followed logging roads to bypass flooded sections of trail. In a freezing downpour somewhere near the Piscataquis River, we splashed along muddy logging roads, neither of us having any real idea where we were going, and decided at that point to leave it up to fate to point us in the right direction. After an hour or two we came upon a man in a pickup who offered us a ride to Monson. We eagerly accepted and tried to explain that we were walking the Appalachian Trail but because it was so flooded there often wasn't a trail and at this point we were just heading to Katahdin whichever way seemed the easiest. The man was nice but apparently a bit confused by the network of unmarked logging roads. While our friend got lost for nearly three hours, we sat shivering in the back of his pickup. The rain washed some of the mud off our boots and bodies and created a mud puddle in the bed. We talked about demoting this man from trail angel to trail demon. He'd stop every so often and apologize profusely. He finally insisted that we join him in the warm cab, regardless of our mud-caked boots. I told Craig he should sit up front, and although he said we could both fit, I really didn't feel like talking to anyone. I remained in the metal bed of the pickup, preferring to listen to my teeth chatter, the wind howl in my ears, and the sheets of rain slap my hood.

I withdrew quite frequently when conditions got that bad. Craig knew I had my own way of coping and he left me alone. Later he wrote, "Today about 5:30 A.M. I saw my third moose while filling my water jug. But the day got worse from there. Thought we had a sunny stretch but we got rained on all day. Raindrop is ready to be done—it is so evident. Tomorrow we will do seventeen miles of nothing but mud. We are out of money, sick of trail food, and the bugs still suck.

But less than two more weeks—we will survive, then celebrate! I want to see her smile again."

I appreciated Craig's optimism, but the fords terrified me, and not all the flooded areas could be avoided. I have a fear of water anyway, and the idea of getting carried away by a river made me shake just thinking about it. We figured a break in Monson would help us clear our minds before the final 100-mile stretch.

Keith and Pat Shaw open their home to hundreds of hikers every year, and their operation is considered a four-star establishment by anyone who knows anything about thru-hiking. Keith greeted us in his green work pants, suspenders, and an engineer's cap which covered his bald head. He looks like the type of man you want as your grandpa. Keith and Pat work hard and make do with what they have. And they're eager to share what they do have with hikers.

After a hot shower to regain feeling in my numb fingers, I joined Craig and ten other hikers around the long wooden table and smiled as Pat carried platters of steaks from the kitchen. The Shaw's home-style dinners are renowned. Eight dollars apiece bought us T-bone steaks from the Shaws' own cattle, potatoes, green beans, fresh bread, apple pie, and excellent company. The next morning we smelled bacon before anyone was out of bed, and they fed us as many pancakes as we could eat.

We sat around that day, out of the rain, swapping stories. The southbounders warned us about more flooding and more swamps, and we warned them of the same. We expected the worst, and for the last 100 miles we got what we expected. There were places on the trail— not in a river, but on the *trail*—where the water was up to my waist. Craig looked at me in disbelief. "We *have* to take a picture of this," he said, "swimming the AT." Our boots never did dry out.

The actual rivers were much deeper than the trail, and I was scared to cross them. Close to Abol Bridge, one felled tree spanned a raging river. Craig shimmied across and waved for me to do the same. I looked upstream and down for slower currents or shallow water, but there was nothing. "You can do it," Craig said, "just try." I began kneeling on the log, sliding along. But I didn't get far. I started to think about falling and getting swept away in the currents. I began to cry and slid back to shore, thinking, If he still wants to marry me after this...

I was angry at my own fear and didn't know how to overcome it, and in retrospect maybe it was a healthy fear. What I lacked in courage I made up for in resourcefulness. I threw down my pack and took out Big Red. I knew I had carried The Most Enormous Therm-a-Rest Ever Made for a reason. Once it was inflated I turned to Craig, "I'll just raft across."

"Okay," he said, and he threw me a rope. I tied the rope to myself, got a running start, and dove into the water. I clutched my Therm-a-Rest like a boogie board and kicked furiously as Craig quickly reeled me in. "Now *that* was fun," I said.

Most thru-hikers say they have mixed feelings about approaching the end of the trail. Personally, another week of rain was about all I could take. Everyone has their own idea of what a thru-hike should be. Some hikers touch every blaze, others hitchhike long distances, some run the trail and have their gear shuttled, others take more than a year to complete it. Every hiker has their own lessons to learn and their own challenges and obstacles to overcome. Craig and I had our relationship put to the test, and we succeeded. For us, maybe the trail was less about hiking and more about staying together.

§

The jewel of Maine and the mountain thru-hikers most look forward to is Katahdin. Today the mountain is so well known it's hard to believe that two hundred years ago few white men knew it existed. Katahdin was so remote and daunting that it wasn't climbed by a white man until 1804, and because most historians agree that Native Americans who lived in the region didn't climb Katahdin, the 1804 ascent is considered the first ever.

The Passamaquoddy and Penobscot tribes of Maine, along with the Micmacs of New Brunswick and the Saint Francis Indians of Canada, call themselves Wabanaki, meaning "white" or "light," signifying that they live closest to the rising sun. Katahdin is mentioned in many of the Wabanaki myths, and a variety of spirits and gods are thought to reside on or in the mountain. The spirit of Katahdin is a friendly force with stone eyebrows who lives inside the mountain and helps the tribes. Pamola, the god of Katahdin who is sometimes depicted as evil, sometimes as harmless, has giant wings that create breezes over the mountain. Occasionally Pamola takes the form of the Stormbird, who throws boulders and creates violent storms and blizzards to keep man off the mountain. Before the arrival of the white man, the Wabanaki both feared and revered the mountain, but their stories indicate that they probably remained below treeline.

The white man's fear of and reverence for the mountain didn't go quite as deep as the Wabanaki's. In the early 1800s, the commonwealth that comprised much of New England decided it should learn more about its lands, so Charles Turner Jr. was hired to survey the area. After a number of years trekking through the North Woods of the interior of Maine, Turner's party canoed up the West Branch of the Penobscot River and found "Catardin" looming above them. They approached the western flanks of the mountain and ascended through thick bramble and boulders. Nine hours later, they arrived at the summit.

Katahdin wasn't climbed again until 1819, when Colin Campbell's survey team was charged with determining the boundary between British Canada and the U.S. Although Campbell's party had an extremely difficult ascent, the real challenge occurred between 1825 and 1833 when politicians in Maine decided to run an east-west transect across the state in order to establish township and property boundaries. A fine idea on paper, the Monument Line was a logistical nightmare. Joseph Norris and his son took the job and headed west from the coast, laying a chain line as they went. Little did they know, their course was headed straight toward Katahdin. They ran the chain up the mountain, making only two miles in one day until they reached the tablelands of Katahdin. All they could see was dense forest, scrub, and near-vertical walls. When father and son returned the following year to continue the line, they elected to skip the sixteen-mile section that would have taken them through the Katahdin region.

The idea of climbing the mountain for pleasure would not enter anyone's mind until much later. During the 1850s, trail work had begun and a handful of guides led hardy souls to the summit. By the late 1800s, paper companies and their logging roads had made the mountain more accessible to recreationists. In 1894, the Bangor and Aroostook Railroad was completed, and steamboats brought visitors to the lakes and river north of Millinocket.

By the early twentieth century, the Katahdin region had received considerable attention from recreationists, but it was used most heavily by the timber industry. A few large paper companies and wealthy individuals owned most of the land, and most of the trees in the Katahdin region had been cut at least once. The people of Maine began to realize that the region would be devastated if it wasn't protected.

For some people, hiking in this part of the country was a spiritual experience. It certainly was for Percival Proctor Baxter. Born into a wealthy family, Percy was able to travel extensively and spent much of his time outdoors. In 1903 he accompanied his father on a fishing trip to Kidney Pond near Katahdin, a trip many people feel inspired Percy to devote his life to preserving that region for the people of Maine. Percy went to the Harvard School of Law and traveled with his father all over the world: Nova Scotia, Africa, Latin America, the Caribbean, Japan, Europe, and Russia. In his twenties, he was elected to the Maine legislature then served as governor of Maine from 1921 to 1924.

The first legislative move to protect Katahdin came in 1905. Baxter introduced a petition from the Maine State Federation of Women's Clubs to preserve the area, but nothing came of it. As a legislator and then again as governor, Baxter tried to establish the area around Katahdin as a state park. He worked for years drafting a protection plan and rallying support. Each time, his proposal failed. Legislators could not understand his desire, not to mention the state's need, to buy land in such a remote area. The president of Great Northern Paper Company, which owned the land, had no desire to sell it; at best he was uncooperative. During the 1930s, various contingencies fought to turn the region into a national park, an idea Baxter adamantly opposed. He feared federal ownership and wanted Katahdin to remain under control of the people of Maine. At the end of his administration, Baxter offered to contribute his two-year salary as governor if the state legislature would create the park and appropriate $10,000 for two years to manage the park. His proposal was rejected.

Finished with politics and content with managing his family's estate, in 1930 Baxter set out as a private citizen to buy nearly 6,000 acres, including most of Katahdin, from the new, more cooperative owner of Great Northern. Over three decades, he continued to buy land from paper companies and large landowners, lobby the state legislature, and fight the logging industry until his personal park included twenty-five individual purchases totaling more than 200,000 acres.

As new parcels were acquired, he deeded the land to Maine as a park and outlined the conditions under which it was to be managed. In 1945 he wrote to the legislature: "Everything in connection with the Park must be left simple and natural, and must remain as nearly as possible as it was when only the Indians and the animals roamed at will through these areas. I want it made available to persons of moderate means who, with their boys and girls, with their packs of bedding and food, can tramp through the woods, cook a steak and make flapjacks by the lakes and brooks. Every section of this area is beautiful, each in its own way. I do not want it locked up and made inaccessible; I want it used to the fullest extent, but in the right, unspoiled way."

His gift, however, didn't come without controversy. Baxter created restrictions and guidelines about how the park was to be managed for fire, flood, hunting, predator control, invasive species, logging, and motorboat and snowmobile use. He wrote, "I seek to provide against commercial exploitation, against hunting, trapping and killing, against lumbering, hotels, advertising, hot-dog stands, motor vehicles, horse-drawn vehicles and other vehicles, air-craft, and the trappings of unpleasant civilization." His vision alienated many users. Hunting groups, for instance, pressured the state not to accept the lands. Sometimes he had to make a number of concessions, including cutting and hunting rights and outfitter camp leases on certain tracts, or the owners wouldn't sell.

Still, as best he could, he stuck to his original plan and tried to convince others of the great need for preservation. He said, "As modern civilization with its trailers and gasoline fumes, its unsightly billboards, its radio and jazz, encroaches on the Maine wilderness, the time yet may come when only the Katahdin region remains undefiled by man." Baxter held steadfastly to his ideals and understood the danger of compromising his guidelines even a little bit. In 1959 the U.S. attorney general asked to cut a Christmas tree from Baxter Park to use at Rockefeller Center. Baxter refused and assured the attorney general that there must be another grand tree somewhere outside the park they could use instead.

Baxter State Park wasn't the only gift Percival Baxter gave to the residents of Maine. He gave paintings to Saint Joseph's Covenant; deeded Mackworth Island to the state of Maine to be used as a home for sick and underprivileged children; gave $625,000 to reconstruct the school for the deaf; enlarged the city of Portland's park system; established a trust fund to manage the library and museum in Gorham; created a fund to manage the animal refuge in Portland; and of course, spent his life acquiring land to preserve the beloved Katahdin region for the people of Maine. He created a trust fund of more than a million dollars to manage the park, and upon his death the park received more than $5 million to add to the fund.

The unusual genesis of the park has created some interesting management situations. In its early years, the Baxter State Park Authority consisted of only a couple individuals. When the area began to receive more use, they realized that there were too few rangers to adequately manage and patrol the area. The MATC and the AMC essentially adopted certain areas of the park; they built and maintained trails, including the Appalachian Trail up Katahdin.

In 1969, park officials realized that visitation had skyrocketed and that the backcountry was getting thoroughly hammered, so they closed certain areas in the park. In the 1970s they instituted strict regulations, most of which are still in effect today. Permits are mandatory for all overnight stays in the park, and visitors are allowed to camp only at designated sites. Upon entering, one must register a detailed itinerary with park officials, and in winter months, rangers check visitors' clothing and equipment to make sure they are prepared. During any month, the park reserves the right to close trails above treeline if weather or trail conditions are particularly threatening, and the park director reserves the right to deny access to anyone, in his or her opinion, who may jeopardize human safety or the protection of the park.

Day use is restricted by the number of parking spaces: 48 spaces at Roaring Brook, 18 at Abol Bridge, and 25 at Katahdin Stream. When the lots are full, visitors are turned away. A special provision allows AT thru-hikers to camp at Daicy Pond without reservations, and, as long as conditions are okay, thru-hikers are permitted to climb Katahdin regardless of the number of day-use visitors.

Every five years, the park evaluates its management plan. The park has had its share of controversies with hunting and motorized use, but it has always attempted to manage the park as Baxter would have liked. Although controversies change with new technology and visitation demands, the ideals that Baxter held for the park have remained the guiding principle in its management. Maine residents get priority for reservations; stereos, televisions, and cell phones are prohibited; no power equipment is allowed in the backcountry; and Leave No Trace guidelines are more than suggestions—they are the rule.

Percival Baxter died in 1962 at the age of ninety-two. Before he died, a grand-niece reported some final words. He said, "Pray for me. It is not that I am afraid of dying, it is just that I have so much left to do." His ashes were scattered over Katahdin in Baxter State Park.

§

The morning for which we had been waiting half a year arrived at the end of July. The mountain that had been a dream, a flicker of light in the dark labyrinth of my mind, had become a dot on the horizon, then a distant peak. This morning, the base of Katahdin, the northern terminus of the Appalachian Trail, was beneath our feet.

We left the ranger station at 7:00 A.M. and began the five-mile climb with excited steps, falling into an energetic rhythm, breathing hard but steady. The trail ascends more than 4,000 feet to the summit, the single largest climb of the trip. "This is it," said Craig, "the final day."

My thoughts reeled back to February 15, the day we saw the first blaze of the AT on Springer Mountain, Georgia. We were so fresh, so naive, so anxious. I remembered how sore I was after the first day, the blisters that plagued my heels for six weeks, and the foot pains that never did go away. I remembered one of the longest and most brutal winters in history. I had flashbacks of numb hands, blinding blizzards, ice storms, sleepless nights, and five-foot snowdrifts. Our relationship was fresh and we worked through the obstacles in good humor. We realized we were stronger as a team than we were alone.

The breeze on Katahdin picked up and cooled off as we approached treeline. My strides were slower now, my legs tiring.

"It's really windy up there," said a man coming down the trail. "I tried to get past the first rock scramble, but the wind was too strong. I had to turn back."

We passed the man and Craig turned to me, "I'm not turning back," he said. "No way."

"Me either," I replied. We approached the windy section and hoisted ourselves up and over the rock ledge. Fully exposed to the elements now, we cinched the hoods of our jackets and kept walking.

The final three miles consisted mostly of steep boulder fields that require hand-over-hand climbing. It reminded me of the rock fields in Pennsylvania and the most challenging sections of trail in New Hampshire and Maine, where I threw my pack down rock faces and scrambled after it. It reminded me of the times that we wanted to quit but somehow convinced each other to stick it out. It was almost always raining.

Today we were lucky. The rangers at Baxter State Park rated the day as Class I, only the fourth "good day" of the entire year.

After a respectable climb, the trail flattened out across the table-lands of Katahdin and the summit came into view. The surrounding mountains were breathtaking: narrow, jagged ridges erupted from a skirt of green. I could feel the sun burning my cheeks.

We kept walking, trying to make out that famous sign atop Katahdin. The sign is more of an end to the trail than the actual peak. The sign is in every thru-hiker's celebratory pose. We had seen it photographed a hundred times. The sign that was branded in my mind was now only twenty yards away. "Give me your hand," I said, and we moved toward it.

After almost six months and more than 2,000 miles, we had walked the Appalachian Trail from Georgia to Maine. With a sigh of relief and teary eyes, I touched the sign. The first line reads KATAHDIN and gives the mileage to southern destinations. Next to an arrow pointing south, the bottom line reads Springer Mt., Georgia—2,135 miles.

I sat up there for two hours, staring south and thinking about our journey, the hardest thing I had ever done. The Appalachian Trail was some of the most unenjoyable hiking I had ever experienced. I remembered the mosquitoes, swamps, rain, biting flies, and burning knees. But I also remembered the trail angels, the good-spirited hikers, the inspiring views, the mountain springs, and falling in love. Good and bad went stride for stride.

The trail taught me about real life, about the reality of the moment. I believe we often get tangled in the fringes and forget where we are and why. The trail forced us to live in the present, to absorb the condition at hand, to live purely and without self-consciousness. It is ironic that some people don't consider that the real world. I often wished I was imagining the cold, the pain, the itching, the wet, but it was no dream. It was real life, as real as it gets.

Craig returned from walking the Knife's Edge, a mile of trail, sometimes only a foot wide, that extends from Katahdin and follows the arc of the ridge. "What an incredible day," I said.

"Sure is," he replied. We sat for another minute looking south at all the miles we had walked, where so many memories were made.

Craig extended his hand to help me up. "Come on, Hon," he said, "let's go home."

"Wait a second," I told him. "I want you to know something."

He paused and looked a little confused.

"I want you to know this was the hardest thing I've ever done, but I'm glad I came along. I also want you to know that next time you ask me on a date, I'd like it to be somewhere that doesn't involve moleskin or pop-tarts or bug spray. Is that fair?"

"Fair enough," he said, helping me to my feet.

We locked elbows and headed south, ready to begin a new journey in a new direction.

# Epilogue

Craig and I traveled from Bangor to Boston on a Greyhound bus while we picked through a package of Oreos on my lap. "So much for giving up chocolate," said Craig. Even though we had stopped exercising, our bodies still craved the quantities of a thru-hiker's diet. Our first challenge in the transition to civilization was to wean ourselves off the Snickers and animal crackers. They were sorely missed. Letting go of the Lipton dinners and pop-tarts, on the other hand, was not nearly as agonizing.

As we sped down the highway I rested my head against the window and watched the landscape pass in a blur. One day after Katahdin I was just beginning to realize the impact the Appalachian Trail would have on my life. During the following months I thought about the trail often. I was proud of that occupation—being a thru-hiker. It was a good way to live. When I was stuck in traffic I missed the silence and stillness of the forest and the simplicity of survival. I missed waking up every morning to the bite of cool air and knowing that I didn't have a to-do list to face. For a while I missed the physical exertion. My legs wanted to fly; an after-work walk or weekend bike ride just wasn't enough. But it was easy to let go of the pain in my knees, and it was a good feeling, six months later, to regain feeling in the bottom of my feet.

I returned from the trail more sensitive to human culture. Eventually I got used to showering two or three times a week, but I still find it strange when people smell like babies and flowers and perfume. I had always thought that ceramic fruit, fine china, and pedicures were a waste of human energy; I feel that way even more now. It was difficult to rationalize driving short distances; I walk or ride my bike whenever I can. I notice waste everywhere and I'm always making mental notes of what we all could do to lighten our loads.

Some changes surprised me. I was terrified to ride in cars. Everything moved so fast; I rode shotgun with my palm braced against the dashboard, prepared for the impending crash. Tired of my screaming, "Watch out!" every thirty seconds, Craig suggested I fasten my seat belt and wear a blindfold until we arrived at our destination.

I became fascinated with drinking fountains. They pop up everywhere—in long corridors at school, in shopping malls, in city parks—just in case you get thirsty in the hour or half-hour or five minutes you're away from home. It's so easy. Just push a button. You don't even have to filter it. For more than a year, I couldn't pass a drinking fountain without taking a sip.

It was a strange feeling when everything that was important in my life suddenly didn't matter: where to pitch the tent, how many days' worth of food to buy, how far until the next water source, how many hours of daylight are left, how to keep a shirt and a pair of socks dry. We worry about different things now: car problems, deadlines, bus schedules, what color to paint the house, where to go for lunch, how to make a Web page, what to buy a friend for his birthday. I often wonder if these things elevate us to a higher level of civilization or if they nudge us closer to nervous breakdowns.

§

Among the important things I gained from the AT was an appreciation for one of our nation's most extraordinary accomplishments. Prior to my hike, I suppose I assumed that the trail had just come into existence out of a legislative document, a few Park Service employees, and a handful of old men with shovels. After my thru-hike, I realized that the Appalachian Trail corridor is more than a line on a map or a dirt path on the ground, and it did not just appear with the signing of an act and a year or two of hacking at the woods. It is the product of a dream shared by thousands of people, by more than just its founder. Backed by the energy of an extraordinary community, the AT flourishes because of the natural beauty in this country and because of the people who fight little battles every day in an effort to manage the trail the best way they know how.

The Appalachian Trail is a symbol of the potential for greatness that exists in this country. Yes, we have done a lot of things wrong. We overbuilt, allowed urban sprawl to encroach too far into the forest interior, elected to provide telecommunications capabilities and sacrifice clear views, caused species to decline and teeter on the brink of extinction, let the air that sustains us become so polluted that it makes us sick, allowed ski areas to develop beyond what's reasonable. But we've also done a lot of things right, and many people are working hard to remedy the mistakes of the past.

The Appalachian Trail ought to be a model for trail projects across the country. It is a success story of a place that meant so much to people they built their lives around it, they lobbied Congress for decades for its protection, they bought entire parks and donated the land to preserve wild spaces, they spend their vacations building trail, they sit on their tailgates waiting for thirsty hikers. It is a success story about American people who work to protect a national treasure when the government won't, and about people who work with the government when government officials are doing the best they can. The Appalachian Trail is a success story about the dreamers in our society. It is about the people who dream of a permanently protected footpath and about the people who dream of hiking it. Every year the trail makes it possible for thousands of people to have their dreams come true.

Because of the pressures of overpopulation in the eastern U.S., management dilemmas surrounding public/private partnerships, user fees and permit systems, reintroducing endangered animals, and fighting exotic species are all amplified in the East. Environmental problems along the Appalachian Trail have been exacerbated by the sheer number of people who live there. The challenges we face in the East may be indicative of what's to come in the West and in other less populated regions. We can learn a lot from the successes and failures in the East, and if we're smart we'll plan to prevent species extinctions, manage land before use becomes a problem, and protect land before ski area expansion and urban sprawl threaten to till every inch of untouched soil. To do this, we must be proactive rather than reactive; we must act sooner than later.

🦋

An unexpected discovery occurred recently. I figured that after hiking for six months I'd be ready to rest for a while, to slow down, to stay in one place. After all, I couldn't wait to finish the trail and go home— it was a long, hard trip and I was worn out. But lately I've felt the need to walk again. I'm restless. There is so much out there to explore, so many things tucked away in the cracks. Annie Dillard writes about finding life in the gaps: "Stalk the gaps. Squeak into a gap in the soil, turn, and unlock...a universe. This is how you spend the afternoon, and tomorrow morning, and tomorrow afternoon. *Spend* the afternoon. You can't take it with you."

My toes are in a crack, prying open a gap, wriggling in. I taste it now. It's wet and salty. I feel a warm breeze lightly brush my cheek, and I squint past the sun in my eyes. I can't tell if there's a stream in there, a canyon in the gap, maybe an ocean. Adventures are tucked in the folds of fabric that create the tapestry of our lives. Paths radiate across the tapestry in every direction. Some paths trace the creases, others part strands of red and gold, some twist and tangle through the tassels. I am certain there is a journey for every one of us; there is a path that awaits our footsteps. I am ready now to blaze my own trail and I've learned the importance of experiencing each moment of the journey to its fullest. It's no easy task, but we must try.

It is up to each of us to choose our path with care and defend it passionately. We all would do well to stalk the gaps, spend afternoons, and fight furiously to ensure that the path we travel will forever lead to the most beautiful places.

# ABOUT THE AUTHOR

Adrienne Hall has not only accomplished the astounding feat of hiking the entire Appalachian Trail, she also has hiked the 500-mile Colorado Trail. Depending on the season, she spends her spare time skiing, snowboarding, hiking, and mountain biking. She is the author of *Backpacking: A Woman's Guide* and *The Essential Backpacker*, and holds an M.S. in environmental studies from the University of Montana.

# About the Appalachian Mountain Club

Since 1876, the Appalachian Mountain Club has helped people experience the majesty and solitude of the Northeast outdoors. We offer outdoor skills workshops, guided trips, and lodging options for all levels of outdoor adventuring. Our conservation programs include trail maintenance, air and water quality research, and advocacy work to preserve the special outdoor places we love and enjoy for future generations.

## Join the Adventure!

Take a hike, ride a bike, paddle a canoe. We believe that people who enjoy breathing fresh air, climbing mountains, splashing in streams, and walking on trails have more fun and take better care of the outdoors. Join the fun today. Call 617-523-0636 for membership information.

## Outdoor Adventures

From beginner backpacking to advanced backcountry skiing, we teach outdoor skills workshops to suit your interest and experience. If you prefer the company of others and skilled leaders, we also offer guided hiking and paddling trips. Our five outdoor education centers guarantee year-round adventures.

## Huts, Lodges, and Visitor Centers

With accommodations throughout the Northeast, you don't have to travel to the ends of the earth to see nature's beauty and experience unique wilderness lodging. Accessible by car or on foot, our lodges and huts are perfect for families, couples, groups, and individuals.

## Books and Maps

We can lead you to the best hiking, biking, skiing, and paddling destinations from Maine to North Carolina. With more than 50 books and maps published, we're your definitive resource for discovering wonderful outdoor places. For ordering information call 1-800-262-4455.

Check us out online at www.outdoors.org, where there's lots going on.

Appalachian Mountain Club
5 Joy Street
Boston, MA 02108-1490
617-523-0636